Between Citizen and State

Great Barrington Books

Bringing the old and new together in the spirit of W. E. B. Du Bois

∽ An imprint edited by Charles Lemert ∽

Titles Available

Between Citizen and State

An Introduction to the Corporation

David A. Westbrook

foreword by Charles Lemert

Paradigm Publishers

Boulder • London

Paradigm Publishers is committed to preserving our environment. This book was printed on recycled paper with 30% postconsumer waste content, saving trees and avoiding the creation of hundreds of gallons of wastewater, tens of pounds of solid waste, more than a hundred pounds of greenhouse gases, and using hundreds fewer kilowatt hours of electricity than if it had been printed on paper manufactured from all virgin fibers.

Published in the United States by Paradigm Publishers, 3360 Mitchell Lane Suite E, Boulder, Colorado 80301 USA.

Paradigm Publishers is the trade name of Birkenkamp & Company, LLC, Dean Birkenkamp, President and Publisher.

Library of Congress Cataloging-in-Publication Data

Westbrook, David A.
    Between citizen and state : an introduction to the corporation / David A. Westbrook.
        p. cm. — (Great Barrington books)
    Includes bibliographical references and index.
    ISBN 978-1-59451-404-3 (hardcover : alk. paper)
    ISBN 978-1-59451-405-0 (paperback : alk. paper)
    1. Corporation law—United States.   2. Corporate governance—United States.
3. Corporations–United States.   I. Title.
KF1414.W47 2007
    346.73'066—dc22

                                                                                        2007010972

Printed and bound in the United States of America on acid-free paper that meets the standards of the American National Standard for Permanence of Paper for Printed Library Materials.

Designed and Typeset by Straight Creek Bookmakers.

12 11 10 09 08   2 3 4 5

Contents

Acknowledgments and Dedication

"IT CAN'T BE DONE," SAID MY VERY GOOD FRIEND JACK, "AND BESIDES, IT'S A waste of your [limited] intellectual capital." "You can't write another book like the last one [I don't have it in me? You'll leave?] until the baby is [safely] out of the house," said my even better friend Amy. "And you should try to write something that can sell," she added, letting me know she was on to my perverse plot to remain unread. Thus suitably encouraged, over a summer so miserable for other reasons that I wasn't having fun anyway, I wrote out, clarified, and elaborated upon my lectures on corporation law. It struck me as quite a rhetorical challenge to sketch academic corporation law in a way that might be interesting to people outside the law, law students, and even my colleagues. I had the supple elegance of Grant Gilmore's prose in mind, and maybe visions of sugar plums dancing in my head, too. But who cares? The book got done; here it is. How badly this effort at a child's garden of corporation law fails I leave to the reader, but I am grateful to have had the chance to try, and this is the part of the book where I say thanks.

Even a quirky little book like this one is a very collaborative effort. Fred Konefsky, Mae Kuykendall, Saul Levmore, Jack Schlegel, and Amy Westbrook, as well as two outside readers, read drafts in their entirety and made useful amendments for which I am very grateful. Dianne Avery, Lauren Breen, Tom Disare, and Marc Miller provided fine comments or other encouragement along the way. Nils Olsen, the dean of my school, has been very supportive. I thank them all.

I also thank the University at Buffalo Law Library, and Jennifer Behrens in particular, for assistance with my many often odd requests for texts or information, which were usually communicated from a distance, in great haste, and for no discernible reason, but cheerfully fulfilled nonetheless. Barb Kennedy once again was a great help with things administrative. Her patience, dedication, good humor, and better sense are appreciated.

My research assistants, Heidi Spalholtz, Gregory Stein, Stephen Trynosky, and Jennifer Tsai, have been wonderful. It is rather a pity that this project is over and they are moving on with their lives. With such players at the heart of the team, I can imagine delegating the labor of writing almost entirely, like a judge, or even certain well-known professors. But for now, I suppose the task of writing is mostly mine, so the ritual shouldering of the cross makes some sense: this text's myriad remaining shortcomings are entirely my own responsibility. Ah, vanity.

This book is addressed mostly to students, and in some ways, this book is really about teaching. It therefore would be common enough, yet noble (and yes, vain) of me to dedicate this book to my students. And I do sometimes care about students, but mostly I hope they don't know that—I'm trying to teach them to take care of themselves. Instead, recalling that paragon of rational self-interest Dr. Johnson ("no man but a blockhead ever wrote, except for money"), I dedicate this book, which I hope will be essentially just an annuity, to my children's education.

Foreword: The Mystery of the Social Betweens

Charles Lemert

SOCIAL STUDIES OF ALL KINDS MUST DEAL WITH THE MYSTERY OF THE SOCIAL betweens. They have not known quite what to say, for example, about the between of the State and individual.

Social sciences as we know them today are indebted to writers like Karl Marx, who in the 1840s faced straight on the massive structures of the modern world and called them what they were. The accomplishment is stunning even today for the simple reason that social structures are, by nature, as hard to pin down as they are powerful in their effects. People will talk about social things like the State as if it were a definite and visible thing. To which Tony Soprano would again be right to wonder, "New Jersey?" Where the State, or for that matter the Market begin and end in the complex life of gathered societies is impossible to say. That they are structures is impossible not to say. But how do structures like the State get down into the heads of individuals? This is the mystery of the Between.

The dilemma of social studies is that, in their quest for science, they drift toward observables—taking, for example, the stock market that can be observed from a balcony somewhere on Wall Street as though it were *the* Market, the center of all capital exchange in the world of economic uncertainties. Psychologists likewise organize themselves according to claims as to what constitutes the core structure of mental activity: brain, mind, the Unconscious, character, behavior, neurological development, psyche, and so on. What they are trying to avoid is cordoning themselves off from each other, not to mention from common sense. But they are not alone.

All social sciences achieve their dubious status by holding fast to particular assumptions that there is one definite structure that organizes the objects that are thought to flourish in this or that social field. Social structures, unlike other structures, being abstract, are fictions that contain a great deal of information of little direct empirical value. This mystery of the Between, as it applies to social things, usually is resolved by appeals to logic, as in: The social is what it is. Social things, thus, comprise all the various happenings that *must* be there if the data are to make sense—if, that is, the numeric calibrations of observations that can be made are to be organized into well-structured wholes like states, markets, and societies.

One of the few credits that my field, sociology, has earned in this respect is that, at its best, it does not even try to stake a precise claim in the Between. Sociology prefers to identify itself as the study not of Mind or Market or State but of Society, whatever that might be. It attempts to raid the fields of other disciplines by the crude method of pretending that there can be a "sociology of … " any group of things so long as it can be named. Hence, the importance of Émile Durkheim, who made the bold move that limited to a degree the endless proliferation of subjects by stipulating that sociology is, simply, the science of social things—facts that cannot be reduced to or explained by the facts of some other field.

But, here, as with Marx, the mystery of the betweens remained acute, still largely unsolved in our time. The Between is, in simple terms, the uncharted empirical territory between structures that are by nature abstract—hence, fictions of a necessary sort—and events that are by nature concrete and local—hence, the zest of generalizations that usually trip in the Between, well before they rise to their proper structural level. Thus, economists beg their own questions by stipulating markets appertaining to some more or less observable economic dynamic like, say, inventories; likewise, psychologists fall off their own wagon when they are satisfied with, say, a neuroscience which has the power of bio-chemistry behind it that leverages itself into an elegantly incomplete science of brain as the necessary Between of well-structured mental lives.

Another of the credits due sociology, among the few it can rightly claim, is that from the beginning the early sociologists were preoccupied by the law; that is to say, they became sociologists only after the fact. Max Weber, having rejected his father's demand that he become a lawyer, became instead a social historian of the law. His doctoral thesis, *On the History of Commercial Partnerships in the Middle Ages*, was influenced by Otto von Gierke's arguments in *Das deutsche Genossenschaftsrecht* (1868–1881) that the medieval idea of corporate association is one of the betweens where isolated individuals join to protect themselves against the, then, as now, sometimes ruthless power of the state.

Likewise, Émile Durkheim, also in the 1890s, having abandoned his rab-binical lineage, turned first off to the sociology of law in complex societies. His doctoral thesis, *The Division of Labor in Society*, distinguished repressive from restitutive legal systems as the central demarcation between ancient societies, which repressed, and modern societies, which, in principle, meant to restore deviants to serviceable partnership in the moral order. In this, Durkheim drew upon the Jewish Covenant with Yahweh as a model for modern ideals of contract, hence of collective life (an extension brilliantly worked out in 1955 by the legal scholar G. F. Mendenhall in *Law and Covenant in Israel and the Ancient Near East*).

To belabor the point, it could be said also that Marx himself, having sought to set Hegel head to toe, cut his eyeteeth in 1843 on Hegel's overdetermined theory of the Between. Marx's *A Contribution to a Critique of Hegel's Philosophy of Right* includes the following: "The idea is made the subject and the *actual* relation of family and civil society to the state is conceived as its internal imaginary." (One would like to have been a fly on the wall when Louis Althusser first read that line.) Marx meant, of course, to distinguish family and civil society from the State—to put them, that is, in the social Between. Like Weber and even Durkheim, the civil Between was viewed as an at least relatively free space supportive of civil associations mysteriously populated by individuals seeking together to resist the power of the State.

David Westbrook's *Between Citizen and State: An Introduction to the Corporation*, with its eye-opening clarity, its verve and humor, and its overall brilliance will serve readers who desire, as one should, to understand the corporations. In a world in which transnational corporations seem to hold upper hand, this would exclude practically no one.

The service this book renders is all the more cultivated by its astonishing kindness. I mean nothing sentimental by this. But it must be noted that this wonderful book takes the long tradition and vexed meditations of social scientists by the scruff of the neck and washes away their failures with fresh warm water.

Though the book will, one supposes, be read first and foremost by students of the law, it should be read by anyone of whatever professional or amateur inclination to understand the residue of virtues that remain in the modern social order. Modern society has suffered in recent decades at the hands of bullies and bombasts of all stripes—from war criminals recklessly running proud modern states back into the feudal grounds from which they arose to involuntary associations of false prophets who are convinced they know better than the moderns when in fact they do not care to know anything more than the crap held in by their ideological sphincters. It is not a happy world, these days in the early 2000s. And it is particular unhappy that new thinking about the Between of citizen and State is so rare.

Between Citizen and State begins to resolve these mysteries. First, and for all students of the social, it establishes a way to fill the Between of social things. Much like the writings of von Gierke and Weber, this book appreciates the strategic role of the corporation in modern life. In terms that would have pleased Erving Goffman, Westbrook characterizes the corporation as theater in which stock characters and ordinary scripts enjoy dynamic and friendly relations. Between and among the principal characters—stockholders, directors, and managers—are obligations and protections meant to serve the good of all.

The book is filled with charming passages such as Westbrook's recapitulation of Benjamin Cardozo's famous opinion in *Meinhard v. Salmon* where Salmon did not disclose to Meinhard the facts of actions that altered their partnership. "Disclosure creates a kind of community, or more precisely, reinforces the community entailed in the business association. People should know where they stand. Cardozo is explicit: if a fiduciary were allowed to take opportunities for himself rather than the beneficiary of his trust, then 'He might steal a march on his comrade under cover of the darkness, and then hold the captured ground. Loyalty and comradeship are not so easily abjured'" (p. 79). The charm in Westbrook's disclosure of Cardozo's elegant regard for the moral basis of the law is that of revealing the best that social relations can be and seldom are.

It is this sort of thinking for which Weber and Durkheim, even Marx, were reaching when they established the modern social sciences on the loose sand of the Between of structures and individuals. The looming power of the structures of modern capitalism was, as Weber put it, an enormous cosmos that clouded the ability of individuals to find their way. The sand did not help.

Like so many who came after them, hope was in the liberation of civil society. But liberty without friction gets you nowhere. Civil society, like civility, its derivative, has too long been a slogan that organizes the failure of liberal thought to fill the Between that, lacking substance, allows states to whack citizens. The trouble with so many of the appeals to civil society is that they leave the civil empty—a kind of open territory in which agents meet to assault states—with what weapons exactly? New Jersey indeed!

What legal theories of corporate law accomplish where most social sciences fall short is to fill that space with real content—in the case of *Between Citizen and State*, with the corporation. It may well be, referring again to von Gierke, that the medieval corporate associations were in fact the bodies that gave birth to the modern idea of liberty. Corporations are first, and perhaps foremost, personalities with duties and responsibilities. In a sense there can be no individuals unless individual personhood is called out in public—and the first instance of that calling out was the corporation.

Not all corporations are kind; most, one supposes, are anything but. But Westbrook allows us to see that the corporation is the concrete and particular form of the possibility of public life and meaningful action. Whether a business partnership or an association of rebels, those who would act require protection. Law is the friction that puts solid ground under the feet of actors. Trust is the fundament of joint action, whether for profit or revolution.

This is such a simple thing. "Disclosure creates community." Trust, whether fiduciary or social, is thus central to community. Erving Goffman would not have been pleased with this conclusion—believing as he did that we are all necessarily dupes and dopes.

I do not assume that David Westbrook is the only lawyer who understands these things. But surely he is among the best at exposing them in ways that we occasional outlaws and regular innocents as to the nature of the Law can understand. Not only that but anyone who tries to figure out what is wrong with most social sciences as they are taught and written would do well to study this book for its contributions to a kind but serious theory of the social Between.

Preface: What about Happiness?

This book has been written for students of corporation law, using "students" in the broadest sense to mean anyone who wishes to gain a more sophisticated understanding of corporation law, more specifically, how legal education imagines the institution of the corporation. Although corporations are everywhere in the United States, thinking about the institution is quite difficult. Perhaps the following story will give the prospective reader some idea of this book's approach to the problem.

I teach the basic law school course on business associations, which introduces students to the corporation and other forms of business organization and to some of the ways in which lawyers work in and with these forms. Versions of this course are taught in every law school in the United States and taken by most law students. Due to this demand, the course is usually offered as a large lecture class. The size of the class, and therefore the range of what students know, presents a problem for any teacher.

Many students arrive knowing a great deal about how business is organized; for many it is the beginning of their commercial education and an important part of their training for practice; but for many it is the only business law course they will take. It is hard to address, much less talk to, such different students simultaneously. At almost any moment, some students are becoming lost while others are getting bored, and my efforts to solve one problem tend to worsen the other.

For this and other reasons my lectures often fall behind "schedule," which means that our discussions over the course of a semester have traveled down paths more roundabout than I had imagined we would take some months earlier when I wrote the syllabus. Failing to stick to the schedule is unsurprising, indeed, it almost always happens if the conversation is good, and in some more advanced classes I barely go through the charade of having a syllabus. Many students in the basic course, however, would find such a refusal to organize disconcerting. Moreover, I've never met anyone who has learned, practiced, or taught the law of corporations without a degree of compulsiveness.

And so I distribute a syllabus on the first day of class, and up through the last day of class I find myself struggling to get back onto my schedule, a schedule that is after all only a figment of my imagination. I'm like a man hurrying to board Thomas the Tank Engine for the summer holiday, simply because I told my students I would, back in February.[1]

On just such a last day, at the end of spring semester and with summer beckoning, I was trying to be a useful engine and "bring it all together" in the few moments of collective attention left to me, when I was abruptly interrupted by a woman sitting in the back of the hall. She looked both unfamiliar and striking; presumably she did not attend class all that often. Perhaps she was a ghost, but she spoke clearly enough: "Sir, with all due respect," [a threatening way to start] "and especially for those of us about to graduate, what does any of this have to do with our happiness?"

Again, I teach the law of business associations, rarely thought of as a "feel-good" course. Once upon a time I was a corporate lawyer, draped in flowing dark woolens. From that vantage, the obvious answer would be that her happiness was simply not a concern of the law of corporations, nor of mine. But since I had after all left corporate practice to become a teacher, such a hard response seemed wrong. Worse, I suspected that she knew that her happiness did not figure in the semester's long march from *respondeat superior* to the faint hope for informationally efficient markets, and she was afraid her happiness would not matter much in the working world she was about to enter. What could I say? The semester was over. I was going into overtime, and a woman on the back row had decided to raise existential issues. For once we had a situation that all of my students could find interesting. So I wrapped up my efforts to tie together the themes of the course and tried to address her question. I cannot remember exactly what I said, but I hope to have conveyed something along the following lines.

"Business associations" are legal abstractions, but they are not simply legal abstractions. People inhabit these forms. There is much to admire in such dramas, what we might generally call commercial virtue: brilliance and creativity, duties faithfully discharged, trust justifiably reposed, and by the way, making money can be lots of fun. On the other hand, it is also true that business folk exhibit a great deal of outright selfishness, incivility, fraud, and so forth. But to

---

1. See Wilbert Awdry and C. Reginald Dalby, *Thomas the Tank Engine: The Complete Collection* (Railway Series) Crescent Reprint Edition (1997/1946).

take a more worldly view, these are all human vices, and who does not have a degree of interest in and sympathy for such vices? Perhaps the right attitude to take toward corporation law thus conceived is dramatic appreciation, hardly an unhappy attitude.

With luck I also said something about the forms of social life, and how "the corporation" is shorthand for a complicated cultural fabric, some basic patterns of which I had been trying to help students see for themselves. Most of law school focuses on the state and the individual, but most of life happens among social institutions. Corporation law is a fundamental aspect of civil society, and, as I hope to show in this little book, provides a way to begin understanding institutions beside the corporation, and even civil society writ large.

To be honest, I don't remember what I actually said. The student later sent me a note thanking me for taking her question seriously. I suppose being taken seriously is better than being mocked, but not as good as being answered. In the years since, I have thought about her question, and about how, in life, we rarely get the chance to go back and say what we afterward realize we should have. But this book attempts to do just that, that is, to respond more appropriately than I was able to on my feet in the dusk of that semester. Which is not to say I intend to answer her question, because I do not. To restate what I believe her question to have been: how do we understand, what do we mean by, and so how do we emotionally respond to this thing called "the corporation" that looms so large in the life of our society? More simply, how should I feel? Although I have written at length about capitalism elsewhere, this book does not really answer that question, for the simple reason that I do not believe it is a teacher's job. This book is an introduction to a modestly complex body of thought, written for students, in the hope that they learn to find their own way, and in graceful fashion. And with that, let me begin this affectionate introduction to corporation law as taught in these United States.

What about happiness, indeed.

Introduction

Corporation Law as Theater

THIS BOOK INTRODUCES A NARROW BUT IMPORTANT TOPIC, THE BASICS OF corporation law as commonly taught in the United States, through an extended metaphor, the theater. As with a play that can be understood on different levels, "the basics" do not mean the same thing to the three different sorts of readers for whom this book is written, namely (1) citizens, including graduate and undergraduate students in various disciplines, who are interested in the corporation; (2) law students, for whom some knowledge of the corporation is required; and (3) corporation law professors. The citizen who is not a lawyer, the student becoming a lawyer, and the professor of law will each read this book in different ways, in part because each will bring different understandings of the law to the text. So one book becomes three, and a few points of clarification here at the outset may minimize confusion about what this book is trying to do and for whom.

Topic

This book is about the law of business corporations, at least as taught in the United States, which is a matter too important to be left to law professors. Part I, "Background," sets the stage by introducing the actors within the governance structure of the corporation (i.e., shareholders, directors, and managers) and discusses some of the reasons that corporation law is considered important. Part I also introduces some basic concepts concerning financing and governing the business enterprise and some idea of how to read appellate court decisions—still the backbone of U.S. legal education—in order to understand corporate relations. Part II, "Internal Struggles," discusses relationships within the corporation and, consequently, the governance of the corporation. Part II is organized around the basic legal doctrines taught in virtually all corporation law classes, doctrines that are illustrated by classic cases. In part III, "External Relations," the focus shifts to relationships between the corporation and citizens, on the one hand, and relations between the corporation and society (often as represented by the state), that is, the corporation "between citizen and state."

This may seem to be a considerable amount of material, but to a business law professor (who spends a great deal of time thinking about these things), this is a very focused book. So a few words about this book's rather narrow scope of coverage may be useful and may also point readers who want to learn more in interesting directions. Most obviously, this book is an introduction and an overview, an account of certain ideas that hold "corporation law" together as a subdiscipline. Corporation law is a well-developed discourse, and there is much, much more to say. But sometimes, and often in teaching, saying less is more helpful. This book introduces a complex of ideas and makes no pretensions to providing a complete exposition of the law, nor even to digesting the reams of materials used to teach students.[1] Therefore, this book is quite short (like life).

Between Citizen and State is primarily concerned with the corporation, even though there are numerous forms of business association aside from the corporation, such as the partnership or the limited liability company. Indeed, basic texts and courses in corporation law are often called "Business Associations," to indicate that they treat forms of business association in addition to the corporation. On the other hand, most of the really large companies that dominate much of the business world, and certainly dominate the U.S. imagination of business and business law, are corporations. Corporations are in many ways the most advanced form of business association, and textbooks are often structured around a progression, from agency to partnership to corporation, that presents the corporation as the culmination of the logic of business associations.

This book is focused on U.S. law, even though, in an increasingly global economy, corporations, and hence corporation law (often called company law), from other countries may be quite important. For students of corporation law in the United States who wish to use this book as an overview, this focus is especially convenient. Despite years of calls for the internationalization of the curriculum, legal education in the United States remains firmly focused on domestic law. And although there are differences, a firm grounding in the laws of one jurisdiction makes it easier to learn the particularities of the laws of other jurisdictions. (Similarly, among state corporation laws, Delaware's laws are routinely printed in teaching materials, and lawyers tend to learn the corporation law of other states as practical need arises.) So, without denying the importance of studying other laws and other legal systems, this book postpones detailed comparison.

Precisely due to its emphasis on the corporation as understood in the United States, I hope this book will be of interest to citizens of other jurisdictions. Many U.S. companies operate multinationally, and U.S. corporation law is, like the U.S. economy more generally, influential elsewhere. Moreover, there is substantial evidence that corporation law within the United States, and worldwide, is converging on a consensus model, or ideal-type, of the corporation, essentially the shareholder-centered model familiar from the basic course.[2] Therefore, in focusing on the conception of the corporation in U.S. law schools, *Between Citizen and State* introduces an understanding of corporation law that is quite important on the global stage, even if hardly the whole story.

It needs to be said that this book is about corporation law *as it is generally taught*, which is not exactly the law in the world. This book is neither economics, nor history, nor sociology, nor some related discipline. This book does not try to answer the question of "how real" the law is at any given moment. Instead, this book is about the law as it is traditionally understood in U.S. law schools, the imagination of law that informs legal education, which, as practicing lawyers never tire of pointing out, is not the same thing as law in the "real world." The corporation law offered here is a specific idealization (what education is not an idealization?) of the legal questions surrounding corporate life. And as with any idealization, the representation of corporate life implicit in academic law is only partial, and, therefore, misleadingly flawed. Practicing lawyers have a point: what one doesn't learn in school is often quite important. But what one *does* learn in school can be important, too, so long as it is kept in perspective. At any rate, the idea of the corporation that law students are taught in law school is the topic of this book.

Finally, because this is an account of orthodox corporation law, this book is not comprised of my opinions, policy preferences, or the like, nor does the text make more than passing reference to current or historical disputes among law professors. This book is not about what the law should be (what I would do if I were made king, or, for my friends on the left, what I plan on doing, come The Revolution). A rather extensive bibliography has been included for those who wish to read more in the academic subfield of U.S. corporation law scholarship.

Method

This book presents law theatrically. In both theater and corporation law, different characters tend to act in familiar, if perhaps not precisely predictable, ways.[3] We understand what heroes and villains typically do, and that understanding allows us, relatively quickly, to understand what the play (or film, television show, or especially, cartoon) is about. Law can be learned in much the same way. Recent shenanigans at Enron, Adelphia, Worldcom, and numerous other companies illustrate that while people do interesting and often funny things inside companies, their actions are rarely truly surprising. Corporate actors have typical motivations and conflicts, and their conflicts tend to be resolved in customary ways. Corporate actors are, in short, stock characters, and their interactions tend to follow familiar plot lines.[4]

Part I, "Background," introduces the characters and their context. Part II, "Internal Struggles," explains some common conflicts in terms of frequently taught cases. Stepping outside the struggles among the actors, dramatic forms presume (and establish) certain broader social relationships. Consider by way of example a detective film that presumes that the state, through its police, may do certain things, that individuals act and are to be treated in certain ways (inevitably violated by the villain, sometimes by the state), and so forth. Similarly, corporation law presumes certain relationships among the company and parties outside of the company, including individuals, other institutions, and the state. This is the subject of part III, "External Relations."

Although students and other members of this commercial society, law students, and law professors can all learn from theatrical consideration of the law of corporations, such different readers do not learn the same things. For citizens in general, a dramatic understanding of the corporation helps to make some sense of civil society. For students of the law in particular, approaching corporations as theater not only makes basic doctrine easy to learn, but such an understanding also makes the tensions within and limitations of the law accessible. For professors, thinking about corporations as if they were plays yields insights into the significance of seemingly banal transactions and the inescapably conflicted nature of law (and therefore the tensions internal to legal scholarship), as well as into what should be rehearsed in class and what should be left for the improvisations of practice. To be more specific, let me address this book's intended readers in turn.

Citizens

For citizens generally, including college and graduate students in disciplines other than law and anyone else interested in policy (others are invited to skip this section), this book provides a straightforward account of the basics of corporation law as taught in U.S. law schools. The book addresses seemingly simple questions like "What is a shareholder?" and more complicated questions like "Why do we care about limited liability?" Such things are important for citizens in a commercial society to understand. At the same time, some readers may find this book overly narrow, and so a word about human questions left unaddressed might be appropriate.

It is true that corporations participate in virtually every aspect of life in the United States. Ordinary life—the hospitals in which we are born, the neighborhoods in which we grow up, our educations and work lives, entertainments and public participation, and in all likelihood the institutions that receive us at the end—would be unimaginable, in anything like their present form, without the institution of the corporation. In light of the importance of corporations to the fabric of our lives, one might think that corporation law deals with a broad range of questions. Actually, the scope of corporation law is surprisingly narrow. Although corporations play huge roles in the U.S. economy and, therefore, participate in almost every aspect of social life, most of what corporations do is not regulated by *corporation* law. Consider, in alphabetical order, antitrust, banking, bankruptcy, consumer protection, contract, discrimination, environmental regulation, government contracting, health and safety regulation, intellectual property, labor law, minimum wage laws, retirement benefits, securities law, taxation, tort, welfare, and zoning. Businesses are affected by all of these laws, and many others. Although such laws often control what a corporation does, they are not part of corporation law strictly construed. Corporation law is an ideal abstract framework that sets the stage and provides the *dramatis personae* (the characters) for the governance of corporations, but contemporary corporation law says very little of substance about the play.

Corporation law strictly construed is primarily concerned with three sorts of actors: shareholders, managers, and directors. Of course many different kinds of people participate in, or are affected by, the activity of a business, such as employees of all sorts, customers, suppliers, lenders, landlords, various service providers (including lawyers), the government that taxes and regulates, neighbors, competitors, and so forth. None of these, however, are actors in the drama of corporation law. It is often argued, mostly by academics, that these various actors, often called "stakeholders" because they have some stake in the affairs of the company, *should* be considered in corporation law. But as a matter of positive law, state corporation law statutes, courts deciding cases about corporation governance, and the overwhelming mass of teaching materials rarely concern themselves with stakeholders, and then only incidentally.

A storied law professor at Yale, the irrepressible Bayless Manning, famously wrote that corporation law was a structure of "empty girders," that is, a framework with no content.[5] Slightly more charitably, we might say that corporation law is perhaps the most formal area of U.S. law. Corporation law is a structure for doing business and little more, a triumph of process over substance. Rather artificially, corporation law has become defined as the law pertaining to the formation, governance, and dissolution of the form as a legal entity. What the corporation may or may not do in the conduct of its business (Does this manufacturing process pollute too much? Is this workplace too unsafe?) is not a matter of the *form* that is the corporation. Such questions have been exiled to other areas of the law and other classes in law schools.

The fact that corporation law is, from a substantive policy perspective, perhaps the most meaningless area of the law, however, does not mean it is without legal interest. As in theater (or basketball), even a few players with well-defined roles operating in a restricted space can play fascinating games of endless subtlety and variation. Shareholders, managers, and directors have different motivations, in both theory and practice, and so conflict among them is to be expected. It is natural, and not entirely wrong, to think of such conflict in personal terms, as conflict among those called shareholders, those called managers, and those titled directors. But the situation is more complicated than that. Shareholders, managers, and directors are legal categories, not proper names. Individual people often fill more than one role. For example, the chief executive officer (CEO) of a company, the leading manager, commonly is also the chairman of the board of directors and a major shareholder. More generally, top managers are almost always directors and shareholders. Founders and other leading shareholders tend to make themselves directors. Conflicts abound. Such conflicts are of immense personal interest to the players, and by extension, to their lawyers.

At a deeper level, one might say that the reason corporation law is so uninteresting, from a policy perspective, is that corporation law has been so successful. Corporation law establishes legal entities, and *such legal entities are generally treated as if they were people.* Thus, if a legislature is concerned about the environment, they need not enact a law that says "corporations cannot [list]." Instead, the legislature is free to write, "No person may [list]" and "person" is understood to include corporations and other forms of business association as well as natural persons. Rephrased, because corporations have been successfully normalized, there is little by way of a distinct legal regime for the regulation of their activities. Much like an individual, a corporation:

may obligate itself in contract;
may be liable in tort;
may be a party to a lawsuit, as either plaintiff or defendant;
may own property, including real estate, securities, and intellectual property;
is taxed (although at a different rate than individuals);
may make charitable donations;
may be regulated;
may petition government.

Perhaps more surprisingly, a corporation:

may be held criminally liable; and
has a right to free expression.

One should be careful not to take this point too far. Corporations are not people, whatever the editorial page of the *Wall Street Journal* might have you believe. Even in the United States, the legal personality of corporations remains different from that of natural persons. A corporation may *not*:

vote or contribute directly to a candidate;
get married; or
serve in the military.

And in countless practical ways, the fact that a corporation has no physical body (cutely enough, the corporation is incorporeal) means that corporations will act and will be treated differently from natural persons. But the critical point for many legal purposes is that a corporation, just like a human, is both a legal subject and an object of the laws. A plaintiff, defendant, party to the contract, tortfeasor, guarantor, and any number of other legal roles may be played either by corporations or by natural persons.

Although corporations may play many of the same legal roles as natural persons, they are not natural persons. Like a play or a game or a market, a corporation often should be understood as an interaction among distinct roles, most notably, the shareholder, manager, and director. To continue our theater metaphor, the lines of various actors are not unrelated. Each line makes sense in the context of the other lines of the play. Similarly, the acts of various players on the corporate stage become "corporate" in their relation to what the other actors do. Each role within the corporation presumes the others. To be a manager or a director presumes a corporation with at least one shareholder, because managers and directors owe fiduciary duties to the corporation and its shareholder(s). Conversely, to be a shareholder, someone who owns but does not run the company, presumes the existence of managers and directors who run the company. Thus, the act of incorporation distinguishes among the business functions of ownership (shareholders), management (managers), and oversight or direction (directors), and reintegrates those functions within a single legal construct, which *as a whole* comprises a legal person. Thus, corporation law does not dictate what corporations do, but instead coordinates the disparate roles to form some sort of whole that the law recognizes as a person and that, therefore, can act in society.

It would be implausible to claim that corporation law's lack of content, its formality, has no political consequences whatsoever. Lawyers tend to believe that form matters, that at some level, process is substance. Much of institutional life in the United States would be unimaginable without corporation law. Corporation law must, then, somehow be politically important, and we have returned to the question with which this section began: how important is corporation law? From this perspective, one's feelings about the corporation as a form of business organization are bound up with one's feelings about social life in America, which has been so influenced by corporations. As a mere introduction, this book takes no particular stand on the social significance of corporation law in the United States, on "what does any of this have to do with our [collective] happiness?" Addressing this question in reasonably sophisticated fashion requires familiarity with that peculiarly modern view of the world we may call financial, or even capitalist, an education that this little book only begins.

Law Students

For law students and anyone else interested in practice (others are invited to skip this section), this book provides a "forest for the trees" overview of the basic course in corporations. Most basic courses are taught through giant textbooks of "cases and materials"—many trees, little forest. Indeed, training students simply to read over and somehow to manage such masses of text is an important aspect of legal education, but oftentimes comes at the cost of much understanding. It is true that various hornbooks and study guides provide digested versions of the basic materials and some guidance on separating the important cases and ideas from less important factoids, incidental cases, and the like. Still, such digests are by their nature derivative, shortcuts to learning a mass of material, rather than a way of thinking about and organizing the material. What this book offers, in contrast, is a self-contained presentation of a traditional way to understand corporation law as a fairly reasonable, if not entirely consistent, intellectual whole.

Particularly for readers who will become lawyers, it again must be stressed that this book is about the ideas basic to corporation law as taught in the law school, which is *not* the same thing as corporation law in practice. Two stories might be helpful in beginning to think about the relationships between learning to be a lawyer (in law school) and actually being a lawyer (after graduating and passing the bar), and hence making some sense out of what is taught and what will have to be learned in due course.

First story, true, happened to a good friend of mine: as a very new and therefore rather bold associate at a major Wall Street law firm, at a training lunch for the corporate group, she asked a bunch of senior lawyers whether they had taken corporate finance in law school. Only half said they had. Not having taken corporate finance herself (and finding herself doing private equity deals and some project finance), she asked what they had done in that class, and they said, "Talk about the efficient capital markets hypothesis."[6] So she asked whether that had anything to do with what they or she were doing now, and they said no, of course not. Since I left practice, of course, I too have taught the efficient capital markets hypothesis and a lot of other financial theory. All of this is great fun, but I have to keep reminding myself that this is what I've done *after* leaving practice, not the bulk of what I did *when* I was a lawyer.

The most obvious point of this story is that what interests legal academics can be quite different from what lawyers actually do. This does not mean, however, that academics should simply teach what lawyers actually do: being a student is not, and can never be, the same as being in practice. Of course law schools should work hard to give students a more realistic understanding of corporate practice and some of the skills that might be useful, but truly lawyers have responsibilities that students do not. Moreover, university study has purposes that are different from the purposes of law firms, government organs (including courts), nonprofit service organizations, and other institutions in which the overwhelming majority of law students eventually go to work. Practical training is important, but it is not the only important thing. By way of an analogy, almost all law students take constitutional law, but not many are expected to litigate constitutional questions. So the deeper question raised by this story is what sort of picture of the world should corporation law *professors* try to give *students* who will one day be *practitioners*?

A simple way to start with this question would be to ask what corporate lawyers do. It has been argued that corporate lawyers are "transactional engineers" who help clients lower the cost of their business plans, particularly strategic objectives such as major acquisitions.[7] The problem with this view is that law is not simply a cost, which may be reduced, even eliminated. Law is always already intrinsic to the problem of collective action. Complicated transactions require lawyers, or more precisely, the enforceable manipulation of complex texts. Whether one wishes to call the people who accomplish such functions "lawyers" is beside the point; the point is that complexity is not external to the business transaction. The documentary work of a major transaction is not some sort of superstructure, but rather it is intrinsic to the transaction, just as architectural designs and blueprints are needed for building a large building. Such textual complexity is a big part of what it means to be in an information economy, part of what it means to understand the corporation as a bureaucracy and its agents, including lawyers, as bureaucrats.

There is, of course, a simpler picture of what corporate lawyers do. It is also often argued that corporate lawyers are merely exploitative, or worse, actually oppressive.[8] Here, too, the character of law is misconceived. Law—particularly the judgments and settlements that litigation produces—determines social life from within realms of conflict, that is, amid contradictory but compelling claims. Precisely because compelling claims are required, law is not simply an instrument of oppression. The truly oppressed have no lawyers. I can also report from personal experience that very few students come to law school intending to be instruments of oppression. And despite the horrible things said about law school, some of them actually true, very few law students leave law school as oppressors.

So what do corporate lawyers do? Another story: once upon a time when I was a lawyer, there was a fairly well-known Delaware corporation with a complicated voting structure designed to meet certain requirements of federal law that such businesses be controlled by U.S. citizens. As you might imagine, what constituted "control" or even "U.S. citizen" was not completely obvious, and there were financial rewards for answering such questions in some ways rather than others, which is where the law firm with which I was then associated came into the picture. Things were working out pretty much to everyone's satisfaction, until one day the founder of the company, who held enormous blocks of stock, died in an airplane crash. Actually, this was the second crash in which he supposedly died—he had disappeared once before—but this time, he was really dead. At his death, much of the stock he controlled was supposed to revert to the company. But, to complicate matters, upon his death many children across the Pacific claimed to be his, some with substantial plausibility. Our problems were that it was unclear whether various blocks of stock could be voted, and if so, by whom, and since those things were unsettled, it was uncertain who, exactly, controlled the board of directors and hence the company. Suffice it to say that a very nasty negotiation ensued, as various members of the board declared that for one reason or another stock could or could not be voted, and therefore one or another of the members of the board was or was not in fact on the board. Somewhere in the midst of this mêlée I was sent by the senior partner with whom I was working to talk to the head of the corporate group, a lawyer with an awe-inspiring reputation. I explained the situation as clearly as I was able, and after a few probing questions, he sat back, looked at me thoughtfully, and said, "Well, it looks like we need corporate counsel."

This, of course, sent me into an existential crisis. I had been working very hard to give the impression that *we* were the corporate counsel. But when I thought about it, I realized that what we actually did, most of the time, was negotiate contracts, deals, and we helped our clients navigate the regulatory coral reef that is so much of modern business life. But this problem was different. This was corporation law as corporate governance, that is, in the sense it is used in the basic class on corporations, and indeed in the sense of much of this book. The question before us was classic: how can board members be elected? Answering this basic question, in this case, turned on a technical and quite uncertain question of how the Delaware courts were likely to decide whether certain stock could be voted, and if so, by whom.

But this was the exception that proved the rule, such an exception that we hired a boutique firm that specialized in guessing what Delaware courts were likely to do in a given situation. Except for such firms, however, few legal practices are concerned with the questions that concern the basic class in corporation law (i.e., how to establish and manage the relationships fundamental to the corporation). Instead, most corporate law practices assume that its lawyers understand such relationships in a general way and expect their lawyers to use that knowledge in order to help clients establish more specific relationships and accomplish particular business objectives. In doing transactional work, corporate lawyers produce detailed scripts for relationships, but work from familiar models. The basic course in corporation law is thus a prelude for corporate practice. The basic course makes students *ready* to be corporate lawyers, but it is not about practice itself.

In different words, the basic course in corporations is a process of acculturation. The issues that arise in a corporation's operation, whether managed through good transactional work or resolved through litigation, produce understandings, usually formalized as texts. These understandings collectively form much of the terrain on which business relations are played out. The basic course in corporations teaches these shared understandings and thereby makes it possible to work with the legal texts that modern business life requires. Not just anyone can read a commercial contract. This is what is meant by the hoary old phrase "learning to think like a lawyer," or the somewhat gentler idea that the law is a language.

Let me be clear: in saying that law school is a process of acculturation, not transmission, I am also claiming that law schools rarely and only accidentally teach "the law" in any *immediately* authoritative sense. We only occasionally and incidentally teach the positive law that controls a situation. (For litigators: "I learned back in law school that the rule is ..." is not an argument that a judge is likely to find compelling.) Law professors do not know where their students are going to practice; do not know the extent to which today's law will be the law tomorrow; do not know the similarity between the facts of the case under discussion and the facts of some case that has not yet arisen, elsewhere. Law professors cannot teach the details that are expected of a practitioner with a particular problem for the simple reason that professors cannot know what specific problems their students will confront when they become lawyers. Instead, professors teach cultural understandings. It is true that such understandings are contained in, expressed, and even sometimes formed by legal acts, and such legal acts occur in some setting—they are "the facts" of the case. But such legal acts, and such "facts," are, within the ivory tower, essentially examples, illustrative, heuristic—not binding—and therefore, in a real sense, not law. Basic business associations textbooks teach the case law from various jurisdictions at various times, and even model acts like the Model Business Corporation Act, rather than the positive law of any jurisdiction, although Delaware receives special attention. But the lawyer who needs to know what Delaware law applies to his or her client better not rely on the memory of a class.

How to handle oneself as a legal professional—what it means to think, read, write, and generally understand the world and act like a contemporary U.S. lawyer—is what law school tries to teach. Legal education inevitably involves the transmittal of knowledge (learning some law, one might call it), and black letter law is fairly easy to test (which is convenient), but those are means to ends. What law schools really do is inculcate, edify, train—legal education is a form of cultural education. Legal education is so profoundly orthodox and, therefore, appropriately understood in theatrical terms precisely because it is cultural education. The purpose of this book is to put this insight into the nature of legal education to use, and I use theatrical modes of thinking to make the learning of one aspect of the orthodoxy, corporation law, easier.

Law Professors

For law professors and anyone else interested in academic theory (others are invited to skip this section), although the substantive terrain covered is familiar, indeed relentlessly traditional, this book willfully violates conventional academic expectations in numerous ways. A few fairly candid words (not too many, and not completely candid, of course) on why it might be interesting.

There is nothing new here, certainly no new paradigm. This book seeks to explain the orthodox understanding of corporation law as taught in the United States, the collective imaginations that the classic cases and especially doctrinal statements presume, embody, and inculcate. This book is neither analysis nor advocacy, but instead a presentation of what the profession commits itself to when teaching. Statements of shared belief, what the theologians call creeds, are by definition not new in substance. Yet a straightforward (as opposed to "critical") presentation of legal education as an orthodoxy is rather unusual in the U.S. legal academy. For starters, teaching in U.S. law schools has been particularistic and inductive (based on "cases and materials"), and professors present their scholarship as original contributions—neither teaching nor scholarship occasion acknowledgment, much less articulation, of law as orthodoxy. Failure to articulate the orthodoxy matters little among professors who have internalized it, nor does it matter for law students, who can be taught through immersion. An articulated orthodoxy is useful, however, for talking to other intellectuals, or even the broader public, should one care to have such conversations.

The rich materials of the social sciences, including the contributions of sociology, history, and especially economics, to our understanding of the corporation, have been largely ignored. Although perhaps written out of a "social" sensibility, this book is not an exercise in law and society scholarship. Neither the operation of law in society nor the "gap" between law on the books and law in action is discussed. By the same token, this book should not be read as history or economics. The book is simply agnostic about the relationships among the foci of the basic course, the actual operation of corporation laws, and the business world.

The relationship between "law" and "social reality"—whatever those terms might mean—is a perennially vexed topic. There have been calls for law to become a social science at least since the late nineteenth century, when Holmes invoked the "man of statistics," but tomorrow never comes. I personally tend to think that there is very little principled connection between the forms of corporation law, at least as understood in academic scholarship, and the particularities of social life in general. At any rate, I have been unable to discern any such structural connection. Sometimes law matters more, and often matters less, to social reality (and hence our evaluation of whether the law is good)—it depends. Were I to discern any principled or general connection between law (or any law) and social life, however, it would constitute a major finding to be set forth and defended in an altogether different kind of book, and not one addressed to students or prospective lawyers.

Moreover, orthodoxy—ideology—is always somewhat independent of its world. Discussions of democracy, justice, or indeed corporation law are not immediately vitiated by the world's failure to embody our abstractions. Legal education is by definition a somewhat abstracted enterprise, taking place as it does within the protected space of the university, about the world as imagined outside. All this book attempts to achieve is a clear statement of a regnant imagination. Indeed, as an articulation of not insignificant social practices and sets of meanings, this book may serve as an artifact upon which the tools of various social sciences may be deployed.

The book seems to take no theoretical stance at all. Again, this book presents the orthodox imagination taught by the professoriate. It does not engage at the level of explicit argument (what law professors argue in articles), but at the level of action, teaching. Consequently, the materials discussed herein are "relentlessly traditional," that is, the book is based on standard materials in basic textbooks, chestnuts, familiar (even hackneyed) arguments. This is a report on how corporation law is taught. This is why the book only uses basic cases, why the coverage is so narrow, ignoring rich materials of other disciplines, why I have not elaborated my own "theory" of "the" corporation, nor even joined up with any of the obvious factions in these fascinating debates. For present purposes, my thinking is irrelevant, and I have suppressed it to the best of my ability. After all, what I think is not what is taught, and certainly what I think is not the law.

The book is not normative; there is no politics here. There is no public policy in the book, except occasionally by accident. The book does not advocate that corporation law ought to be changed to do X. This is admittedly odd, because most legal scholarship is intensely normative. Legal scholars argue from a relatively coherent set of ideas (a theory), which ideas are said to compel (at least among right thinking folks) a determinate course of action. That is, the vast majority of legal scholarship, whether written from the right, often in the language of law and economics, or the "progressive" language in which the left expresses itself, aspires to a practical politics that flows from an intellectual stance.[9] Indeed, texts that do not take a normative stance tend to be viewed within the legal academy as incomplete, irresponsible, or even an accommodation to this intolerable world.

This book, however, has different intentions and, therefore, is written differently. *Between Citizen and State* presents a general and explicit account of the orthodoxy that often implicitly organizes most corporation law teaching and scholarship. This book is written in the hope that gaining an objective understanding of this orthodoxy is worth the while of various readers. The extent to which a reader professionally or even personally subscribes to this orthodoxy, much less tries to change it, is his or her own business.

Part I

Background

Chapter 1

Stock Characters and Ordinary Scripts

Characters

As in many dramatic genres, the principal actors in a corporation tend to be easily recognizable characters who do familiar things for
common motivations. Corporation law is constructed around three basic
characters, namely shareholders, directors, and managers, who are expected
to play certain roles. Traditionally, the three principal roles these actors
play are:

> *Shareholders* own the company. They invest money (or sometimes other assets,
> such as their labor) into the company. In return for their investment, shareholders
> receive ownership interests in the company, called "shares," or "stock," or some-
> times "equity." Shareholders, as such, do not run the company, but participate
> in the governance of the corporation in a number of legally defined ways. Most
> importantly, shareholders elect directors. Shareholders generally expect to make
> money from their investment.

Directors direct. They are concerned with the company's business strategy. Directors must agree to major corporate decisions. Directors oversee, and may hire and fire, the managers. Like managers, directors are supposed to work for the benefit of the corporation and its shareholders.

Managers are employed by the company to run the day-to-day operations of the business. Managers are supposed to work for the benefit, and under the ultimate control, of the corporation and its shareholders, usually as determined by the directors.

In the very traditional understanding that this book teaches (albeit in an untraditional way), corporation law establishes a formal structure for the governance of a business. It is important to remember that this structure bears only a limited relation to business life. The question of whether this formal structure can be maintained in an often messy real world underlies much of what is interesting in corporate law. Will people mind their manners, play their appointed roles? Or will they be tempted to do something else?

What are the motivations of our three main characters?

Shareholders expect to make money from their investments; shareholders often are said to be "rationally self-interested." To that end, one might think that shareholders will keep tabs on "their" company, monitor the performance of managers, understand the company's business, and exercise their rights as shareholders (most importantly, vote for directors) in order to ensure that the company is well run. But shareholders are widely understood to be unwilling or simply unable to evaluate the business. For a small and relatively powerless shareholder, getting involved may be a waste of effort. Many shareholders (including the author) tend toward apathy, laziness, and incomprehension. After all, at least some shareholders hope to make money, in a famous phrase, "solely from the efforts of others," that is, simply because they have invested wisely.[1] In fact, most shareholders do not participate in the governance of the company in any meaningful way. Although this passivity may be rationally self-interested as a matter of individual psychology (a matter best left out of corporation law), passivity is neither rational nor interested as a matter of corporate governance.

The common understanding of "the shareholder" is thus somewhat inconsistent or at least embraces very different kinds of people. On the one hand, judicial and academic corporation law frameworks assume that the passive investor is a fair description of most actual shareholders. On the other, although courts expect shareholders to have little knowledge about or power over the affairs of "their" corporation, they also expect shareholders to act in their own economic self-interest, or at least so courts say.

Desires for active involvement and laziness, however, are not the only motivations found in corporation law cases, nor the only motivations found in actual humans who play roles in the governance of corporations. *Managers* are expected to lead, to make things happen, for the benefit of the corporation and its investors, the shareholders. Doctrinally phrased, the law requires managers to be fiduciaries, to hold positions of trust, in which managers are required to place the interests of others before their own self-interest. In acting for the benefit of and (nominally) under the control of another, managers are often called agents. However, the idea of the agent—the older, more honest word is "servant"—hardly fits with the common and not incorrect image of the business leader. As noted above, business leaders are often presumed to be strong willed, ambitious, perhaps even autocratic—hardly servants. If managers who are supposed to be leaders, on the one hand, are also required to be servants, on the other hand, then corporation law would seem to breed conflict. And as a matter of fact, business history and litigation are filled with stories of managers who succumb to the temptation to gratify their own interests. (This cannot be surprising. Laws often are intended to thwart some desire, but frequently, the desire wins.) Rephrased more heroically, many managers refuse to be servants and therefore use their control of the corporation to benefit themselves. Thus, from the perspective of traditional corporation law, the self-interest of managers is quite different from the self-interest of investors. The self-interest of managers is likely to be a bad thing, a betrayal of and a rebellion against their obligations to serve the corporation and its shareholders.

But this, of course, is overly dramatic. In fact, the conflict between the manager as fiduciary and as self-interested economic actor is to some degree universal. Surely one cannot imagine a business leader who had no ambition, no self-interest. Thus, the question for the law is drawing the line between acceptable and unacceptable self-interest in the context of a manager who is required to look out for the interests of the corporation and its shareholders. How far is too far? For a simple example, we expect a chief financial officer (CFO) to be paid, and often handsomely. We do not expect a CFO to construct opaque transactions between his or her company and entities under the CFO's control, funneling millions of the company's dollars into his or her own pocket, as Andrew Fastow did at Enron.[2]

Managers' ambition, their desire to exercise and maintain their power, can be phrased in relatively rational language: managers have a stake in being managers in addition to their easily quantifiable economic interests. So one might say that managers, like shareholders, are rationally self-interested, thereby obscuring the differences in motivation among the actors. (It would be rather empty to claim that every actor has a rational interest in doing whatever it is he or she wants to do.) The rationality of shareholders is different from that of managers and directors in terms of corporation law because they lead to different actions and different ways of running the business. For example, managers tend to resist takeovers, long after it ceases to be in the economic interest of shareholders to do so.[3]

And there is no reason to presume economic rationality among either shareholders or managers; there is massive evidence to the contrary.[4] Indeed, as a psychological matter, many managers should be understood more like celebrities than accountants or insurance actuaries: many managers are not particularly rational, and their successes are socially rather than individualistically defined. Throughout business history, flamboyant managers have caused "their" corporations to engage in risky, often ostentatious, activities. Such managers frequently bring their companies and themselves to the edge, and sometimes over the edge, of bankruptcy. The very language of high-level business is deeply political, social, even military. Consider the phrases robber baron, tycoon, captain of industry, master of the universe, big swinging dick. Less dramatically, it is quite common for a chief executive officer (CEO) to engage in "empire building," to urge that his or her company buy another company, thereby making the CEO the manager of a larger (often deeply indebted) enterprise. This happens all the time, even though it is widely known that a minority of mergers are economically successful. Such empires frequently have to be unwound later, as they prove to be, well, unmanageable.

Turning to *directors*, we find that their motivations are conflicted, too. The law requires directors to oversee the corporation, and especially the activities of managers, in the interest of the corporation and its shareholders. Directors are supposed to set a long-term strategy for the business, which usually means agreeing to management's ideas about what the long-term strategy should be. More to the point, directors are supposed to monitor the performance of managers, set their salaries, and fire them when necessary. This may be difficult because directors are often chosen by management. In fulfilling their duties to the corporation and its shareholders, directors, like managers, are expected to be loyal to the company, and careful. Directors are supposed to be respectable, worthy, perhaps a little boring.

If the weakness of shareholders is understood to be sheep-like helplessness in the face of more energetic forces, and the temptation of managers results from their ability to misuse their power over the company, then the temptation of directors boils down to comfort. Directors often desire to preserve their privileged (and sometimes well paying) positions, hope to get along with their colleagues (who were instrumental in their appointment), and prefer not to work too hard or to make unnecessary waves. And who would want membership on a company's board of directors to interfere with other aspects of life? Certainly being a director should not entail much sacrifice, except perhaps a little time, and by all accounts should not require one to give up a business opportunity—or so one might hope.

We thus have a menu of quite inconsistent motivations typically found in corporation law or in the lives of corporate actors, including sturdy self-reliance and involvement (associated with shareholders); helplessness (also shareholders); the obligation to run the company on behalf of others (required of managers); the temptation to abuse their power over the company (feared of managers); the obligation to oversee the company, make sure its affairs are in order, on behalf of the corporation and its shareholders (hoped from directors); and the desire to fall into a prestigious lethargy (cynically expected of directors). This list of motivations is merely by way of introduction and is none too precise. Obviously the abuse of power by managers, or the desire for comfort that directors sometimes display, could describe a range of particular impulses or behaviors. Even the desire for wealth maximization is more complicated than it looks—different kinds of investors need to be paid in different ways (to foreshadow: creating documents that structure deals so different investors will be paid in different ways is enormously complicated, and lucrative, work for lawyers).

Setting the Stage

As with television, when we focus on the activities of a corporation we usually find that the show has already begun. And if we change the channel, or turn the pages in the financial press, we find that much the same is happening elsewhere. How are such productions started? How are corporations made? There are numerous variations, most of which are slight, but in general, corporations are formed as follows.

Corporations are creatures of state law.[5] All states have a corporation law statute. The most influential is Delaware's General Corporation Law. In addition, the Committee on Corporate Laws of the American Bar Association has promulgated a Model Business Corporation Act (MBCA), which is not itself law, but which has been used by many states as a model for drafting legislation.

Corporation law statutes set forth the requirements for establishing a corporation in that state. A person or persons (called the "incorporator") files documents with the state that (1) ask for permission to use the corporate form to do business, and (2) provide the information required by the statute, and the incorporator (3) pays a modest filing fee. The incorporator is often a young lawyer or paralegal at the firm hired by the businessperson establishing the company. Filings are usually made with the office of the Secretary of State.

The heart of a filing is the "articles of incorporation" of the proposed corporation. (Sometimes the articles are called the "charter," or the "certificate of incorporation.") The articles are the basic rules under which the incorporator proposes the corporation will do business. By way of analogy, one may think of the articles of incorporation as somewhat like a constitution for the company. Articles of incorporation are required by law to include basic information about the company. Some of these items may be mystifying at this juncture; much is discussed later in the book. And again, this is a generalization—there are variations and some additional requirements from state to state. Those things said, the articles of incorporation include:

- the name of the corporation. The name must not cause confusion with an existing firm, and the name must indicate that this corporation is a corporation;
- the names and addresses of the incorporators;
- the number of directors, and sometimes the names and addresses of the initial directors of the corporation;
- the "registered office" and "registered agent" of the corporation (i.e., where it can be served papers and the like, important for taxing or suing);
- the purpose for which the corporation is being established (generally, some version of "any lawful purpose");
- the duration of the corporation's existence (generally, "perpetual");
- the basic capital structure of the corporation, including the number of shares authorized and the rights and preferences of each share.

As one would expect from a constitution, the articles of incorporation also establish, with varying degrees of specificity, how the enterprise is to govern itself. Many states allow the articles of incorporation a sort of choice of law: should the business be governed by specifically drafted "custom" rules or by "off the shelf" rules of state law?[6] The articles may also set forth specific rules and constraints for the conduct of the business going forward. As with a constitution, however, the provisions of the articles of incorporation are procedurally difficult to change. Consequently, the modern practice is to make the articles short and very general. Specific understandings of how the business is to be conducted are made in an additional set of rules called the bylaws, which usually can be changed relatively easily, often by a simple majority vote of the board of directors.

Assuming that the articles of incorporation comply with the requirements of state law, state governments routinely accept filings for incorporation. The state must indicate to the incorporators, and to the public, that it has accepted the articles of incorporation. Some states issue a traditional "charter" or "certificate of incorporation," in either case incorporating the articles. Some states simply make a notation on the copy of the articles returned to the incorporators and issue a receipt for the filing fee. The particular formalities do not matter; the important point is that the state acknowledges acceptance of the proposed structure for doing business. Also, once the state has accepted the articles of incorporation, the articles of incorporation become a public document.

Once the incorporator receives the certificate back from the state government, he or she calls a meeting of the initial directors (in some states, the incorporators). The purpose of the meeting is to begin governing the business as a corporation. More specifically, at initial meetings, corporations elect directors if this has not been done; adopt the bylaws; issue stock and accept contracts relating to stock; make initial resolutions regarding the company's operations, and begin ordinary governance of the company. In order to accomplish this, the incorporator (or a lawyer hired by the company, if a lawyer is not serving as incorporator) typically obtains or drafts the following sorts of documents prior to the initial meeting.

The *bylaws* are the rules by which the corporation governs itself. Bylaws are not generally a matter of public record, although the bylaws may contain the articles of incorporation, and even laws, documents that are in the public domain. The bylaws are a sort of binding guidebook for the directors, who must abide by the company's bylaws for their actions to be official, that is, actions of the corporation. Therefore, the directors consult (or should consult) the bylaws for guidance on how to go about their business.

Especially in small companies, investors receive *stock certificates* (often printed on special paper that cannot be easily copied or altered, much like the paper on which currency is printed) that indicate the investor's share of ownership in the company. Stock, as already mentioned, carries with it the right to vote on placement of directors and certain other important matters. At the initial meeting, directors often issue stock to investors. Moreover, at the initial meeting both the company and shareholders may make agreements relating to the purchase, sale, or voting of stock. Such agreements are drafted in advance.

Corporations take specific important decisions by *resolution* of the board of directors. Examples of such decisions at an initial meeting might include hiring of a CEO, instructing him or her to proceed with transactions such as the lease of office space, authorizing the opening of bank accounts, and the like. Such resolutions are also typically negotiated and drafted in advance.

Finally, the incorporator usually drafts the *minutes* of the first meeting (i.e., the record of a meeting that has not happened yet). At no point is the scripted character of corporate governance more obvious. Corporate actions are proper (and legally binding on the corporation) only if they are done according to certain procedures. For example, if a decision requires a vote by the board of directors, then the directors must so vote, and they must do so in an acceptable way. Failure to have such a vote means that the decision has not been authorized by the corporation. Because the propriety of corporate actions depends on the fact that proper procedures were followed, then corporations must keep a record of what was done, of the fact that procedures were followed. This insistence on maintaining a record of procedure is why companies must maintain minutes of board meetings, and more generally, keep *books and records.* (For the same reason, board meetings traditionally begin by voting to accept the minutes of the last meeting, thereby creating a chain of procedural propriety.) At the initial meeting, however, there is no prior corporate action. Thus, minutes are drawn up of the current meeting, which are treated as an agenda, that is, a script. And having voted to accept the items in the script, the enterprise is now being managed in an official, business-like way, that is, the business is now functioning as a corporation. In fact, the business is a corporation.[7] Corporations—even small startup corporations—thus exist as legal entities distinct from their owners, and indeed, distinct from their personnel.

Genre (the Corporation as a Legal Entity)

The notion of the corporation as an entity is so engrained in U.S. culture that it often passes unremarked. But imagine a large corporation, call it "Largeco," and further imagine owning, perhaps in a retirement account, some shares in this company. The following points probably seem like common sense, but are worth articulating.

1. You would assume that Largeco would buy things, own property, hire people, make various financial arrangements—you would expect, in short, that Largeco has the *legal powers* necessary to do business. Corporations are legal persons. They can contract, sue and be sued, and so forth.

2. You would expect Largeco to make business decisions without asking you or the other shareholders. Corporations have *centralized management,* instead of being managed by their owners.

3. Since Largeco runs its affairs without your involvement, you would expect Largeco to be responsible for its liabilities. Specifically, you are likely to assume that Largeco will pay for its contractual obligations, for harms it might cause, for its obligations to the government, and the like. If Largeco fails to do so, you would not expect to be sued for the unpaid obligation. This is called the *limited liability* of shareholders.

4. You would probably assume that, if you needed the money (say, for retirement or some emergency) or even if you just found a better investment, you could sell your stock in Largeco. You would not need Largeco's permission to transfer your shares (they are, after all, your shares) in the business. In the jargon, shareholders in a corporation, absent special circumstances, are assumed to have *freely transferable interests,* which means that they can buy and sell their shares without restriction.

5. Assuming that Largeco is a well-established institution, you would expect that, absent a disaster of some sort, the company would continue to exist. If we look at the shareholders of Largeco as a group, then we see that the company's shares are constantly being bought and sold. Largeco, however, remains the same company, even though its shareholders—its owners—are constantly changing. Moreover, recall that owners vote for directors, directors hire and fire senior managers, senior managers hire and fire junior employees. All of this happens continually, over time. Thus, just as Hamlet is Hamlet regardless of which actors play the roles, Largeco remains Largeco even if all the individuals involved change. Corporations are assumed to have *continuity of existence.*

6. If continuity of existence means that people can come and go, even die, without changing the character of the corporation, then there is no biological limit on the "life" of the corporation. In principle, the corporation has *perpetual duration.* In the real world, a particular corporation may cease to exist in all sorts of ways: it may be wound up by its owners when the business ceases to be profitable; it may be dissolved or taken over by creditors in bankruptcy; or the business may be bought by another

business and cease its separate existence, in a merger or other acquisition. But nothing about the corporation per se requires the entity to cease existence.

One more point may be slightly less obvious. The basic law school course, and so this book, focuses on relationships within the corporation, among shareholders, directors, and managers. There is a tendency, if one is engrossed in a movie, to forget that one is watching a movie. Most drama is intended to make the audience forget the stage. We see "the hero," not "an actor whose job it is to play the hero." Although I have no illusions that the matters covered by this book are that interesting, the book's focus on the characters (shareholders, directors, managers) may induce forgetfulness of the context, the corporation itself. That would be a mistake. It is important to remember that shareholders, directors, and managers do not exist in isolation; one is a shareholder, director, or manager *in a corporation*. The corporation is no more dispensable to understanding the relationships of the people in the company than the production company of a movie is dispensable for understanding who plays what role in a film. Or, to shift the analogy slightly, it makes no more sense to understand shareholders, directors, and managers without corporations than it does to understand soldiers without the army, priests without the church, or for that matter, professors without the university.

* * *

Perhaps unsurprisingly in light of their structural similarity, both drama and corporation law can be understood in similar ways. In both contexts, we need to be able to think through the characteristics, motivations, and the relative situations of the different actors. We need to consider the dynamic tensions among them: what does this or that person (or institution) want? Or need? What constitutes a win, or a failure? If we pull back from the action a bit, we can think about broader questions, the social context in which the action takes place, the history that shapes the action, the ideals or values that, not only motivate the actors, but that allow us to judge their actions. People from all walks of life, media savvy as they are, engage in this sort of (usually subconscious) analysis whenever they watch television, see a film, or otherwise enjoy a dramatic entertainment. Without such analysis, even a simple movie would be incomprehensible. The same sort of multifaceted, dynamic analysis makes sense for understanding the business corporation. Indeed business folk, including lawyers, unselfconsciously think like this every working day.

Chapter 2

Why Corporation Law Matters

Competing Visions of Collective Action

AT THE BEGINNING OF THE TWENTIETH CENTURY, SOMETIMES CALLED THE progressive era, the modern business corporation was viewed by some people as a key instrument of progress, and especially of industrialization. In 1911, president of Columbia University Nicholas Murray Butler famously remarked that "I weigh my words when I say that in my judgment the limited liability corporation is the greatest single discovery of modern times.... Even steam and electricity are far less important than the limited liability corporation, and they would be reduced to comparative impotence without it."[1] Corporations, and the far-flung coordination of activities that they permit, have become so ubiquitous that it is difficult to recover the excitement then felt for the relatively new institutional possibilities of working together. An analogy perhaps useful today might be the excitement felt by many people at the possibilities of working at a distance enabled by mobile phones, videoconferencing, email, and similar advances in communication.

In the nineteenth century and since, the business corporation has also been reviled as an instrument of oppression that benefited the owners of corporations, the capitalist class. Although full-blown Marxist analysis has become somewhat unfashionable, many people remain suspicious of corporate greed, in politics and in social life more generally. For a present-day analogy to the late nineteenth-century suspicion of corporations, consider the suspicions of corporate activity conducted internationally, discussed and often protested under the heading "globalization." Indeed the contemporary U.S. corporation still has its critics, and of course its defenders, among scholars.[2]

Why all this excitement, both pro and con, over the corporation? To be very general: incorporation provides an institutional mechanism that can collect, organize, and focus the energies of many people. The corporation is a way of working together. Consider a very simple example: a motorist buys fuel at a local gas station—how many thousands of people, spread out over the globe, worked together to deliver the fuel? In a capitalist economy the delivery of gasoline is generally understood to be a function of markets, which is not untrue. One pays for fuel. At the same time, most of the myriad tasks entailed by the exploration, recovery, distillation, and delivery of fuel are not accomplished by people working together on the basis of arm's length bargains. Of the thousands of jobs required to convert crude oil on one side of the planet to highly refined gasoline available for retail sale on the other side of the planet, very few were priced in a marketplace. Title to the fuel does not change very often; the fuel remains the property of relatively few large concerns (oil companies) throughout most of the process. Moreover, an enormous amount of work must be done to maintain the existence of such companies. Consider the jobs—from management to the human resources department to the people who clean the offices—that have nothing directly to do with oil. With a little thought, we see that understanding fuel to be the product of a market for a good is a gross simplification. Between some undersea reserve of crude oil and gasoline in an automobile's tank, there are relatively few moments at which activity was coordinated through a price mechanism. Instead, much of the oil business is actually comprised of corporate, rather than marketplace, activity.

This is a major problem in economics, which can be stated rather simply. What activities are organized within firms, and what activities are priced on a market? For his work on the problem, which led to the field of transaction cost economics, Ronald Coase received what is commonly called the Nobel Prize in Economics.[3] Coase argued that some exchanges are relatively difficult to negotiate; the "transaction costs" of reaching a bargain and completing a sale are high. Such exchanges are ill suited to markets, but may be organized by firms. Suppose, for example, that Ronald wants Milton to be a secretarial assistant, a job that requires the performance of a broad range of tasks on an ongoing basis. If Ronald and Milton have to haggle over each task (so, how much is that sharpened pencil worth to you?), then little work will get done. So Ronald hires Milton for a salary, and in exchange, Ronald gets the right to organize Milton's time and behavior. There is, of course, much more to be said, but for present purposes it suffices to remember that much of the economy, especially large-scale aggregate actions, is not organized directly by the market. No negotiation, no sale, no transfer of money or title takes place. One way to understand corporation law is as a legal (formal) articulation of social mechanisms that enable actions in the commercial environment that are not priced. From this perspective, corporation law would seem to be a major determinant of social order and, hence, politically vital.

Difficulties in Evaluating the Corporation

Academic theories of the corporation are very briefly discussed in chapter 11, but as a matter of social and historical analysis, it is difficult to show how scholarly theories of the nature of the corporation matter to the political beliefs of academics. Members of what we might conveniently call the left and the right have espoused various theories of the corporation. Nor is it clear how, if at all, academic proposals for reform affect the positive law of corporate governance, although occasionally some lines of influence may be discerned. Nor is it clear how the "law on the books," the positive law of corporate governance (e.g., duties expected of managers and directors), affects life in corporations, or society more generally. In sum, the chain from legal theory, to doctrine, to positive law, to institutional structure, to business practice, to social life is so long and so much else must be considered that more than tentative conclusions are unlikely and quite beyond the scope of this book. For present purposes it is enough to flag such problems.

Although the connections between legal imagination, actual institutional development, and social evolution are all very unclear, grand stories about the historical significance of the corporation (or any large institution) are almost unavoidable. People like Butler, who are excited about the direction civil society seems to be taking, tend to be enthusiastic about the institution of the corporation as they understand it; those who are dismayed about what they perceive to be the direction of civil society tend to be hostile to the corporation, again, as they understand it. A sense of history, and of the corporation's role in history, is built into the structure of feeling about the corporation.

As a professional matter, this unruly historical sensibility, this insistence on importance, is annoying. The historian Robert Gordon cautioned against such an "evolutionary functionalist" approach to legal history, in which we understand legal developments as the logical expression of social and especially economic developments.[4] So, for a pertinent example and to foreshadow the discussion below, it is very easy to understand the development of the modern business corporation as the legal aspect of, and prerequisite for, the development of the capital-intensive modern factory.

Such appeals to history, however, rarely end arguments altogether. In particular, legal history told in this fashion rather unselfconsciously takes on a triumphalist bias (i.e., that which happened was destined to happen). As well as bad form, such bias obscures important complexities. There are a lot of good reasons to believe the actual history of the business corporation was not nearly so simple as the story suggested above or the slightly more detailed stories told below. Current legal history on the topic is both vast and deep.[5] The industrial revolution in some places preceded the limited liability corporation; many early industrial firms were not incorporated. Jurisdictions that adopted the legal form often did so without a clear economic need; and jurisdictions that adopted the form did not all industrialize thereafter. Understandings (and so use) of equity, debt, the operation of businesses (especially the conditions of competition), and the creation of markets differed from place to place, from market to market, and varied across the past 200 years. The financing of U.S. railroads with European debt is not the same thing as the financing of mills in Lowell, Massachusetts, with equity—and so forth.

On the other hand, some sort of historical understanding seems to be unavoidable. Some things simply are understood in narrative fashion, even by people with no intention of becoming professional historians. So what is worth saying, for present purposes, about the development of the contemporary business corporation? What might a sensibly ideological account of the contemporary institution look like?

A Narrative Account

The modern—as contrasted with the medieval—political imagination is dominated by the tension between individuals and the state. In the United States, the state is thought to be established by the people and to represent the people as a whole. In contrast, the Middle Ages were more concerned with the idea that groups of people could form a single body, a "*corpus*" in Latin (hence "corporation"). The preeminent example of such a body was the church, the "body of Christ." The church was understood to form a community—a unity—despite the fact that its members lived thousands of miles apart and under the laws of many different temporal governments. But the church was not the only corporate body. Cities were also incorporated, as were universities, guilds, orders of knights, charitable foundations, and trade associations. Many early legislatures were conceived of in terms of orders, that is, social groups rather than individuals were represented. Such corporate associations all had legal powers, if not all the same legal powers. At a minimum, however, such associations were groups of people who, collectively, were legal actors.[6]

If the legal entity is the first step in the development of the modern business corporation that Butler loved so much, intentionally establishing such an entity for the purpose of making a profit is the second. Although the English Crown had long been in the business of chartering towns and universities, in the early modern period the English Crown began establishing entities for frankly commercial purposes. The Russia Company and the Africa Company, both chartered in 1553, seem to have been created as joint stock companies for the purpose of developing trade with those areas.[7] The Bank of England (1694) and the South Seas Company (1711) are not just important examples of early companies, they are experiments in economic organization with national scope and impact.[8] The development of corporation law in England is widely believed to have been retarded by the spectacular failure of the South Seas Company in 1720, and the associated passage of the Bubble Act, which required all joint stock companies to be chartered by the Crown.[9] By the end of the eighteenth century, however, the development of the corporation in English law had resumed.[10] Corporations—joint stock companies—were formed for the exploration, colonization, and exploitation of foreign lands, including the East India Company (1600), the Hudson Bay Company (1670), and the Virginia Company (1609).

Chartering companies raised money for the Crown. As importantly, chartered companies accomplished important state objectives without requiring the state to spend its resources. Government could either raise money in the ordinary way (i.e., tax), and then spend tax revenues on accomplishing the government's purpose (e.g., establishing a colony), or one could authorize others to risk themselves and their fortunes to establish the colony, thereby spreading the Crown's influence with a minimum of up-front expenditure. In America, some of the colonies were founded by the Crown directly (e.g.,

Maryland or Virginia), and some were chartered (e.g., Massachusetts or Rhode Island).

Understanding the benefit of the corporation to the investors—an issue that remains relevant to understanding corporations today—requires a bit of basic finance. By way of quasihistorical example, consider two scenarios for the launch of a sailing ship in the overseas trade. Almost all the facts are the same. If the voyage is successful, the ship's owner will be wildly rich. But building a suitable ship, hiring officers and crew, and provisioning the ship will cost a great deal of money. The ship will be gone at least a year, probably more than two years, so there will be no immediate return on the owner's investment. Worse, there is a substantial likelihood that the voyage will fail altogether. Ships often sink; are captured by pirates or seized by foreign governments; crews mutiny or die of thirst, starvation, or sickness; and for other reasons simply do not return.

In the first scenario, the only way to own a ship is as an individual, a sole proprietor. In light of the risks of the voyage, even very wealthy individuals would refuse to put up the money to build the ship or hire the crew, and even potentially very profitable voyages would not happen. Perhaps a few extremely wealthy people would fund voyages, but in the aggregate, relatively few voyages would be undertaken. Moreover, the owners of what few ships did sail would be likely to take few risks, and the ships would stay close to the coasts.

In the second scenario, suppose that some sort of corporation (historically, often a so-called joint stock company) was founded to build and operate the ship. Several individuals invested their capital in the corporation, creating a pool of money with which to build the ship, hire a crew, and so forth. By investing in the company, each investor put up a share of the cost of equipping a ship for the voyage. If the voyage was successful, each investor would partake in the profits according to their share of the investment. The risk of loss of the ship would remain, but any such loss would not be devastating to any one investor.

Most people, and so most investors, are unwilling to risk losing substantial portions of their wealth, even in return for a chance at substantial gain. Most people are, in the jargon, "risk averse." To provide an example: most people would rather (1) invest 10 percent of their wealth with a 70 percent chance of doubling their money and a 30 percent chance of losing their investment, than (2) invest 100 percent of their wealth with a 70 percent chance of tripling their money and a 30 percent chance of losing their investment, that is, everything. Therefore, to return to our shipbuilding example, if a corporation can be used to make it possible to invest only a relatively small portion of one's wealth in this risky shipping business, then many people would be willing to participate.

Moreover, if ship ownership is by shares, then an investor might participate in the launching of several ships, thereby diversifying his risks. Let us assume that all voyages take one year and that 30 percent of ships sink and 20 percent are captured by pirates, thereby all investment is lost. Let us also assume that 50 percent of the ships come home laden with spices or furs and return, on average, 200 percent on investment. Thus, if one has to invest in a single ship, one has a 50 percent chance of losing the investment, and a 50 percent chance of making a 200 percent profit. Although the expected return on such an investment is 100 percent, the actual return will be either 0 percent or 200 percent. If, however, one can invest the same amount of money in fractional shares of ten ships, one can be reasonably certain of a 100 percent return on total investment. Although one ship is likely to sink and another will probably be captured by pirates, other ships will be successful. The money made from successful voyages should more than cover the money lost on unsuccessful voyages, leaving the investor with a profit. The ability to diversify lowers the risk to investors, which also encourages them to invest.[11]

If ships are owned and operated by companies, in which investors buy shares, then less money is required to invest in sea trading. In consequence, not only the rich, but also people with relatively modest fortunes, may invest. (One might consider the recent phenomenon of sales of fractional ownership in business jets, or, less glamorously, simply owning shares in some giant corporation.) Because the wealthy and the not-so wealthy together control far more money than do the wealthy alone, the total pool of capital available for outfitting sea voyages is much larger under the second scenario, corporate ownership, than under the first scenario, sole proprietorship.

Although the establishment of joint stock companies in seventeenth-century England was certainly motivated by profit, conquering and colonizing new lands should not be understood as an exclusively *private* enterprise. The corporation existed in order to fulfill specific purposes—indeed geopolitical strategy—of the Crown. At a high level of abstraction, one might draw an analogy between the British establishment of joint stock companies and privateering (authorized piracy against the shipping of other states, generally Spain and France), and the granting of patent rights on inventions and technologies stolen from other countries (especially the Netherlands): the Crown encouraged private initiatives that furthered national interests. Joint stock companies were created by acts of parliament. They were made by law, and in that sense, essentially public.

The specific contours of eighteenth-century British and colonial associations varied, so that some were more, and others less, like contemporary notions of the corporation. Joint stock companies themselves were often given exclusive rights to a business. Again, as with the grant of patents, the government did not expect joint stock companies to compete for customers in a marketplace. Both patents and joint stock companies were intended to secure monopolies over presumably valuable trades. This is hardly the contemporary conception of the private corporation—as an exclusive grant to a valuable resource, the establishment of a joint stock corporation is similar to granting land to a noble in reward for services to the Crown.

In the colonies and in the early United States, in the late eighteenth and into the nineteenth centuries, the corporation continued to be understood as a mechanism for the achievement of government objectives. Municipalities, schools, churches, and institutions of higher learning were incorporated. Corporations were also established, usually upon petition by investors, for the building of bridges, and the construction of roads, and the survey/development of land. And banks were chartered, on both the state and federal levels, as corporations.[12] And in keeping with tradition, in order to ensure the success of the enterprise, corporations were given exclusive rights and monopolies, and thereby sheltered from competition. Obviously, such arrangements were intended to benefit both the public and the individuals who invested in and ran the business.

Over time, as the corporation became increasingly understood to be an essentially private enterprise, that is, as a business undertaken for the benefit of its owners, the legal process of incorporation changed. Until the middle of the nineteenth century, state legislatures, like the British parliament, passed laws establishing individual corporations. Such laws were referred to as private bills, in part reflecting the fact that they were passed to benefit what would today be called special interests. Just getting a bill sponsored in the legislature required time and influence on the part of the businessmen who sought to incorporate. Once sponsored, such bills tended to be passed without extensive consideration by the legislature and often as a favor to the sponsoring legislators, but of course even favors must be repaid. In short, the practice of establishing corporations through the passage of private bills fostered corruption and favored the rich.[13]

From the 1830s onward, the practice of incorporation via private bill came under increasing attack as part of the wave of reform known as Jacksonian democracy. Generally, the reformers sought the passage of "general incorporation" laws, which made the corporate form widely and fairly available. Under such laws, anybody who filed basic information with the state government regarding the business to be undertaken by the corporation, and who paid a nominal flat fee to the state, would be granted corporate status without specific consideration by the legislature. The idea was not to limit the use of the corporate form, but to extend its use to merchants and other small businessmen, what might loosely be called the middle class.[14] In the course of the nineteenth century, general incorporation statutes were adopted throughout the United States.

Perhaps even more important than the increasing ease of incorporation was the increasing availability of investment opportunities, spurred by "limited liability" (i.e., limitations on the liability of shareholders for the obligations of the business to third parties). In contrast, in the older and simpler form of business association, the partnership, the partners had (and generally speaking have) unlimited personal liability for the obligations of the business. In the course of the nineteenth century, it became increasingly common to restrict the liability of shareholders in corporate enterprises—although the restrictions varied from time to time, place to place, and business to business.

Looking back over nineteenth-century developments from the early years of the twentieth century, Butler compared the limited liability of shareholders to electricity and steam, the technological marvels of the age. To Butler, limited liability was progressive. The general idea (probably then and certainly now) was that limiting liability encouraged investment. Limited liability lowered the risks of investing in distant enterprises, or in other situations in which it was difficult to monitor the performance of, and the risks facing, the business. Lowering the risks of investing encouraged investing. In the aggregate, for Butler and others, more investment meant more corporate activity, and more corporate activity meant more progress. Thus, limited liability could be conceptually integrated into a progressive view of business. If anything, this association of a tight relationship among limited shareholder liability, investment, business, and progress has grown more strongly held over the past century, at least within the academy—what was once an argument has become an assumption.[15]

The other characteristics of what is now unselfconsciously thought of as "the corporation"—a suite of legal attributes—were only gradually reached over time. For example, in 1810 it was argued that, while a corporation could sue in tort, it could not be sued in tort because the cause of action was defined in terms of its enforcement, seizure of the person, and since a corporation could not be seized, an action in tort afforded no remedy. And because the common law is defined by remedies—no writ without a remedy—there could be no case here. Already by 1810, the court thought this too clever by half.[16] But the broader point is that the various legal capacities of the corporation were acquired only gradually. So, for another example, it was not until late in the nineteenth century that corporations were allowed to hold stock in other corporations, thereby allowing the construction of modern conglomerates.[17]

As the corporation became an ordinary way of doing business and a common investment, the social function of the institution shifted: what had been a way to achieve the particular interests of the government became more of an institutional vehicle for the conduct of private enterprise. Widely available incorporation meant that groups of businessmen with competing interests would seek to incorporate, and that the state, which granted incorporation to all reasonable applicants, would not grant one or the other group exclusive rights. Although the vagaries of fortune, finance, and human fallibility hardly disappeared, the success or failure of a given company came to be seen as largely a question of competition with other corporations in the private arena (who will build a better mousetrap?). The business corporation thus began to be seen—as it is still widely seen—as a fundamentally private entity, whose immediate interests and survival are divorced from the state or the public as a whole, except insofar as the state and the public have a general interest in a thriving private sector.

There was a doctrinal corollary to this shift in perception, the so-called death of *ultra vires*. The phrase is law Latin: *ultra*, beyond, and *vires*, powers (plural of *vis*). The doctrine held that certain corporate acts were unlawful because the corporation did not have the legal power so to act, as a matter either of its charter or of state corporation law. Entailed in the idea of *ultra vires* is the notion that corporations are established for specific purposes, that corporations are created to get particular jobs done. As we have seen, in back of this idea is the notion that corporations are instruments of state power. And, throughout the nineteenth century and into the twentieth, states required incorporators to file the purpose of the corporation, to state the planned business.

Under general incorporation statutes, however, states do not scrutinize or choose among the various parties and purposes incorporating businesses. As suggested above, with the passage of such statutes, the purpose of the business corporation came to be seen as essentially private, as making money for its owners. And once corporations came to be understood to be merely a way of organizing private business, it was not clear why the incorporators should state, in advance, what the business was to be. At a deeper level, in a competitive society marked by technological change, business must be adaptable.

In contemporary language, business models are constantly evolving. Thus, although a business could probably be described with broad and vague language (XYZ Corp. manufactures, distributes, markets, and retails household products), business itself came to be seen as a more flexible, adaptive, and in that sense, reactive activity. Reflecting this shift, state incorporation laws began to require merely that the business be incorporated for "lawful" purposes.[18] (It would be a bit much to expect states to establish corporations for criminal purposes.) But if a business is established with the power to engage in all lawful acts, then the bounds of permissible activity are set by the general laws of the state, not the charter or corporation law. Thus, there is little need for the doctrine of *ultra vires*.[19]

The issue of corporate purpose, however, is not always resolved by reference to "the interests of shareholders." Assuming that all shareholders just want to make money (a standard assumption in the basic course) hardly determines whether particular activities are in the interests of the company and its shareholders. Investors in a business corporation are assumed to want to earn a return on their investment, and the corporation is easily if vaguely enough understood as existing in order to earn money for the investors. But earn money doing what? Discussion over just what the substance of a given business is, and so what constitutes the interest of shareholders, is interminable. Circumstances continually change, subjective judgments must be made, people are fallible when much is at stake—for these and other reasons, businesspeople often disagree. Stepping back a bit, however, the larger point is fairly clear: corporation law is designed to establish entities with the legal powers necessary to do business. The substance of that business, within very broad bounds, is not the concern of corporation law. Corporation law just sets the ground rules; actually playing the game is what businesspeople do.

And yet, even today, one should not exaggerate the private character of the corporation. In order to form a corporation, a private petition still must be granted by a government official, acting under the authority of the legislature. A corporation does not exist without an act of the state.[20] Corporations—even corporations established in order to make private parties wealthier—thus have an essentially public aspect. The state recognizes the corporation as a legal actor. Indeed, to speak of the corporation as a legal entity requires such recognition, for the simple reason that no actor could function legally (sue and be sued, contract, own property, and the rest) if the actor was not recognized by the law, that is, did not exist in the eyes of the state. And as we saw in the previous chapter, corporations will enjoy legal rights and be obliged to fulfill legal duties much like natural persons. But it cannot be denied that the state's ongoing involvement with the corporation is quite small. We thus return to Bayless Manning's idea that corporation law is profoundly empty.[21]

This emptiness can be unsettling. A large corporation collects the energies and resources of thousands, even tens of thousands, of individuals and countless investors. Corporations act purposefully, but their purposes are indefinite, and so seem directionless. Like other businesses, corporations are supposed to make money for their owners, the shareholders. But the words "make money" hardly tell us anything. As we shall discuss in great detail, corporation law is concerned with the possibility that corporations act for the benefit of managers rather than shareholders, but this tells us no more about what a corporation is likely to do. Corporations seem to have no compass; they will move in whatever direction is likely to make money. It is true that corporations are regulated by state and federal laws, but without an internal compass, is there any reason to expect the corporation not to try to get away with as much as possible? Corporations do have different cultures, and some cultures seem more responsible than others, but where, as a matter of law, do such cultures reside?

As we have seen in this chapter, the state has abdicated its traditional role of determining the substance of a company. Yet no one outside the corporation has assumed ultimate responsibility for the corporation. As we shall see, the limited liability of corporate actors means that neither the shareholders, the managers, nor the directors are at all likely to be personally responsible for the corporation's activities. Corporations are thus actors that are not themselves responsible (at least not for any reason that leaves legal traces), and for which nobody legally need be responsible, either. The corporation is like Frankenstein's monster, or the golem of Jewish legend, a creature with the power to act, and an inchoate desire to serve, but clumsy, maybe even dangerous.[22]

Chapter 3

Capital Structure,
Dramatic Structure

Finance

ALL BUSINESS REQUIRES INVESTMENT IN THE BROADEST SENSE OF AN ACTIVity undertaken in the expectation of a future return. The temporal structure of investment makes drama possible, indeed unavoidable. It does not matter whether an investment is of cash, some other form of capital, or labor. It does not matter how the investor reckons the return (as a profit, a reduction of costs, an increase to equity, or otherwise). What matters is that the investor has put something of value at risk. Like all forms of gambling and theater, investment has a soon-to-be resolved question at its heart: is the future on the side of the investor? Will the sea captain return?

Now imagine, as in the previous chapter, that the sea captain establishes a company and sells shares in the company. The sea captain has *financed* the enterprise, that is, used other people's money in order to build, outfit, and provision a ship for a long voyage. Although different sorts of transaction have different vocabularies, all finance has the same basic structure. Someone wishes to do something for which they have insufficient savings. Perhaps a student wishes to become a lawyer; a family wishes to buy a house; a business wishes to build a new facility; a corporation wishes to buy another corporation. It does not matter. In each of these situations, someone seeks a dramatic change in his or her status. Indeed, if the financing is successful, names may change: not a student but a lawyer; no longer a renter but a homeowner; not a small operation but a big company. Financing may be transformative.[1]

In order to realize the wish, money is sought from a third party. Perhaps the federal government sponsors a student loan program; a bank makes a mortgage loan; a company issues bonds; shares are exchanged in a merger. There are many species of financing and hence lots of different names. Depending on the type of transaction and local conventions, the party using the capital may be called borrower, debtor, issuer, or company. Again, depending on the transaction, the party providing the capital may be called various things, including bank, lender, creditor, bondholder, share- or stockholder, or the investor. Thus, a financing establishes a relationship, between, for example, borrower and lender, debtor and creditor, issuer and shareholder, or whatever the case may be. In order to be as general as possible, let us call the party who receives the money the capital user, and the party who provides the money the capital provider.

A financing is not a gift. In finance, capital is provided (investments are made) in exchange for some set of legal rights given to the capital provider. The capital provider's rights fall into two basic classes: debt and equity. For example, a bank lends money in exchange for a right of repayment of the sum lent (the principal), plus a profit (the interest). This is a *debt financing*. For another example, imagine that a company sells stock, sometimes more descriptively called *shares*. The capital provider, in buying stock, becomes an owner of the company, and hence shares or participates in the company. This is an *equity financing*. The combinations are endless, but conceptually speaking, debt establishes relationships of contractual obligation from one party to another. The capital user *owes* the capital provider. Equity merges the two parties. The capital provider *owns* the capital user, and thus in some sense *becomes* the capital user, hence merges.

Another example: imagine a business, perhaps a single restaurant, with two owners, partners. In order to cover expenses as they arise, the business establishes and uses a line of credit with a local bank and is therefore obligated to make monthly payments to the bank in repayment of its borrowings. This is debt. Nobody thinks, however, that the bank is in the restaurant business, or that the restaurant is in the banking business. Now imagine that the restaurant is successful, and the partners consider expanding. In order to open two new restaurants, the partners seek money from several affluent friends. In exchange for their investment, the friends become co-owners of the combined business. This is an equity transaction. The friends, now, are in the restaurant business—they own restaurants.[2]

In either a debt or an equity financing, the capital provider receives rights expected to be of greater value in the future.[3] Most obviously, if a bank lends money, the borrower is obligated to repay, over time, the sum borrowed (the principal) along with some additional amount (the interest). The bank does not make a profit until time has passed. In an equity financing, the company is expected to grow (that is usually why the capital user wanted to raise money in the first place). Assuming this expectation proves to be correct, the ownership rights that the investor receives in exchange for his or her investment will be more valuable in the future. To be a bit redundant for the sake of clarity: finance, like all investment, is a bet on the future. And bets sometimes fail. Hence the drama—investors bear risks. Indeed, modern finance theory makes this truism into a definition: what investors are paid to do is "bear risk."

It is important to realize that in the corporate world, a financing is a bet, not just on a future event, but on the future of a relationship.[4] Will the capital user be successful and, hence, able and inclined to repay the capital provider's investment? Will the student become a lawyer and repay his or her student loans? Will the family be able to make the mortgage note on the house? Will the company's big new facility make enough money to enable it to pay off the debt it undertook (the bonds it sold) in order to build the facility? Will the merger of two companies work to create a single company worth more, on a per share basis?

The relationship may not work out as expected. Many of the rights that capital providers receive from capital users are intended to protect capital providers against the possibility that the financing will not work out. Imagine, for an example familiar in our culture, that a bank lends money to a family to buy a farm. Once it makes the loan, the bank is at risk—it has already turned over its money, and the farmer may not repay. As a result, as a condition of making the loan, the bank demands the right, in the event the family does not repay the loan, to take the farm. Rephrased, the bank receives a mortgage on the farm, so that the farm is security for the loan. Such security, however, is often inadequate. Suppose the farmer defaults, and the bank takes the farm. Bankers are not usually farmers, and the bank is likely to find itself in the unenviable position of attempting to resell a farm that has just failed. Of course, the farmer is at risk, too, because life and especially farming are uncertain. Moreover, if many farmers default on their loans (if weather is very bad, for common instance), then banks that lend to farmers may fail (unless the government steps in to help, again, hardly ideal). Thus, as with many relationships, capital users and providers, farmers and the banks that lend to them, both tend to hope that things work out, that the future unfolds as planned.

The specific terms on which the capital provider and the capital user enter their relationship are open to negotiation, if often only the tacit negotiation represented by having to meet competing offers in the marketplace. Like all negotiations, financings depend on any number of factors, including not only the availability of alternatives, but also the strengths of desire and fear that each party brings to the table. (I realize that neither farmers nor bankers often talk like this; they are farmers and bankers.) The simple example of a farm loan, however, illustrates how financing—the need for capital users to realize wishes, and from the provider's side, the need to make capital work—creates relationships. The farmer's need to borrow money requires him or her to grant a mortgage to the bank; the bank's need to invest capital requires it to take the risk of making loans. And so farmer and banker become borrower and lender, whose fortunes are intertwined. More generally, as we shall explore, finance creates the "capital structure" of a business enterprise.

What Is a Share of Stock?

A primer on the specifics of the financial instrument known as a share of stock may be useful to some readers. (Other readers are invited to skip forward to the section "Capital Relations" later in this chapter, where the regularly scheduled programming is now in progress.) What does a shareholder typically receive in exchange for investing in a corporation, and what sort of legal relationships are thereby created? What does it mean to own a share of "common stock"?

A share of common stock is a fractional ownership interest in the corporation as a whole. Let's start with "fractional." A stockholder "shares" the ownership of the company with the other stockholders. If there are a hundred shares, then each share represents 1/100, or 1 percent, of the ownership of the corporation. Each share is exactly equal to every other share of the same class, that is, all shares of the same class must be treated in the same way.

The idea of fractional ownership implies not just the numerator, the number of shares in question, but also logically requires the denominator, the corporation "as a whole." A shareholder as such has no right to any particular asset of the company, nor, for that matter, is a shareholder responsible for any liability (in the broad accounting sense of obligation) of the company. Title to the assets of the corporation is held, and the liabilities of the corporation are owed, by the corporation, not by the shareholders. The corporation, again, as a whole, is owned by the shareholders.

To make the same point in a different way: if individual investors could dispose of particular assets unilaterally and at will, then such investors would have undivided ownership over (have control over) particular assets, but would not own the enterprise by shares. An example should make this clear: suppose ABC company has some real estate, some machinery, and a few delivery vehicles, and five shareholders, each with 20 percent of the company. If Bob could take the trucks within "his" 20 percent, then presumably Carmen can sell off some machinery, under the same logic. But at this point, Carmen would have no claim to Bob's trucks, and Bob would have no claim to the money from Carmen's machinery. Instead of owning 20 percent of the company, they each would own 100 percent of certain fixed assets. Thus, just as no numerator exists without a denominator, the notion of fractional ownership entails the idea of the whole. The notion of fractional ownership (and hence the notion that the corporation is a vehicle for the aggregation of capital discussed in the last chapter) logically requires the notion of the corporation as an entity.[5]

What does it mean to say that a share is an "ownership interest" in the corporation? In the common law tradition, ownership is usually understood through two inquiries: first, questions concerning the right to profit and the obligation to pay losses on the thing, and second, questions concerning rights to control, manage, and dispose of the thing. Owners typically benefit economically from owning property, at least property bought as an investment. Typically, owners are responsible (liable) for their property. This is called beneficial or sometimes economic ownership. In general, the owner of a property also has rights to do whatever he or she wants with the property: use it, move it, change it, sell it, give it away—whatever one may do legally. This is usually called the right to control, "quiet enjoyment," or sometimes simply "legal" ownership of a thing.[6] So, using this conceptual division between rights to benefit and rights to control, what can we say about owning stock in a corporation?

To begin with beneficial ownership: shareholders do not get much in the way of a physical asset. Traditionally, but today usually only by request, the shareholder receives a "certificate of stock ownership," a piece of paper evidencing the number of shares purchased by the shareholder. In large publicly traded companies, however, stock ownership is recorded on the books of companies whose business it is to keep track of such things, much as title to land is established by county registries. Such companies do not have "certificated" stock.

How does a shareholder benefit economically from owning stock (i.e., make money on his or her investment)? There are three basic ways a shareholder can make money from his or her shares: as "residual claimant" to the assets of the corporation, through a "dividend," and through a sale of the share. The idea of the "residual claimant" is simpler than it sounds. Imagine a small business whose owners decide to retire and close the business. Suppose that, after all the costs of operating the business have been paid (rent, salaries and benefits, supplies, marketing and distribution costs, everything), and after all the outstanding obligations of the business have been paid (including taxes, loans, credit extended by suppliers and other businesses, everything), there is money left over. That money belongs to the owners, who are the "residual claimants" of the business, that is, the claimants who remain last in line, after all other claims on the business have been paid. In a business structured as a corporation, shareholders are the residual claimants. If the business were to be wound up, and after all costs and debts had been paid, the shareholder would receive the proceeds, on a number of shares owned, or *pro rata*, basis (not on a per person, or *per capita* basis) of the remaining assets.

This is what is meant by the statement that shareholders are "the owners" of the corporation. The difference between the assets of the company (the things it owns) and the liability of the company (the things it owes) is what the shareholders own. On a corporate balance sheet, this difference is called equity or shareholders' equity. It is one view of what the company—the shareholder's property—is worth. And, to turn the language around one more time, the word *equity* is often used to refer to the ownership interests in the corporation: an equity financing, introduced above, does not just create cash or assets *for* the company, it creates owners *of* the company (i.e., the same transaction must be understood in terms of the company's finances and its governance).

A second way for a shareholder to make money from owning stock is through a dividend, sometimes called a "distribution." A company may decide that it is reasonably profitable, and it may decide to return a portion of its profits to its shareholders. A company may distribute cash, stock, or some other asset. If the corporation declares a dividend on its stock, a shareholder has a right to the dividend for each share of stock owned by the shareholder. Thus, if the corporation decides to pay a dividend of $1.50/share on its common stock, and a shareholder owns 2,000 such shares, the shareholder receives $3,000. Each share of common stock must receive the same dividend.[7] So, if the company has a million shares of common stock outstanding, then the company must distribute $1.5 million.

Third, a shareholder may make money by selling his or her shares. Shares are said to be "freely transferable," absent particular legal circumstances restricting their transfer. And, as with any market, a sale of stock presumes the existence of a buyer. But in general, shareholders make most or all of their profits through the sale of their stock. Suppose that a woman named Alex buys 10,000 shares in 1to3 Inc., an up-and-coming little company with one million shares outstanding, and gross revenues of $100 million a year. Alex owns 1 percent of the company. Suppose that, true to its name, 1to3's revenues triple in three years, but the company issues no more stock, pays no dividends on its outstanding stock. On these facts, Alex's shares are worth considerably more money than they were when she purchased them; she owns the same percentage of a substantially larger company.[8]

The fact that common stock is a fractional ownership interest that is freely transferable does much to define what it means to be an owner and the way the shareholders relate to the company and other shareholders. At least for many companies (almost all of the companies with familiar names), stock in the company is easily sold. Such stock is traded in markets that are "liquid," that is, markets that allow assets to be easily translated into cash, the most liquid of assets because it flows most easily. Moreover, because an individual share of stock is such a small fraction of the company, the extent of Alex's ownership is very flexible. She may become a more important owner by buying more stock, or a less important owner by selling some stock, or she may cease being an owner altogether by selling all of her stock. Alex is certainly invested (i.e., she has bought an asset with the expectation of profit). But the extent of her commitment to the company—another sense of "investment"—remains to be seen.

Ordinarily, ownership implies responsibility. Intuitively, if the owner is entitled to all the benefits of a property, it seems logical that he or she should be responsible for the obligations associated with owning the property. So, for a familiar example, the owner of a house is entitled to all the benefits of ownership, but is also responsible for the costs of keeping the house in legally safe condition, paying insurance and taxes, and so forth. Rephrased in a corporate context: if the shareholders are the residual claimants, entitled to keep whatever remains after the obligations of the company have been paid, then it might seem logical that the obligations of the company should be paid by the owners.

As mentioned in chapters 1 and 2, however, the corporation is a "limited liability" form of association (i.e., the owners of the company are not responsible for the obligations of the company beyond their original investment). Suppose that a corporation finds itself insolvent, that is, the company's debts exceed its assets. In general, creditors of the company cannot seek payment from the shareholders of the company. So, in our foregoing example, suppose that instead of tripling its revenues, 1to3 Inc. files for bankruptcy and begins to liquidate its assets. Can a creditor of 1to3 who will not be fully satisfied by the bankruptcy proceeding seek the rest of the money it is owed from Alex, who is, after all, an owner of 1to3? No.

There is a great deal to be said about the limitation of liability; the topic will be addressed in some detail in chapter 10. For present purposes, however, the important point is that limitation of liability is thought to increase the willingness of parties with capital to buy stock. Shareholders enjoy the benefits of ownership, as described above, but their risk is limited to the amount of their original investment. As a result, one may invest in a company even if one does not understand the company's business very well, or otherwise is not in a position to keep very close tabs on the company. The very worst thing (from the investor's perspective) that is likely to happen is that the investment will be lost. In light of the fact that stock can be bought in relatively small quantities, even a total loss need not be too disastrous for the shareholder.

So much for the beneficial ownership of stock; what about the legal ownership of stock? How can a shareholder exercise control over his or her property, thereby protecting that shareholder's investment? Shareholders have rights to participate in the governance of the company, usually limited to voting. Specifically and most importantly, shareholders have the right to vote for directors, usually on an annual basis. Directors hire and fire the management of the company. Thus, shareholders participate, albeit quite indirectly, in the choice of a company's management. Shareholders also vote for certain major changes to the structure of the corporation: changes to the articles of incorporation and decisions to merge the company into another, sell all the assets, or dissolve the company. Shareholders may also vote on proposals brought by other shareholders or by management.[9]

Although the foregoing pretty much describes the main features of the most typical form of common stock, there is nothing in theory, and little in practice, that requires the ownership interests of a corporation to be configured in precisely this way. Statutory corporation law requires that some shareholders be able to vote, so that directors may be elected and for other purposes, but that said, ownership interests can be configured in many ways. In a famous metaphor, the institution of property is likened to a bundle of sticks. Each stick in the bundle is a right to do something. Different sticks may be bundled together to form bundles; different bundles may be comprised of different property rights. In particular, a corporation may issue different classes of stock, with somewhat different rights.

This is usually described in the language of "preferences," as in preferred stock. Over what is preferred stock favored? Over common stock—companies usually issue common stock with the typical and traditional characteristics described above, and then may issue one or more classes of preferred stock, which have some additional rights.[10] The special features of the preferred stock are intended to make it more attractive to investors (or perhaps attractive to a different investor from the sort that would be interested in the common stock).

Probably the most common preference is for dividends. Instead of receiving a dividend in an amount and whenever the company (here meaning the board of directors) may decide profits are sufficient and circumstances warrant, a customary practice has been to promise holders of the preferred stock an annual dividend in a fixed amount. The dividend on preferred stock must be paid before dividends can be paid to the holders of the common stock—hence, the preferred stockholders are "preferred" over the holders of the common stock. In addition, such dividends may be "cumulative" (i.e., if business conditions prevent the payment of the dividend in a given year, then any such unpaid dividends must be distributed before a new dividend is paid on the common stock). But this is just one traditional bundle of rights.

Other bundles are possible; one can create stock with other preferences. A class of stock can have a preference over common stock with regard to the assets of the company at its dissolution, that is, a company can issue stock that, upon the winding up of the company's business, has a right to receive any proceeds from the company's assets after creditors are paid (debt gets paid before equity), but before holders of common stock. Holders of preferred stock can be granted rights to have their stock redeemed (bought back) by the company (very handy if the business is in trouble). Traditionally, preferred stock does not vote. But *convertible preferred* stock, which converts into some specified number of voting common stock upon the occurrence of some event or perhaps at the option of the holder of the stock, is also a traditional instrument.

Capital Relations

To repeat: financing creates the capital structure of a business and, hence, the relations among its principal actors. A financing, therefore, is a bet not only on the economic success of the enterprise, but, in terms of corporate governance and politics, a bet on the future of the relationships that must carry the enterprise forward. So what sorts of relationships are created by the corporation's issuance of common stock?

In the United States, countless investors are willing to buy stock, often in distant, huge companies. Consider the millions of people who own shares of Microsoft or General Electric. In comparison with starting and operating a business of any kind (consider, for example, the virtual impossibility of starting a business like Boeing, which manufactures commercial aircraft), owning shares in a corporation is *easy*. As discussed above, the company does the work, and if all goes well, the shareholder profits. Nor does investing have to be expensive. Shares are usually issued in such large numbers, each representing only a small fraction of the enterprise, that individual shares do not cost very much.[11] Finally, there is little downside to stock ownership: the owner's financial exposure is limited to the amount of the individual investment. By 2002 approximately 50 percent of Americans were invested in the market for equities, either directly or through mutual funds or other intermediaries.[12]

It is often said that because shareholding creates such manageable opportunities to participate in enterprises, the limited liability corporation increased the total amount of capital available. As noted in the previous chapter, as a matter of history, the precise relations between the corporation and the industrial revolution (to say nothing of the emergence of an industrial economy and now an information economy) are unclear. The causal questions, the extent to which enterprises could have been created without a legal institution that resembled the business corporation, need not be answered here. For present purposes, it seems enough to suggest that the business corporation has facilitated the creation of truly mass organizations.[13] And it is uncontested, moreover, that this society collectivizes and organizes complex economic processes through business corporations. The corporation is thus contemporary in the sense of participating in the construction of this society.

The constitutive role of the corporation raises political issues. Corporations that become huge become powerful. One might consider Ford at the beginning of the twentieth century, or Microsoft today. How is such power controlled? This was the problem confronted by Adolf Berle, a lawyer, and Gardiner Means, an economist, in their landmark 1932 book, *The Modern Corporation and Private Property*.[14] Berle and Means noted that as of 1930, 200 corporations, comprising less than seven hundredths of 1 percent of all nonfinancial corporations in the country, controlled nearly half of the corporate wealth in the United States.[15] This, for a nation that thought of itself as a democracy, and indeed as a constitutional republic, where political power was limited, was a problem. (It still is.)

Even on purely economic grounds, in the 1930s it was far from clear that markets comprised of giant corporations were socially desirable. Berle and Means wrote in the depths of the Depression. The economy was in crisis; growth was negative; unemployment was high; human misery was widespread. Capitalism was widely thought to have failed, not just in the United States but also around the world. The Soviet Union was openly communist and appeared quite successful. In this light, the giant corporation appeared to be part of the problem. But what, precisely, was the nature of the problem?

Berle and Means argued that the distinctive feature of the large business corporation was the separation of ownership from control. In a sole proprietorship, the owner operates the business and so makes business decisions, manages. In a partnership (such as a traditional law firm), the partners make business decisions jointly, unless the partnership agreement provides otherwise. In contrast, the owners of a corporation, the shareholders, do *not* manage the business. As noted in chapter 1, the corporation has centralized management, that is, corporations hire professional managers whose jobs are to run the business. More precisely, the board of directors hires the top managers of a corporation, who in turn hire middle and lower managers, who in turn hire other employees.

Conversely, and in contrast to the owners of businesses structured in simpler forms, the shareholders of a corporation have no role in the day-to-day management of the company. The shareholders' legal rights to participate in the governance of the company (notably the annual election of directors) are indirect and almost purely formal. The vast majority of shareholders, each owning only a tiny percentage of the company's stock, have no practical influence over the direction of the company. The existence of similarly situated shareholders makes little difference. Powerless shareholders tend to be both politically and geographically dispersed, and so organization is generally impractical. Shareholders are, therefore, rationally passive; shareholders leave the field of corporate governance almost entirely to managers and the few other shareholders who control significant blocks of stock.[16]

The problem for shareholders is that the company's managers may act in their own interests, rather than in the best interest of the corporation and its shareholders. To begin with, the most obvious conflict between owners and managers is that of executive compensation. Put simply: if the salary of a company's chief executive officer (CEO) is raised from $1 million a year to $2 million a year, the additional million dollars is money that the company—that is, the shareholders—will not keep. Of course, the same could be said of any cost that the corporation bears. The difference is that top managers influence the board of directors, which sets management's compensation using shareholders' money. And the managers of major corporations are often stunningly well paid, in many ways: cash; lines of credit; stock and stock options; cars; luxury travel; use of company planes; decorating budgets for office and home; entertainment expenses; control over charitable and political donations; and long-term economic security in the form of rich severance and retirement packages. It is good to be king, but it is almost as good to be CEO of a major corporation.[17]

More subtly, the corporation itself may be managed in some way not in the interests of the shareholders. Managers profit from their status as managers. Shareholders, in contrast, profit when the company makes money over and above the costs of doing business, including salaries and other executive compensation. Thus, managers value stability of the business as a whole, and stability in the executive suite in particular. Corporations, which have been justified as vehicles for taking risks (return to our ship captain), tend to become risk-averse and conservative, because the people actually running corporations, the managers, do not want to lose their very nice jobs. In particular, managers are unlikely to agree to mergers that would increase the value of shareholders' equity, but would result in the elimination of their positions. More subtly, and probably pervasively, managers just take little risk.

This conflict of interest between shareholders and managers has come to be called the "agency problem" of corporation law. An *agent* is defined as someone who agrees to work for the benefit of, under the control of, another person, who is called the *principal*.[18] The most familiar agency relationship is a job. Agents owe a duty to try and help their principals. In the employment context this is often called *loyalty*; in agency law this is called the *fiduciary duty* of the agent. Managers are employed by corporations and, therefore, are agents of the corporation, and indirectly, its owners, the shareholders. But as we have seen, managers have incentives to work for themselves rather than for their employer. And because shareholders are passive and often distant, it is often very difficult for shareholders to monitor the activities of their agents, the managers. Managers may take advantage of shareholders without shareholders ever knowing. In short, shareholders have a serious agency problem.

Yet the fact that most shareholders participate in the corporate enterprise in only limited and passive fashion must also be understood positively. Indeed the entire point of the business corporation—the story of the previous two chapters—is that the combination of fractional ownership and limited liability, and, hence, large pools of capital placed at the service of professional managers, can accomplish great things. If the owners must play an active, involved part in the management of the company, then owners cannot invest in things for which they have little time, aptitude, or physical opportunity to participate, and the pool of capital and the scale of enterprises might be expected to shrink accordingly. Rephrased, requiring owners to have an active role in the corporation would in effect convert corporations into partnerships and might reduce the amount of capital available to enterprise.

Berle and Means thus understood the modern corporation to be situated between a rock and a hard place: how to facilitate the aggregation of capital while ensuring that the resulting entity is managed to the benefit of its owners, that is, responsibly. This is the central problem of corporation law; the academic subdiscipline can be understood as a series of efforts to address this durable tension. Berle and Means wrote over seventy years ago. Corporation laws (and securities laws) have developed in the interim, and still we have scandals—such as Enron—in which managers abuse their power over the corporation, and investors are ruined. Law manages the problem, but does not appear capable of solving it.[19] Creating a pool of money, an economic tool, inevitably raises the question of how the tool is to be used and the possibility of misuse. The tension between ownership and management that Berle and Means did so much to articulate can no more finally be resolved than romance or the conflicts among generations or any of the other fundamental human tensions explored by theater.

Even in situations for which there is no solution, one may take sides. Berle and Means began, and many corporation law scholars since have begun, from the proposition that shareholders need protection from managers. The law and institutions of the corporation are structured to protect the shareholders, without—and this is just a restatement of the fundamental problem—impeding the ability of the business, that is, the managers, to make money for the shareholders (and themselves). Other scholars, many operating under the banner of "law and economics," are relatively unconcerned about the abuse of managerial power over shareholders and are more concerned that the medicine, the regulation of managers, is worse than the disease. Without resolving this question, and wherever one stands, the basic structure of the question has remained unchanged since the 1930s, although some of the vocabulary has changed.[20]

The shareholder's first line of defense against the misbehavior of managers is the institution of the board of directors. The board is supposed to ensure that the company is run in the best interest of its owners, the shareholders.

More specifically, directors monitor the performance of the business and its managers. Directors vote on major corporate decisions, including the compensation to be paid to managers. And most importantly, directors have the power to hire and fire top management. In short, at least as a legal and formal matter, directors have strategic control over the corporation.

Shareholders vote on the board of directors, usually annually. Shareholders thus have the legal power to require that directors do their job of ensuring that the corporation is managed for the benefit of the shareholders. Moreover, the directors (and managers) owe fiduciary duties to the shareholders. Such duties are legally enforceable by an individual shareholder. Finally, companies that are badly run may be vulnerable to a takeover, that is, discontented shareholders will be willing to sell their positions to a "raider" who will elect a new board and, hence, a new management. The threat of such a "hostile takeover" may discipline boards of directors and management.

Yet businesses are founded by managers. Corporations are incorporated by people who often make themselves CEOs. Moreover, such founders tend to reserve considerable shares and, hence, a fair degree of voting control for themselves. From their perspective, shareholders are merely capital providers, sources of money like banks, not part of the company itself. Similarly, founders and subsequent managers tend to have two types of people on their boards: employees of the company, and "outside" directors with whom the management is friendly. Finally, and most importantly, the management knows more about the business, and its challenges and opportunities, than other directors, and much more than ordinary shareholders. Most of the information possessed by the board of directors is provided by the management. It is, therefore, very difficult for the board of directors to exercise strategic control over the management. In practice, the board is often a tool of management rather than of the shareholders.

* * *

Again, these dynamics will be articulated in greater detail in the next part of this book. But at this point, we have our three roles—shareholder, manager, and director—understood in relation to the financial structure of the corporation. Shareholders create a pool of capital, which is placed at the service of managers, who are subject to the oversight of directors.

Chapter 4

Understanding the Moral (Learning from Cases)

Since the late nineteenth century, basic legal education in U.S. law schools has focused on cases, more precisely, on the explanations of their decisions written by appeals court judges and their law clerks. Although varying proportions of policy, theory, several social sciences, and whatnot have been added over the years, judicial "opinions" remain the backbone of basic legal education in the United States. Even corporation law is taught largely through appellate decisions, despite the fact that corporations generally are formed, operate, and governed, and are dissolved, merged, or otherwise cease to exist without much litigation, and appellate opinions, relative to the mass of corporate activity in this country, are rare. Most lawyers who consider themselves "corporate lawyers" are not so much litigators as negotiators, transactional lawyers, and regulatory lawyers. Nonetheless, corporation law is taught largely through a limited set of cases, most of which appear in most basic textbooks.[1] Parts II and III of this book, therefore, discuss many of these classic cases, traditionally called "chestnuts," and a few words about what meaning to draw from cases might be in order.

Appellate cases are often argued, and opinions are rendered, in terms of an actor's compliance, or failure to comply, with preexisting legal rules: did X break general rule Y, which applies to such cases, or not? And the idea of a general framework of rules that can be stated in abstract terms that constrain particular behavior is central to most understandings of what the law is. Therefore, in introducing students to the law, and in giving students a conceptual framework with which to confront the countless specific questions that practicing law presents, law professors tend to emphasize the "blackletter" doctrines exemplified by the cases, general and abstract statements of rules that work together to form a certain conceptual framework—the framework, it is presumed, that actually operates in the minds of those charged with conducting the institutions of the law. So law students (who must be presumed to want to learn the law), therefore, study cases in order to learn what the doctrine is.

Knowledge of even a few cases, however, reveals that courts are hardly consistent. One rule is said to be applied in one case, but another rule is said to be applied in another case that would seem to be substantially similar. Such conflicting cases are often printed side by side in textbooks, highlighting the inconsistencies. In the late nineteenth-century model of legal education (forever associated with Harvard Law School's Dean, Christopher Columbus Langdell), the job of the student was to learn how to distinguish similar cases and to formulate a statement of the applicable legal rule so that the cases were seen to be correctly decided under the rule. This method of pedagogy was an important aspect of the broader jurisprudential stance that, after the fact, was called legal classicism (also commonly associated with the majority of the U.S. Supreme Court in the famous *Lochner* decision).[2] This is a simplification: there was more to legal classicism than distilling the essence of legal doctrine from the mash of judicial opinions, a process which much later came to be derided as "rationalizing legal analysis." Moreover, in important ways the "classical" legal mind of the late nineteenth and early twentieth centuries is, as one might expect, different from the understanding of a contemporary lawyer. Those things said, law students in the United States still read cases in a fashion not entirely unlike that taught by Langdell at Harvard in the 1880s.[3] Almost as importantly, rationalizing the decisions of courts and government agencies informs what one might call practical legal scholarship, that is, the reportage, analysis, and commentary produced for the practicing lawyers and other interested parties, often in the context of continuing legal education (CLE) requirements imposed by state bar associations. And rationalizing legal analysis remains an unavoidable aspect of academic scholarship devoted to the decisions of courts or government agencies.[4]

As has been suggested, in the course of the twentieth century, rationalizing legal analysis lost much of its intellectual prestige, at least among law professors. Indeed, the rise and long fall of legal classicism is perhaps the dominant way to understand the intellectual history of the U.S. law school. Although the details are surprisingly interesting and endlessly debated by cognoscenti, for present purposes it suffices to say that, by the time that American Legal Realists such as Yale law professor Karl Lewellyn wrote in the early 1930s, the classical enterprise had come to seem implausible.[5] The Realists were right that good arguments can be made for both sides of a court's decision; presumably the lawyers did make arguments for each side. Today, even first-year law students are trained to argue on both sides of a legal proposition. Moreover, cases were distinguishable (or comparable) pretty much at will. Thus, the idea that analysis of cases would lead to a statement of "the law" that controlled the cases was simply not believable. And law, therefore, was not a science, at least not a science based on the data afforded by the cases. As the saying goes, "we are all Realists now."[6]

This union between rather classical teaching and anticlassical scholarly prejudices is not a very happy one. Confronted with inconsistency among cases and the malleability of arguments, law students often become cynical about legal doctrine, or even law more generally: what was thought to be a legal rule is often seen as merely the formalization of the preferences (sometimes called "politics") of a judge. Students discover that law is not a constraint upon politics, but is instead an exercise of power. Many idealistic students—those who had put the most hope in law to redeem politics and even social life more broadly—experience this realization as depressing indeed.

Cynicism and depression are somewhat sophomoric, if not entirely wrong headed, responses to law. Cases, and even statements of legal doctrine, can make considerable sense if one has appropriately modest expectations. Classical legal science claimed, and legal education all too often still claims, that reading cases can deliver abstractly principled yet determinate, even controlling, statements of the law. But it now seems clear that judges do not work that way. Judgment does not work that way. A more modest approach would be to consider legal doctrine in the past tense, as a summation, rather than in the future tense, as a prediction or cause. (The past, of course, is often highly suggestive of the future, except when it is not.) Statements of legal doctrine make sense if they are understood to be formal and general descriptions of a class of decisions taken in a given society with regard to certain sorts of cases, rather than a statement of some abstract principle that mechanically dictates the outcome of particular conflicts.

For example, it is uncontested that a corporation's directors owe fiduciary duties to the corporation and its shareholders. The question for litigation is not to specify some complete list of the actions that constitute fulfillment of that duty. Such a list would be impossible to finish.[7] Litigation concerns whether a particular action, or perhaps failure to act, constituted a breach of a certain director's fiduciary duty. Of obvious relevance to answering this question—a question slightly different in each case—are the familiar considerations of forensic argument, including how this court, or other courts, decided more or less similar cases; the direction, if any, provided by the legislative or executive branches of the government; the general sense of what seems appropriate in the relevant communities; the social consequences of generalizing the court's decision, and the like. Thus, fiduciary duty is defined negatively (by its breach) and after the fact. A doctrinal statement (e.g., taking of a corporate opportunity by a director) without notice to, or ratification by, the board or shareholders is a breach of fiduciary duty sounds like a rule. But the statement is also (and is more defensible as) a summation of a class of cases in which courts found the behavior of directors to be inappropriate.

For another example, take the simple doctrine of *respondeat superior.* The black letter "rule" is that masters are liable for the torts of their servants. Students tend to approach the question in doctrinal (abstract and deductive) fashion: if A meets the definition of a master, and B meets the definition of a servant, and B hurts C, then C can recover damages from A. This is merely logical, but as Holmes famously said, the life of the law has been experience rather than logic.[8] A case is likely to look more like this: a business hires a person to perform a job. The person (for these purposes, the "agent," or in old fashioned language, the "servant") harms someone, and the victim sues the business (the "principal" or "master"), because the agent does not have enough money to pay the damages. The practical question before the court is who is going to pay? More generally, is this sort of thing something for which the business ought to be held liable? Further questions would be asked. Was this a full-time employee or a subcontactor? Was the agent's harmful action within the scope of his agency?[9] How has this court, or other courts, decided similar cases? If the court decides that the principal should pay, then the principal is a master and the agent is a servant, to which the doctrine of *respondeat superior* applies, that is, masters answer (are liable) for the actions of their servants. But one cannot say that the labels "master" and "servant," and therefore the doctrine of *respondeat superior,* apply until the case has been decided. *The doctrine announces the outcome rather than controls it.*

The vast majority of cases are plausibly decided, that is, there are unsurprising reasons for the decision. From this perspective, legal doctrines are abstracted and, hence, highly articulated, even principled, statements of rather more inchoate commitments held by judges (and implicitly by the legal community, and less directly, society at large). In this context, the job of the law student is to learn the mores of the law profession. This is not to say that all cases are correctly decided; it is in fact to suggest the opposite. Presumably any student of the law (or any lawyer, professor, or judge) would, if somehow given the chance, decide some cases in ways differently from the judge who in fact decided the case. However, this is roughly equivalent to saying that one might call certain balls strikes. The professorial tendency to declare certain decisions "wrongly" decided should be looked upon with a bit of indulgence. No doubt, were I emperor, the law would be different. But until then, it would be adult to recognize that politics, including law, does not always work out as we (might think we) wish, or even believe to be true.

One of the central purposes in this book's urging of a dramatic understanding of law is that such understanding fosters the comprehension of antagonisms. The "felt necessities" of a society, indeed of a life, are not logically consistent.[10] And neither are the morals to stories nor those collective and enforced morals we call legal doctrines. And once we accept the need to work with such inconsistency, we may begin to cobble together a sophisticated understanding—this is called being worldly, a useful thing for anyone, but especially for a lawyer.

Part II

Internal Struggles

Chapter 5

Directors' Fiduciary Duties

Loyalty

In General

As passive and distant owners of the corporation, shareholders have little ability to monitor how their business is being conducted. In particular, shareholders cannot determine whether the managers of the company are operating the business in their own interests or doing what they were hired to do, which is to operate the business on behalf of the corporation and its shareholders. Shareholders not only have little opportunity to learn of mismanagement, they have few legal rights to do anything about whatever mismanagement they might discover. Shareholders have limited capacity to monitor or respond; shareholders are positioned as victims.

Directors are supposed to protect the corporation and its shareholders. How? Directors are supposed to establish a strategy for the business, to hire managers who can execute that strategy, and to monitor the performance of managers and of the business as a whole. More practically speaking, directors are supposed to ensure the good conduct of the business through the exercise of their power to set the pay of, and to fire, managers. To indulge a fancy: if shareholders are damsels in distress (as retail investors, shareholders are often called "widows and orphans"), then directors are knights. But knights face temptations; Lancelot sleeps with King Arthur's wife, Guinevere. The reality is less salacious, of course. Institutional investors like mutual funds are not too much like damsels, and the quite mature men and women who sit on the nation's corporate boards rarely come off as gallant young warriors. But like knights, directors are obliged to serve and are perennially, and subtly, tempted.

Although business actors are often thought to be motivated purely by self-interest, a view no doubt encouraged by the discipline of economics, in fact the business world commonly expects and even legally requires persons to act on behalf of others. A person required to act on behalf of another is often called a *fiduciary,* one who has fiduciary duties or fiduciary obligations toward the other. So, for an obvious example, directors have fiduciary duties to the corporation and its shareholders. Fiduciary relationships are everywhere in business. Agents are fiduciaries for their principals, which means that managers are fiduciaries for their corporations and its shareholders, and lawyers are fiduciaries for their clients, as are brokers, banks, and other financial intermediaries. Partners and joint venturers are fiduciaries for each other. Executors of estates and receivers in bankruptcy are fiduciaries. And paradigmatically, trustees are fiduciaries for the beneficiaries of the trust.

This is circular and vague and just not very helpful. One might want to know, what must be done in order to fulfill the fiduciary duty? Rephrased, what is the substance of the fiduciary relationship? Such questions are understandable but naive; matters are not so simple. The very term *fiduciary duty* is somewhat misleading, as it suggests a concrete obligation that can be specified in the abstract. To say that a person is a fiduciary, however, says nothing about what his or her particular job is. What, specifically, a given fiduciary's obligations are depends on the relationship in question. Bankers and lawyers may both be fiduciaries, but they do different things and, hence, fulfill their duties toward others in different ways. As U.S. Supreme Court Justice Felix Frankfurter put it: "[T]o say that a man is a fiduciary only begins analysis; it gives direction to further inquiry. To whom is he a fiduciary? What obligations does he owe as a fiduciary? In what respect has he failed to discharge these obligations? And what are the consequences of his deviation from duty?"[1] Instead of specifying tasks, to call someone a fiduciary is to say that he or she is expected to have a certain attitude or stance, and consequently, to behave in ways akin to (if not the same as) what is expected from trustees, who are the model fiduciaries.

The medieval English institution of the trust was developed as a way to settle variously defined rights to land over time, a problem that arose in a bewildering variety of ways. But consider, by way of an overdramatized but not baseless example, unpleasant biological facts that have yet to be overcome, the mortality of men and the foolishness of their sons.[2] A nobleman who wished to secure his estate and pass it along to his heirs had to worry that he would die before his son was old enough to manage the estate. Worse, a hotheaded youth might mortgage the estate, spend the cash whoring and gambling in London, and lose the castle, thereby reducing not only his own prospects, but also the status of the family. The solution to this problem was the trust, an institution whereby "legal ownership," that is, control of a body of assets (the "corpus" of the trust) would be conveyed to a sensible friend, the trustee, who was expected to manage things for the benefit of the heir, "the beneficiary" of the trust, who retained "beneficial ownership." When the young heir reached a certain age, when it was hoped he would be mature enough to be responsible for the family's fortunes, the trust would expire, and the legal ownership of the corpus (i.e., control over the baron's castle) would go to the heir. The trust accomplished its intended purpose and is indeed still used for transferring assets to the young and therefore irresponsible, as well as for numerous other business and charitable purposes.

The person establishing a trust (the "grantor") places great confidence in the trustee. The trustee must be absolutely trustworthy. To go back to our baron: once the trustee had gained legal control over the baron's estate, the trustee could ignore it, mismanage it, or in the extreme case, take it for himself—in any event, harming the intended beneficiary of the trust, the baron's son and heir. The grantor, the baron, was already dead, and apart from haunting, was powerless to do anything to help his heir. The son was probably also powerless, and law, then as now, is a tricky and often inaccessible path. As a practical matter, therefore, in establishing a trust, the baron had to believe that the friend to whom the trust was given simply would do the right thing. Thus, the creation of a trust was, and is, a sign of utmost confidence. Trustees are expected to do right by someone else, even though they are given legal powers that present them with the opportunity to do otherwise. And doing the right thing by others is what is expected of fiduciaries more generally, including the directors of a corporation.

The Duty of Loyalty

As every virtue implies a vice, loyalty implies its opposite, disloyalty (what Sir Lancelot would call infidelity).[3] The fiduciary is in a position to use (or sometimes fail to use) the power of his or her office in such a way that he or she personally benefits, rather than the party to whom he or she owes fiduciary duties. If we presume that virtually all fiduciaries have a degree of self-interest, then conflict of interest is the structure in which the fiduciary exists, and which defines him or her: the choice to be loyal or not. The choice may present itself in countless ways; there are countless forms of temptation. A few patterns, however, are familiar and discussed in commonly taught cases.

A corporation may do business with one of its directors or with a company controlled by one of its directors. Imagine that a real estate development corporation buys land from one of its directors. Such deals are often called interested director transactions, because the director has a personal interest in the deal. In this example, the director is on both sides of the transaction. The director is on the side of the development corporation, because he or she is a director, who supposedly has the interests of the corporation at heart and, therefore, should want the transaction to occur at *a low price*. At the same time, as the seller, our director has a personal interest in seeing that the land fetches *a high price*. Our director, in short, has a quite specific conflict of interest.

A shareholder in the real estate development corporation would want to know whether the company had overpaid for the land. In the nineteenth century, interested director transactions could be voided by the corporation (or a shareholder acting in the name of the corporation), regardless of the fairness of the transaction.[4] In the twentieth century, courts became somewhat reluctant to void contracts made by corporations with their own directors. It is often in the interest of a corporation (and its shareholders) to have directors who have some understanding, stake, and degree of influence in the business environment in which the company does business. So, in our example, it makes sense for a real estate development company to have directors who understand the real estate business and who are influential in the community in which the company operates. Such people are likely to own land and may well control related, even competing, businesses. Thus, the corporation has somewhat of a conflict of interest, too: on the one hand, the corporation has an interest in directors who fulfill their fiduciary duties; on the other hand, the corporation has an interest in business opportunities brought to it by its own directors.

The Business Judgment Rule and Other Complicati

Courts have become hesitant to void interested director transactions, or to hold directors liable for losses, because, more generally, courts have become reluctant to second-guess business decisions. This reluctance is not historically constant. Berle and Means, in the 1930s, argued for extensive review of business decisions.[5] In the years since, however, courts generally have become somewhat more modest, reasoning roughly as follows. Litigation is different from business; judges weighing arguments are not making business decisions. Perhaps even more importantly, business requires taking risks and making decisions about the future, which is always more or less unknown. Even a good board of directors will make bad business decisions. It seems wrong to allow shareholders to sue merely because the decision turned out to be incorrect. And if shareholders were allowed to sue merely because decisions taken on their behalf turned out to be wrong, then directors might be expected to be very cautious. But as discussed in chapters 2 and 3, a central benefit of the corporation is that it allows people to work together to take risks.

Therefore, when shareholders sue directors, courts are inclined to say that the decision of the director is protected from judicial review by the "business judgment rule" and dismiss the case. The doctrinal contours of the business judgment rule are less than perfectly clear; there is academic literature on the subject. For present purposes, however, it suffices to say that courts are very hesitant to review the substance of the business decisions made by boards of directors. In order to avoid being dismissed out of hand, shareholders must show considerably more than the error of a board's decision. Shareholders must show that the decision breached the board's fiduciary duty. For these purposes, the fiduciary duties of directors are commonly discussed under two general headings: the duty of loyalty, discussed in this chapter; and the duty to make decisions consciously and carefully, the duty of due care, discussed in the next chapter.

So, in our example, suppose our shareholder sues on behalf of the corporation, claiming that the real estate development company paid too much for the land.[6] The shareholder can, without much difficulty, demonstrate what certainly looks like a conflict of interest: the corporation would like to buy land for a low price, and the director, as seller, would like to sell the land for a high price. Based on such a *prima facie* (Latin for first glance) showing of a conflict of interest, courts would not apply the business judgment rule. Instead, the burden would shift to the director, who would have to show the "entire fairness" of the transaction. If the directors cannot show that the transaction was entirely fair, then the directors would be personally liable.

A word of caution is in order. Again, this is a book about the law as taught. Skirting the edge of the basic course in business associations (and other basic courses) are legal and business realities that complicate questions of responsibility and liability. As noted, legal education focuses on appellate opinions, although litigation is the exception, and appeals more so. Criminal law focuses on trials, even though few people who are indicted are tried—they plea. And corporation law discusses oversight of the corporation in terms of the liability of directors, although directors very rarely pay for breaches of fiduciary duty or any other obligations incurred while fulfilling their responsibilities as directors.

Companies generally indemnify (pay for) directors and officers against the costs of lawsuits; most corporate charters are written so that the corporation indemnifies its directors to the fullest extent permissible under the law. In addition, corporations carry insurance on directors and officers, sensibly enough called directors and officers (D&O) insurance. Typically, companies carry policies both on the company's obligation to indemnify and on the directors and officers themselves, for situations in which indemnification is not permissible. Thus, the picture painted by the basic cases—of personal director liability for breaches of fiduciary duty—is a substantial simplification.[7]

Confronted with an interested director transaction, the corporation could seek to have the transaction ratified. A disinterested portion of the board (usually, the disinterested independent directors, those directors who are neither on both sides of the transaction nor employed by the company) may vote that the transaction is fair. Courts generally give such ratified board decisions the benefit of the business judgment rule. Or the shareholders as a whole may ratify the transaction, at which point the dissenting shareholder's argument that the transaction was not to the benefit of the corporation and its shareholders collapses of its own weight.

There are, of course, other ways in which conflicts of interest may arise. As mentioned in chapter 3, directors set the compensation paid to top management, and many top managers are also directors. (Particularly in the United States, it is common for the chief executive officer to be the chairman of the board of directors.) Thus, traditionally, many top managers, while wearing their director hats, voted on their own salaries. Even when managers do not vote on their salaries, most directors are nominated to the board (and perfunctorily approved by the shareholders) because of preexisting relationships with management. In such an environment, compensation is likely to be, to put matters diplomatically, very generous. And indeed executive compensation among U.S. executives has been rising—relative to inflation, ordinary employee compensation, size of firm, practices of other industrialized nations—for decades. Criticism has been substantial.[8] In the wake of Enron and other accounting scandals, the Sarbanes-Oxley Act of 2002 requires the boards of all publicly traded (and a few privately held) companies to have compensation committees comprised exclusively of independent directors.[9] As of this writing, such oversight has not dampened the inflation of executive compensation.

Less dramatically, directors also set their own compensation. To be a director is not a full-time job, and the compensation of directors is dwarfed by that received by managers. Nonetheless, directors are well compensated for the amount of time they devote to the corporation. And there are other benefits: board meetings are often held in luxurious settings, travel expenses are handsomely reimbursed, a degree of prestige comes with membership on the board of a major corporation, and so forth. The conflict of interest at issue here is not that directors will pay themselves too much, but that directors who enjoy their status as directors will not jeopardize their positions by making themselves uncomfortable to management and the other members of the board.

Meinhard v. Salmon and Disclosure

Other conflicts of interest are less subtle. A director may be in a business that directly competes with the corporation.[10] Or a director may take an opportunity for a future business that, at least in the opinion of some shareholders, should have been offered to the corporation.[11] Indeed, a fiduciary who takes a business opportunity for himself or herself alone gave rise to what is probably the most famous opinion in the corporation law canon, *Meinhard v. Salmon.*[12] In point of fact, *Meinhard v. Salmon* involves a joint venture, not a corporation, but no matter: the case teaches a great deal about fiduciary duties and is universally taught, cited, and occasionally criticized as overly moralistic.

Meinhard and Salmon had a joint venture to lease and refurbish the Bristol hotel, on the corner of 42nd Street and 5th Avenue in midtown Manhattan, converting the property into a mixed-use commercial building. They agreed to operate this property for twenty years, from 1902 until 1922. Salmon leased the building, oversaw its refurbishment, and managed the property. Meinhard provided the money. They shared in profits and in the risk of loss, according to an agreed formula. In time, one Elbridge Gerry came to own the Bristol hotel that Meinhard and Salmon were operating under a lease, as well as other buildings along 42nd Street. Gerry wanted someone to lease his property, destroy the existing buildings, and redevelop the entire site. Gerry approached Salmon with the idea. Since Salmon had leased the building in his own name, rather than in the name of the joint venture, Gerry was not on notice that Salmon "held [the lease] as a fiduciary, for himself and another, sharers in a common venture."[13] Salmon agreed to be the developer after the joint venture with Meinhard expired. Therefore, and without telling Meinhard, Salmon entered into a new lease for the Bristol hotel, and for the other properties. This was a grand proposal. The lease could be extended for up to eighty years, and so was in effect much like a sale, and it covered a swath of increasingly prime Manhattan real estate. On eventually learning of the massive new project, Meinhard demanded that the new lease be held as an asset of his joint venture with Salmon. When Salmon refused, Meinhard sued.

Judge Benjamin Cardozo, then of the New York Court of Appeals, later of the Supreme Court, and for whom Yeshiva University's law school is named, wrote perhaps his most famous opinion.[14] Cardozo distinguished between the self-interest often expected in the business world and the regard for another that is expected of a fiduciary.

> Many forms of conduct permissible in a workaday world for those acting at arm's length, are forbidden to those bound by fiduciary ties. A trustee is held to something stricter than the morals of the market place. Not honesty alone, but the punctilio of an honor the most sensitive, is then the standard of behavior.[15]

But what, in this situation, should Salmon have done to fulfill that standard? A punctilious fiduciary would not keep a business opportunity, which he had received solely because he was the fiduciary, secret from the person to whom he owed the duty. Cardozo was angry that "Salmon appropriated to himself [the opportunity to participate in the next project] in secrecy and silence."[16] Cardozo expected Salmon to tell Meinhard about the opportunity, so that Meinhard could either participate in the development with Meinhard or at least offer a competing bid to Gerry. "The very fact that Salmon was in control with exclusive powers of direction charged him the more obviously with the duty of disclosure, since only through disclosure could opportunity be equalized."[17]

Since Salmon did not disclose, "he excluded his coadventurer from any chance to compete, from any chance to enjoy the opportunity for benefit that had come to him alone by virtue of his agency. This chance, if nothing more, he was under a duty to concede. The price of its denial is an extension of the trust at the option and for the benefit of the one whom he excluded."[18] Thus, because Salmon did not disclose, a share of the benefit of the new lease was held in trust for Meinhard.[19]

Loyalty and Community

What have we learned about the roles of directors from being led, even if only vicariously, into temptation? First and most obviously, the possibility of temptation requires the expectation of virtue; the business world is not comprised solely of greed, sometimes called rational self-interest. Many people, notably the directors of corporations (and lawyers) are expected to serve others, even sometimes when such service may be against their economic interest. Second, what directors or other fiduciaries are supposed to do is defined by the specific character of the relationship in question. Third, in uncertain situations, particularly potential conflicts of interest, fiduciaries should disclose. Fourth, oftentimes a decision that might otherwise appear to be self-interested and in breach of a fiduciary duty can be ratified after the fact. Otherwise, courts may require a fiduciary to prove that an action, taken in his or her own interest, was inherently fair to the party to whom the fiduciary owed a duty—which can be difficult and looks bad.

Disclosure, and its cousin, ratification, do not eliminate self-interest, but tend to legitimate it, a matter that will be explored in greater detail in chapter 13. That Salmon wished to make money developing in Manhattan was not the problem. Nor did Cardozo suggest that Salmon had to give Meinhard the chance to participate in Gerry's development scheme, or that Salmon could not participate. All Salmon had to do was disclose to Meinhard the existence of the project, so that Meinhard had a chance to compete. Disclosure tends to prove good faith. Disclosure thus creates a certain kind of community, or more precisely, reinforces the community entailed in the business association. People should know where they stand. Cardozo is explicit: if a fiduciary were allowed to take opportunities for himself rather than the beneficiary of his trust, then "He might steal a march on his comrade under cover of the darkness, and then hold the captured ground. Loyalty and comradeship are not so easily abjured."[20] Rational self-interest, perhaps, but bounded by some sense of propriety, and in at least that limited sense, community.

Chapter 6

Directors' Fiduciary Duties

Due Care

Due Care and the Business Judgment Rule

FROM THE PERSPECTIVE OF SHAREHOLDERS, WHO LOOK TO DIRECTORS TO oversee their business, it is not enough that directors be loyal. Making decisions believed to be in the best interest of the corporation and its shareholders does little good if the board makes bad decisions. Decisions need to be well made. Therefore directors need to take "due care" in making decisions. But to what extent is taking due care a legally enforceable fiduciary duty? That is, to what extent can courts require that directors make good decisions (i.e., hold directors personally liable for bad decisions)? As discussed in the previous chapter, courts are not inclined to correct the decisions of boards of directors. Indeed, under the business judgment rule, courts defer to the business judgment of boards of directors, even when those decisions turn out badly.

For example, in *Kamin v. American Express,* a shareholder sued the board of directors of the American Express Company (Amex), arguing that the

73

directors had made a decision demonstrably not in the best economic interest of the shareholders.[1] Amex bought Donaldson, Lufkin, Jenrette (DLJ). The stock of DLJ, and also of Amex, had subsequently declined in value. One possible course of action was for Amex to sell the DLJ stock and take its losses. Amex could count the losses made on the DLJ acquisition against its profits from other operations (i.e., Amex would pay less corporate tax), but formally admitting the investment was bad would have been embarrassing for Amex's management.

Another possible course of action was to distribute the DLJ stock as a dividend to Amex shareholders. Under this course of action, Amex would not take a loss on its investment in DLJ, and, therefore, Amex would pay more corporate tax, but Amex's management would not have to admit that it had made a mistake. Amex chose the second possibility, and Kamin, a shareholder, sued, arguing that the value of Amex stock under the first course of action was demonstrably greater than the value of the Amex plus DLJ stock shareholders would receive under the second course of action. Under the first course of action, the company got a tax break. Under the second course of action, the company did not get the tax break. So, Kamin argued, the director's decision was clearly wrong and injured the shareholders of Amex by the amount of the tax difference.[2] On a motion for summary judgment, the Delaware court held that this was not a violation of the duty of due care. In such cases the issue is not whether the court would agree with the substance of the decision; the issue is whether the board violated its duty of due care in making the decision. The decision to grant a dividend is in the discretion of the board; courts will almost never review the substance of a board's decision to grant a dividend.[3] Granting a dividend is a business judgment and not the province of courts.

What Do Directors Do?

What qualifies as a decision taken with due care? Answering this question requires some notion of what directors are expected to do, and in particular, some more nuanced sense of the context in which directors are asked to make decisions, and some more nuanced sense of how they work. Being a director is a part-time job. Directors meet periodically, usually at least quarterly. It is preferable for board meetings to be held live, face to face, but sometimes directors meet through electronic media such as a conference call or video conferencing. Information is often distributed and sometimes understood beforehand, but in the nature of things, relevant considerations and further information come forth at the meeting itself. At least for medium to large companies, full board meetings are often held at a good hotel. The directors come together for the meeting; their normal lives are spent apart. A board meeting is thus a discrete occasion, literally a meeting, at which issues thought to be confronting the company are decided.

Board meetings are about issues *"thought to be* confronting the company" because a board meeting cannot simply be about all the issues *actually* confronting the company. The company is a vast collective enterprise and more than a little ephemeral. To be flippant, the corporation as such cannot travel to Palm Springs or the Bahamas or even corporate headquarters or wherever the board's meeting might be. Therefore, of necessity, a board meeting is about the issues confronting the company as the company is portrayed, usually by management, at the meeting.

The fact that directors deal with representations of what a company may be shapes the work of directors in at least three ways. First, the scale of even a medium-sized operation is vastly larger than can be discussed in a meeting. The company's affairs are out there, in the world. The meeting is about the tips of whatever icebergs seem worthy of attention. Management is likely to seek board approval for what management itself considers to be major decisions. Some issues—personnel changes among upper level management or the board itself, proposed changes to the capital structure of the business, and other major financings, the budget—are perennial, if somewhat unpredictable in detail. Other problems ("challenges") arise in the course of doing business, on a random basis: changes in key commercial relationships, major liabilities, opportunities for new business directions, and so forth may all be brought to the board's attention. Although some issues must be brought to the board's attention, management almost always controls how issues are presented. And selection is unavoidable—management may decide not to put an issue on the table, and that issue may later prove to be important.

Recall that directors are supposed to protect shareholders (who are understood to be distant and passive) from management. In light of the discretion given to managers to set the agenda and present the issues, however, it is hard to see how even very capable and committed directors, meeting for a few days a year to discuss the affairs of a company that may operate 24/7 on several continents, can really know what the management is up to. That is, for the largest companies that concerned Berle and Means, and for that matter, even for companies quite a bit smaller, the hope that directors can address the problems of scale confronted by shareholders is a bit wishful. Board meetings are *partial*.

Second, and to a great extent as a result of the problem of scale, the representations of a company presented to directors are necessarily very *abstract*. Significant matters are placed on an agenda and discussed in orderly fashion. Papers are distributed, and the very round numbers more or less add up. Assumptions are made, more or less tacitly, and the resulting facts are reported. Oftentimes experts (usually accountants or lawyers) vouch for some aspect of what is reported, although never all. Committees of the board meet intermittently, and the outcomes of such discussions are summarized for the full board, and sometimes discussed by the full board. Issues confronting the company are presented; what management plans to do is announced; and more or less satisfying reasons are given. If a committee has met on the issue, it may make a recommendation. Votes are called, and management's proposals almost always pass. But, as a board member, what has one really learned? One has heard a great many representations, with no easily corroborated connection to their objects (i.e., board meetings deal in abstractions from their companies). The most obvious example is a projected budget.

Such abstractions are necessary to getting a meeting done, of course, but the abstract quality of representations poses substantial problems for directors. How deeply should a director expect to be satisfied by a business presentation? Surely one must immediately recognize that with regard to any number of questions—consider currency risk, for example—there is no way the management knows what will happen. One may, of course, ask questions. But as a practical matter, the ability to ask questions at a board meeting is limited, far more limited than the ability of a student to ask questions in a class. Unless one actively suspects that management is lying—in which case one should work to remove management, or not remain a member of the board—there is much to be said for helping to get the work of the board done, for being a team player.

An anecdote may clarify the problem: shortly after the Enron scandal broke, I had several conversations with the late Barber Conable, who had been both a president of the World Bank and a longtime member of Congress (notably on the House Ways and Means Committee), and who was good enough to speak to one of my classes. At the time, Conable was on the board of American International Group (AIG), the world's largest insurance concern.[4] AIG was then run by the brilliant Maurice "Hank" Greenberg. Conable reported that the board had no practical choice but to listen to Greenberg describe the maneuvers currently being undertaken by the group's many interconnected entities, and

what Greenberg thought the risks and opportunities to be. It was
listen to the man, Conable said, but who could know, or judge, it
right? A few years after Conable died, AIG came under considerab
from the New York attorney general's office and the Security and Exchange
Commission, beginning with the accounting for a transaction with a unit of
Warren Buffett's Berkshire Hathaway group. Greenberg was forced from office,
and litigation ensued.[5] Had Conable not fulfilled his duty of care? I doubt it.
He certainly knew an enormous amount about what large institutions did with
their money, and he was always known as a hardworking man.

The third point to be made about how a company's affairs are represented at a
board meeting has already been suggested: management presents the company
and its issues to the board. Things are somewhat different if a company is in
crisis, when institutions such as the courts, the press, a hostile bidder, or the
financial markets may seize the power to represent a company's affairs from its
management. Or management may lose its ability to account for the business of
the company or even cease to function altogether. In such crises, the board may
(often should) seize control, although, by the time the crisis becomes evident,
it may be too late to save the company. Until such crisis, however, the board as
a practical matter is forced to trust management. Most everything the directors
know about the company (about what a great job management is doing for
the corporation and its shareholders), they learn from management—which
is not exactly what Berle and Means had in mind. Board meetings, in short,
are *biased*—management's view predominates. It must immediately be added
that "biased" is meant here as an objective characterization, not necessarily
as a condemnation. Many managers are admirable business leaders and even
good people. But whatever virtues managers possess does not change the fact
that, even when they are as conscientious as can be, managers have a distinct
perspective, and hardly a disinterested one.

Taken together, we can see that board meetings are occasional events at
which a group of people pay attention to management's *partial, abstract,*
and *biased* presentations of a company's situation, prospects, and their own
performance. In this context, how do we expect boards of directors to work,
and what do we expect them to do? With its history in tort law, "duty of care"
conjures up an image of a director who undertakes a specific task and accom-
plishes or fails to accomplish that task according to some widely agreed upon
(and so judicially enforceable) standard of care. So what is the task that the
law expects directors to do, to perform with due care?

The problem is that the question, posed in this way, is bad. (Don't believe
that "there are no bad questions.") The question presumes a most inaccurate

understanding of the directors' job, and then asks whether they have done that job well.[6] First, directors are asked for their business judgment. Uncertainty and incomplete information—even uncertainty about how incomplete the information is—are the order of the day. How broadly and deeply to inquire, in order to try and resolve such uncertainty, in a world where knowledge is costly and often unobtainable, especially in time, are likewise matters of business judgment. And business, by its nature, involves taking risks. The question is not "Is it safe?," but "Does the company adequately understand the risks of its situation in order to move forward in this way as opposed to some other?" Situations are complex. Business leaders must coordinate a constellation of issues, often in the face of various sorts of opposition, both from constituents (financiers, consumers, employees) and of course competition and a generally recalcitrant world. Thus, while "due care" suggests that directors are accomplishing a discrete task, deciding some clear-cut issue, in fact the issues that are put before boards are almost never discrete or well defined, but instead tend to be strategic and diffuse.

Second, single directors do not make corporate decisions; *boards* of directors do. Boards are collective bodies. The members must work together and, to some significant degree, trust one another. As with any collective body, a degree of compromise and deference is required in order to get anything done; those who cannot get along over time will not be allowed to participate. Boards operate by consensus—the vast majority of votes are unanimous—but it is not the consensus of homogeneity. A well-constructed board is diverse, in the sense that directors have various levels of knowledge and experience of particular aspects of the company's business. Considerable deference to particular expertise within the board is sensible. Thus, while the negligence concept of a duty of care presumes a typical board member, there is no typical board member. Different people are on the board precisely because they bring different qualities to the table.

Third, boards make, or even authorize, very few of the countless decisions that any company must take on an ongoing basis. The vast majority of a board's decisions are of a routine, housekeeping or procedural character. Very few issues are, or could be, put to the collective consideration of the full board as focused questions to be discussed, argued over, and ultimately decided by vote. On rare occasions a company comes to a crossroads, and a decision must be made by the board standing more or less alone (e.g., over whether to replace a failing chief executive officer). Much more frequently, however, management reaches a tentative decision but cannot go forward without the legal approval of the board. Management may even want the opportunity to review its thinking in a supportive, yet critical, forum. Instead of make decisions on free-standing questions, what the board does is monitor, approve, suggest, amend, and caution. Bayless Manning spoke of the board's duty of attention.[7] Melvin Eisenberg wrote of the board as *monitoring* the company and its management.[8] One might say that boards force management to account for themselves to their peers, often a rather sobering enterprise. Thus, rather than an individual actor who is expected to conduct a particular task with a certain degree of care, a board of directors is expected, as a collectivity, to maintain a certain stance toward the corporation, and in doing so, to incline the business toward appropriate conduct.

Inside and Independent Directors

So what can be done to create a board—and thus a corporate environment—that is most likely to influence management in a positive direction? This question is traditionally discussed as a choice between *inside directors,* who work as managers of the corporation, and *independent directors,* who have no other relationship to the company. The advantages of inside directors are derived from the understanding of the company and its problems these individuals bring to the board. Managers work at the company full time; they spend their days concerned with the company's business. No independent director can hope to match the depth and breadth of understanding of an inside director, for the simple reason that an independent director is, by definition, outside the company most of the time.

The disadvantages of inside directors are equally obvious and essentially are derived from conflicts of interest. Managers have vested interest in high salaries, rich severance packages, and job security. The board sets the salaries and severance packages of managers. The board hires and fires managers. The board votes to recommend mergers, which often result in the dismissal of managers. In such situations, the interests of inside directors may well be opposed to the interests of shareholders. More subtly, managers have a distinct perspective, which may be quite different from the perspective of especially diversified shareholders. Such differences in perspective may not be perceived as conflicts of interest. So, for example, managers may cause the company to diversify away, or insure against, risks that an otherwise diversified shareholder might find attractive.[9] In short, the fact that inside directors are employed by the company often compromises their ability to direct the corporation in the interests of shareholders. Such compromises make outside directors look more attractive.

The idea of the director is thus somewhat self-contradictory. On the one hand, the ideal director is deeply interested in, and knowledgeable about, the company's business. As a practical matter, however, such a director would not acquire and maintain such understanding without a personal interest in the company, and therefore is likely to be knowledgeable, but not disinterested. On the other hand, but by the same token, a truly disinterested director is unlikely to be very knowledgeable. To state the same problem rather more doctrinally: fiduciary duties can be understood in terms of two senses of the word trust—trustworthy because well intentioned (the motivation of the fiduciary, doctrinally expressed as the duty of loyalty); and trustworthy because reliable or attentive (the quality of the fiduciary's decision, doctrinally expressed as the duty of care). This makes a certain amount of sense, if we recall the idea of a fiduciary is rooted in the law of trusts: one would want the holder of a trust to exemplify both meanings of "trust."[10] At least in the context of monitoring sizable corporations on behalf of their boards, however, the meanings of "trust" are in tension: the director who has no conflict of interest and is likely to be trustworthy is also likely to be rather ignorant; the director who works with the company daily is therefore deeply knowledgable but unlikely to have objective judgment.

In the wake of Enron and other accounting scandals, Congress passed the Sarbanes-Oxley Act of 2002, among other things requiring publicly traded corporations (and some privately held entities) to have an audit committee, and a compensation committee, comprised exclusively of independent directors.[11] Thus, with regard to the most obvious conflict of interest, the compensation committee, and with regard to the most obvious source of information, accounting, Congress required disinterest from corporate directors, even if presumably giving up a degree of knowledge.[12] After Enron, trustworthiness evidently seemed the more important aspect of the problem. But the board of Enron itself had a fair number of independent directors and nonetheless failed spectacularly. The Sarbanes-Oxley Act does little to ameliorate the fundamental fact that, as a structural matter, boards of directors must trust the very people, management, they are supposed to be monitoring.

Smith v. Van Gorkom

For many years, the tensions within the doctrine of due care were unproblematic, for the simple reason that courts did not employ the doctrine to evaluate the performance of directors loyally doing their job. In a few cases, courts condemned directors who completely abdicated their responsibilities for failure to exercise due care, but in such cases it was often more correct to say the directors had not exercised any care whatsoever. And courts condemned directors whose judgment was tainted by self-interest, but such cases could be understood as at least in part failures to fulfill the duty of loyalty.

The doctrine of "duty of care" in its pure form was employed hardly, if at all, until the famous case of *Smith v. Van Gorkom*.[13] The chief executive officer of Trans Union Corporation, Van Gorkom, approached the financier Jay Pritzker and offered to sell Trans Union for some $55 per share. Trans Union had tax credits that were valuable to Pritzker. At the time, the company was trading around $38 per share. With the addition of a few additional terms, Pritzker agreed in principle to buy Trans Union through a leveraged buy out, in which borrowed funds would be used to buy out existing Trans Union sharehold-ers, and control of the firm would be transferred to a company controlled by Pritzker via a statutory merger.

Under the Delaware Code, the merger required the approval of Trans Union's shareholders. In announcing Pritzker's offer, the board needed to recommend to the shareholders that they accept, or reject, the offer. Van Gorkom, there-fore, took the proposal to his board of directors. The duties of the board in recommending a merger, or any transaction in which the shareholders will be bought out and therefore cease to be shareholders, are somewhat ambiguous. On the one hand, the board is recommending that the shareholders should take the cash (i.e., that the compensation offered is worth more than the company will be worth). On the other hand, the buyer must think that the company can be worth more or else the transaction would not take place.[14] After an oral presentation and a relatively short meeting, Trans Union's board voted to recommend shareholder approval of the merger, effectively transferring control of the company to Pritzker.

A dissenting shareholder sued, arguing that Trans Union's board had not fulfilled its duty of care in assessing whether Pritzker's offer was in the best interest of existing Trans Union shareholders. No financial data was considered. In particular, no opinion from an investment bank, stating that the offer was reasonable, was presented to the board. Not only was there no serious effort to find a competing offer for Trans Union, but in fact, Van Gorkom had agreed not to shop Trans Union to other potential buyers, and had, moreover, agreed to a "breakup fee" to be paid to Pritzker in the event that Trans Union were nonetheless sold to someone else. Thus, neither the company's own numbers, nor an independent bank, nor the marketplace lent authority to the board's decision that Pritzker's offer was in the best interest of Trans Union's existing shareholders. The Delaware court held that this process of decision was a breach of the duty of due care, and held the directors personally liable to the shareholders for the difference in the price received from Pritzker and a price to be determined by a judicial proceeding.

The corporate world was rather shocked. As discussed in a strong dissent from the Delaware Court's decision, Trans Union's board was very experienced with both this company and in business generally. Trans Union's stock price and its business had lagged for years. Pritzker had made a generous offer, because he had a business opportunity (to use the tax credits) that neither Trans Union nor any other buyer on the horizon could use. The Delaware legislature also strongly disagreed with the decision in *Smith v. Van Gorkom* and passed legislation allowing a Delaware corporation to include, in its certificate of incorporation, a provision making directors not liable for breaches of the duty of due care (except in certain defined situations).[15]

There was a social aspect to the case as well. Pritzker and many of the board members of Trans Union were prominent members of the Chicago business establishment and had known each other for years. The principals in this deal trusted each other and so were able to do business on a relatively informal basis.[16] Trust, after all, is how much business gets done. For his part, Pritzker thought he had made a fair deal for Trans Union and resented the Delaware Court's implication that he had pulled the wool over the eyes of the Trans Union board. In a period of hostile takeovers, when financiers were widely reviled, perhaps Pritzker did not want to be considered a corporate raider who took unfair advantage of the weakness of others. Whatever his reasons, after the decision Pritzker made an extraordinarily generous offer: he required each of the Trans Union directors to make a $130,000 contribution to a charity of their choice, while Pritzker himself agreed to pay the damages (i.e., he allowed the Delaware Court to renegotiate the price of Trans Union).[17]

Nonetheless, *Smith v. Van Gorkom* has remained influential. The court emphasized the process of decision and found that process wanting because there was no presentation of written documents or of numbers. No board today would presume to discuss a merger without a "fairness opinion" generated by an investment bank, and indeed without a heavily documented presentation of why the merger is a good idea and in the financial interest of shareholders. Investment banks and law firms active in this area have become, to put it diplomatically, adroit at generating such documentation so quickly that it doesn't impede the flow of their client's business.[18] Thus, while *Smith v. Van Gorkom* has undeniably generated work for investment banks and law firms, it is not obvious that such documentation improves the decisions made by boards of directors. Perhaps merger decisions are better because of *Smith*'s insistence on more documentation, or at least maybe sometimes they are. What seems beyond doubt, however, is that here as elsewhere, the law acts to increase the formality, and hence the documentation, of transactions.

Chapter 7

Managers as Heroes

The Managerial Perspective

THE CORPORATION LAWS OF DELAWARE AND OTHER JURISDICTIONS, AS WELL as the Model Business Corporation Act (MBCA), pay their respects to the idea of protecting shareholders. A superficial reading of such laws, along with the Berle and Means tradition of solicitude for the shareholder, might lead one to imagine shareholders as ordinary folks, spread across the land, who require the law's protection from rapacious managers. Unsurprisingly, managers understand the corporate drama a little bit differently. (The big bad wolf has a few things to say about those little pigs, too.)

In the tales managers tell, a businessman—the more dramatic "entrepreneur" is appropriate—envisioned and founded the company. It was his idea, and he worked at it. Like most people, our entrepreneur did not want to risk everything he owned in order to run his business. Although nobody plans on disaster, bad things could happen, and he had a family and a personal life, too. So our model entrepreneur incorporated his business in order to receive limited liability; if the business went under, he would not personally be ruined. In the process, our entrepreneur needed a leader, and so he made himself chief executive officer (CEO), president, and sole director. The young company also needed financing, and so it borrowed money when it could. But borrowing only works in some circumstances, and oftentimes those are not the circumstances of a start-up company. So the founder of the company sold some of his company to investors, that is, he sold them stock in the company. As a result of such transactions, directors were added to the company. By law, all shareholders vote on directors, but his investors believed in him and in his business plans, and, therefore, they were willing to accept the entrepreneur's suggestions for additions to the board of directors, and so on.

From the founder's perspective, shareholders are only a source of financing. No financing is free; that is what it means to have financial obligations. Sooner or later shareholders must begin to earn a return on investment; the advantage of equity over debt financing (of selling shares as opposed to borrowing from a bank) is that the young company generally has longer to begin earning a return to shareholders than debt holders would tolerate. Although shareholders are patient, they still need to be reassured that the business is making progress and will eventually make money. Shareholders need oversight precisely because they are not demanding cash flow. So having equity investors means that one has to have directors. The other downside of equity investors is that they claim to own the company and, therefore, feel the company should be run for their benefit. And so the charade starts: shareholders are absentee owners; managers are merely employees who operate the company under the watchful eye of the board of directors, who actually run the company—set its strategy—for the benefit of the corporation itself (whatever that means) and its shareholders.

In a famous case, *Dodge v. Ford,* Henry Ford breached the etiquette.[1] Ford Motor Company had made enormous profits on its operations, and despite price cutting, raising wages, and massive expansion of its operations, had a large surplus of cash. The Dodge brothers, major shareholders, wanted Ford to distribute much of this surplus as a cash dividend. In fact, the Dodge boys wanted the cash in order to build a car company of their own, which they eventually did.[2] In open court, Ford maintained that his shareholders, including the Dodge brothers, already had made a fine return on their investment, and that he was not going to issue any further dividends. Instead, he was going to use the enormous surplus built up by Ford to lower the price of his products even further, thereby improving the life of many Americans.[3] The Michigan Supreme Court pointed out that the company was supposed to be run in the interests of its owners, the shareholders, not in the interests of Ford's idea of a better society, and ordered Ford's board (acknowledged to be under Ford's control) to issue a dividend.[4]

Dodge v. Ford is an exceptional case in many ways, including legally. The decision of whether to retain surplus cash, reinvest it, or return it to shareholders in the form of a dividend, is an almost purely business decision. Note that the shareholders benefit either way. If the cash is retained by the company, then the company has a valuable asset and is better able to meet future challenges, and as a result, the shares are that much more valuable. If the cash is invested by the company, then the company presumably acquires another asset and benefits from the return on the investment, and as a result, the shares are that much more valuable. If, on the other hand, the cash is distributed to the investors, then they have shares plus cash, which is good, too. There is no law regarding what would be better in a given situation: that is a business decision and hence hardly decidable by a court, which is not running the business. Thus, in order to win his case, all Ford had to do was provide the court with a plausible business reason for his actions, that is, to explain his actions in terms of an economic benefit, however long term, for the shareholders. (For example, Ford could have claimed he was offering cars so cheaply, and reinvesting rather than distributing profits, in order to capture market share.) In refusing to couch his answers in terms of the interest of shareholders, Ford rebelled against the mores of corporation law. For whatever reason of his own (and ego must have played some role), Ford had exposed the charade, which is bad manners if good theater.

Ordinarily, the founder of a company runs the company as CEO. It is his company. He works at it every day; he makes plans for the future and copes with the present; he answers for the company. If the company is successful and at least moderately long lived, then eventually a new CEO will replace the founder. The new CEO, presumably, is also a man with great energy and ambition, who has worked hard for the chance to lead the company. It is almost inconceivable that such a manager would not identify with "his" company—and numerous cases (and not a few scandals) indicate that managers regard themselves, rather than the shareholders and certainly not the directors, as the center of gravity of a company.

The conventional story taught in the law schools and elsewhere is as wrong about shareholders as it is about managers. Proponents of regulation half jokingly refer to shareholders as helpless "widows and orphans," but many shareholders are themselves large corporations, or fabulously wealthy individuals who can be expected to take good care of themselves. Even shareholders of more modest means, that is, members of the middle class, tend to have their interests represented by powerful institutions such as mutual funds, pension trustees, and insurance companies. A philosophically minded manager in a bitter mood might realize that a capitalist society is quite likely to use the law to protect the interests of capital providers, not just widows and orphans, but mutual funds and insurance companies.

Reassessing Corporation Law from the Managerial Perspective

In a cheerier mood, however, our philosophical manager might realize that things, especially in the law, are not always what they profess to be. Although corporation law is superficially concerned with shareholder protection, in practice, corporation law rarely presents much of an obstacle for directors and hence for management. Doctrines that initially appear to provide stout protection of shareholder interests are usually something less. For example, while it is true that directors are required to fulfill their fiduciary duties to the corporation and its shareholders, it is also true that fiduciary duties are very difficult to enforce. Under the business judgment rule, courts provide no redress for the vast majority of directors' decisions, even costly decisions. What constitutes fulfillment of their fiduciary duties by directors and managers is, of course, contested from case to case, and shifts slightly with the judicial climate, but in general, courts do not require much of managers.

For example, after years and years of litigation, the Delaware Supreme Court upheld the Chancery Court's decision that Disney CEO and Chairman of the Board Michael Eisner, and the rest of the Disney board of directors, did not breach their fiduciary duties in hiring Eisner's friend, Michael Ovitz, to be president of Disney.[5] The terms of Ovitz's employment agreement were complex, evidently not completely understood by the board at the time the agreement was approved, but in fact stunningly beneficial to Ovitz. When it became clear that Ovitz was not going to work out as president of Disney, the Disney board approved a "no fault termination," causing a veritable waterfall of wealth to fall upon Ovitz. The trial court, upheld on appeal, decided that while the decisions surrounding the hiring and firing of Ovitz fell far short of corporate governance "best practices," no breach of fiduciary duty occurred. A lot seems to have been at stake: the court declaimed that if it were to hold managers liable for bad decisions taken in good faith, "the entire advantage of the risk-taking, innovative, wealth-creating engine that is the Delaware corporation would cease to exist, with disastrous results for shareholders and society alike."[6] Thus, perhaps surprisingly, the Delaware courts have maintained that the fact that the law, in doing little to protect shareholders, actually benefits shareholders, because it encourages risk taking by managers. Tough love.

As important as they may be to legal education, legal doctrines articulated through appellate litigation are relatively insignificant in the day-to-day operations of a business. The very fabric of corporate life is structured to give managers a free hand in running their businesses. Perhaps this is as it should be, as suggested in chapter 3 and by the *Disney* court. But it means that the public image of corporation law, a titanic struggle between shareholders and directors (the Berle and Means story), is quite inauthentic, even fabulous. What corporation law is really about—and this alternative account comes through in the basic course by the end of the semester—is letting managers work.[7]

From this managerial perspective, the idea of a contest between shareholders and managers for the soul of the board of directors, the contest that has structured the past two chapters, and in some sense, this entire book, is overheated. Start with shareholders. Shareholders come in two sizes—small and large. Many small shareholders are much as Berle and Means portrayed them, relatively passive and uninvolved. At least in publicly traded companies, if such shareholders are unhappy, they may sell their shares. Shareholders who pay any attention to their investments, or shareholders who are appropriately diversified (have a range of investments), bear little risk of loss. Therefore, the argument of Berle and Means, and much corporation law scholarship since, that the dispersed, passive shareholder relies on good corporate governance for protection of his investment, is overdone.[8]

Although shareholders certainly may, in some situations, be victimized, it also must be remembered that not all small investors are passive. Even a shareholder who owns only a single share has the right to put questions to all other shareholders (and have the company pay for distribution of the question).[9] More importantly, shareholders can bring class action or derivative suits, as discussed in the next chapter, thereby challenging corporate power. Although it is difficult to win such suits, it is not difficult to get the attention of management. Major shareholders can do all these things, too, but much more importantly, major shareholders can engage meaningfully in contests for control of the board of directors, also as discussed in the next chapter. So the picture of the poor little shareholder from which corporation law traditionally starts is one-sided, to say the least.

Managers often have a somewhat different perspective on directors, too. Of course directors want what is best for shareholders. They are elected by shareholders; most of them are shareholders themselves. But at the same time, top managers—who meet with directors—also know that directors are part of the corporation, part of the team. Many directors are employees of the company. As noted already, traditionally in America, the chairman of the board is also the CEO, and in a young company, often the founder. Even outside directors, who are not employed by the corporation, tend to be nominated by management. Unsurprisingly, managers tend to choose people, often much like themselves, who are likely to understand the issues confronting management.[10]

At a deeper level, however, the problem with the idea of board meetings as contests between managers and directors on behalf of shareholders is that it deeply misunderstands the activity of management, an enterprise in which both "managers" and "directors" participate. As discussed in the preceding chapter, boards of directors are collective bodies, charged with attending to how the business as a whole is faring, and managers are on boards. Some managers are also directors and vote at meetings. Other managers are not directors but attend board meetings and participate in other ways. But the emphasis on "voting," and by implication, on adversarial debate, is misplaced. As discussed in the previous chapter, while they vote occasionally, boards work by consensus. Decisions made by boards (and even more importantly, matters ignored by boards) tend to be based on collective judgment, politics, rather than logical demonstration and debate. Trust and a high degree of collegiality are required to get anything done. Trust and collegiality can break down, of course—boards can fight among themselves. But boards remain boards. Infighting does not somehow transform board meetings into the scenes of logically structured opposition and interrogation suggested by the previous two chapters.[11]

As mentioned in chapter 1, the corporations at which they work are deeply significant for managers and other businesspeople. Indeed the proposition that "corporations are significant" may seem ridiculously obvious—their significance permeates the cases and indeed ordinary perceptions of life in the United States. As will briefly discussed in chapter 12, however, for some legal scholars "the corporation" has posed a substantial theoretical problem, and some have even concluded that it does not exist. But this is an academic problem; for business folk, the reality of the corporation is not seriously questionable. Managers, who may also be inside directors, devote significant portions of their lives to success as measured by position on the company's organizational chart (and by the status of the company as a whole). The corporation achieves success in the world by improving its business; the manager achieves individual success within the corporation by being promoted. The manager desires both sorts of success, and by the same token, fears the decline of the corporation's fortune (bankruptcy) or his own career (termination). Achieving corporate success is the dominant challenge for managers, not as Berle and Means would have it, the conversion of corporate assets (i.e., some sort of conspiracy against the company's true owners, the passive shareholders). Directors, too, want to see the success of "the corporation and its shareholders" to which they owe fiduciary duties. Directors are not the agents of shareholders, for the simple reason that shareholders do not control directors. Instead, directors direct, oversee the strategy of the business—directors are engaged in an enterprise, which, while less day to day and operational, is nonetheless part of the management of the enterprise.

Even in terms of purely individual self-interest (as opposed to self-interest socially defined as status within the corporate collective), the interests of managers and shareholders tend to be aligned, not opposed. Management is forced to look out for shareholders for three reasons: first, the "market for corporate control," especially the remote but important possibility of a hostile takeover; second, "performance-based compensation"; and third but most subtly, what it means to be a manager. As a result of these institutions, the agency problem might be considered exaggerated, at least from a managerial perspective.

First, as discussed in more detail in the next two chapters, there is a market for managers, just as there are markets for other sorts of workers. This market is quite competitive. Every corporation has access, both inside the company and outside, to more people with the skills, desire, and other qualifications to make them top managers than there are upper level positions. And boards are not hesitant to fire managers whose companies are not doing well; the average tenure of a CEO is not particularly long. Boards are not hesitant to fire managers in part because if management (including the board) does not do well enough, the company becomes vulnerable to a proxy fight or a hostile takeover, in the course of which the board will be replaced with another board, who will then replace management.

Second, managers are themselves shareholders. Founders of companies, such as Henry Ford, were always major shareholders as well as managers. But in recent years, it has become standard practice to compensate managers with equity in the company, in addition to their cash salaries. The idea behind such *performance-based compensation* schemes is that if a manager owned stock, or owned the right to buy stock (an option), then the manager has an incentive to run the company in such a way as to make the stock as valuable as possible. If the manager were successful and the stock price rose, then the manager might be very well paid indeed. Shareholders should not be dismayed, however, because by definition their own holdings had increased in value as well. Thus performance-based compensation can be used as an institutional mechanism for bridging the antagonism between owners and managers diagnosed by Berle and Means.[12]

Third, sometimes business folk use "ownership" in a rather emotional sense, as in "ownership of a project"—to mean responsibility for, commitment to, and personal identity. Quite apart from the sticks of the market for corporate control, or the carrots provided by performance-based compensation, many managers are deeply committed to their companies.[13] After all, they often devote much of their professional lives—their lives, full stop—and their reputations to the success of their employer. It is hardly surprising to learn that managers regard themselves as the real owners of a company. They make it go; they give it life. In theatrical terms, managers, not shareholders and certainly not directors, are the protagonists.

Chapter 8

Shareholders as Strategic Actors

Domination

IT IS COMMON AND NOT WRONG TO THINK ABOUT LAW IN TERMS OF LITIGA-
tion, as a formal process of deciding a conflict that arises somehow and is
then brought to the law's attention. Legal education fosters an imagination of
law as not just above the fray, but as a peacemaker—law is about the peaceful resolution of conflict. This view is commonly held by law students, who
learn through reading the opinions of appellate courts. In order to situate the
reader, courts usually begin by recounting "the facts" of a case (i.e., telling a
short and highly selective story, one that will make the court's resolution of the
case seem sensible) about who these parties are, the nature of their conflict,
how they came before this court, and what they seek from the court. Then the
opinion proceeds to discuss reasons for why the court has decided as it has.
In the narrative structure of an appellate opinion, conflict arises in the world,
and the parties come to the court to resolve the conflict. Law is thus portrayed
as existing above the hurly-burly of conflict.

But this is not the only view of law, not even the only view in the basic course on business associations. Law also is about *doing* things, transactions, and indeed it is this aspect of law that fashions the commercial world. In particular, corporation law defines certain kinds of legal actors (manager, director, shareholder) and gives each certain powers. The right to exercise such powers are, if it comes to that, legally enforceable, that is, guaranteed by the power of society acting through the state. Hence, law forges weapons and is hardly innocent. Indeed, law is involved in most conflicts, and perhaps all commercial conflicts, from the beginning: struggles are waged with powers, and over privileges, created and enforced by law.

Once people are granted legal powers, then just as surely as night follows day, someone will exercise his or her powers in a way that seems abusive. The task for the law, then, is to decide which exercises of power are to be countenanced and which are to be condemned. This task is not as easy as "abusive" implies. Corporation law creates dynamic structures, in which people have various sorts of authority over one another, that is, in which people are not equal. Corporations (and other business structures) create opportunities for strategic behavior, less clinically phrased, for one party to take advantage of another. Even when authority is exercised entirely appropriately, bitterness may result. An obvious example from previous chapters is that directors may make a bad decision, the company may go bankrupt, and shareholders may lose their investment. Shareholders are powerless to prevent the decision, and judicial remedy is extremely unlikely. Tough world.

Even shareholders, whom corporation law generally portrays as victims, may be in a position to take advantage of others. Consider two not uncommon situations that receive considerable (probably undue) attention in the basic course on corporation law: first, the dominant shareholder in a small corporation, and second, a shareholder who brings a shareholder derivative suit, or in the alternative, a class action suit on behalf of similarly situated shareholders. As discussed below, both shareholder dominance and shareholder litigation afford chances to abuse power. In both situations, however, it seems important that individuals have such powers. A shareholder who has invested more in a company should, it would seem, have more influence over the company than a shareholder who has invested less. Similarly, if we are at all serious about the possibility that managers and directors may take advantage of shareholders, then it would seem that shareholders should have the ability to sue for judicial protection of shareholder rights. So neither shareholder dominance nor litigation is going away. The law has responded by attempting to fashion ways of allowing shareholders to dominate their companies and to sue directors and managers, while at the same time preventing, remedying, or at least limiting abuses of such shareholder power.

Close Corporations

By way of example of the potential for abuse presented by shareholder dominance, consider a small corporation, formed to run a pizza restaurant, with only two shareholders, one who owns 51 percent, and one who owns 49 percent of the shares.[1] For these purposes such a corporation is often called a "close" or "closely held" corporation. The 51 percent shareholder is a "dominant" or "majority" shareholder; the 49 percent shareholder is a "minority" shareholder. The company has three directors; the dominant shareholder elects himself and two friends. The directors hire the dominant shareholder as a financial "consultant" who charges handsome fees. The pizza business generates positive cash flow, but only meets expenses, including consulting fees. Consequently, the business makes no profit and issues no dividends. The minority shareholder receives no benefit from his investment. Essentially, the dominant shareholder has appropriated the minority shareholder's investment in the company. But what can the minority shareholder do? He cannot elect a member of the board of directors; this board will not issue a dividend. Nor will he be hired. He cannot sell his shares—who would want to buy into this situation? The only thing the minority shareholder can do is sell his shares to his fellow shareholder (or back to the company), presumably at a low price.[2] This is colloquially known as a "squeeze out" or a "freeze out."

This basic structure—and hence the potential for abuse of a minority shareholder—is common. When a small or medium-sized business is incorporated, shareholder voting control often resides in a single person or a small group, oftentimes a family. Indeed, voting control may be centralized in some quite large companies. Ford, BMW, and Fiat, for examples in the automotive industry, are controlled by the Ford, Quandt, and Agnelli families, respectively. Voting control is power to choose, and hence control over, the board of directors, who in turn have any number of mechanisms through which they can benefit one shareholder at the expense of others. In *Donahue v. Rodd Electrotype Co.*, the controlling shareholder demanded that some of his shares be purchased by the company, essentially giving himself a dividend that was not available to all shareholders.[3] Or, as in *Alaska Plastics, Inc., v. Coppock*, the dominant shareholders can make themselves directors, and then award themselves director's fees.[4] And perhaps the most common method, as in the pizza example above or *Wilkes v. Springside Nursing Home, Inc.,*[5] is to use the power of the board of directors to pay salaries to some, but not all, shareholders. In response to this problem, many states have enacted laws regulating the relations among close corporations,[6] and many courts have imposed partner-like duties on shareholders in close corporations.[7]

Differential treatment is not, however, wrong per se. Most obviously, in a situation in which some employees are also shareholders, and some shareholders are not employees, one would expect the employees to receive a salary. In our example of the pizza restaurant, the text strongly implied that the "consulting fee" was really just a disguised dividend impermissibly made to only one shareholder, that the dominant shareholder did not work for the money, and that the corporation did not need consulting services. But consider a slightly different scenario: the dominant shareholder makes himself sole chef and general manager, and pays himself the going rate for such work, and there are no profits left for the minority shareholder. This case would be different, even though a dominant shareholder had benefited himself at the expense of fellow shareholders. The question, then, is whether a particular exercise of dominant shareholder power is permissible.

As the structure of the question suggests, the answer is "it depends." There is a great deal of law here, and this chapter will make no attempt to canvass the attempts that various legislatures and courts have made to allow people to run the businesses they control, on the one hand, without abusing their fellow owners, on the other.[8] Any such distinction, however, turns on essentially cultural assessments of what uses of power are acceptable. Courts often signal the fact that they are making such assessments with soft and vague terms like fiduciary duty, fair dealing, good faith, practice in the industry, and community norms.[9]

Shareholder Derivative Suits

Shareholders may sue on behalf of their corporations; this is called a shareholder derivative suit. In the classic sort of case, a corporation has a cause of action, but for some reason does not attempt to vindicate its rights in court. In that situation, a shareholder may initiate a suit on behalf of the corporation. Technically (and this gets technical very fast), a shareholder derivative suit is a suit in equity (seeking an order rather than money damages) against the corporation (as nominal defendant, because the corporation refused to bring suit) and its board of directors (as real defendants), asking for a court order directing the board to file a lawsuit. The suit is called "derivative" because the shareholder's standing is derived from that of the corporation whose directors and managers will not file suit. Recovery is to the corporation rather than the shareholder.

An example should help clarify: consider a bad director, who breaches his duty of loyalty, perhaps by taking a corporate opportunity. The board of directors decides that it does not want to sue the bad director. This might be a sound business judgment. Perhaps nothing was done wrong, perhaps litigation is too expensive, or there is no hope of recovery; but maybe the board of directors does not want to sue the misbehaving director because he was also the chief executive officer (CEO). Let us thus assume that the board is itself being disloyal.

Let us further assume that the corporation has been hurt: had the bad director/CEO not taken the corporate opportunity, the corporation would have made more money. The corporation, however, is owned by its shareholders, so we might be tempted to say that the shareholders have been injured as well. The shareholders have not, however, suffered any *legal* injury. A shareholder who owned 100 shares of XYZ Corp. before the CEO breached his duty still owns the same 100 shares. His rights have not been injured, even though the value of those rights has been diminished. Therefore, the shareholder, as an individual, has no "standing" to bring a suit. Courts do not hear cases about things going badly. To have standing (a right to bring suit and be heard in court), a party must allege that it has suffered a legal injury, that a right has been impaired. One has no right to valuable shares. Lots of things may cause shares to lose value: business downturns, problems in the broader economy, simple incompetence, or superior competitors—but such unfortunate events do not impair legal rights, do not create causes of action, and courts offer no remedy.

What does it mean to say that this is a suit "in equity"? Once upon a time (meaning in England before the late nineteenth century), there was a distinction between suits "at law" and suits "in equity." There were separate court systems. The so-called common law courts were royal courts administering the king's justice, that is, the law common to all England. And there were the courts of equity, ultimately organized under the royal chancery, and strongly influenced by Roman and canon law. Classically, the remedy in the common law courts was a money judgment; the remedy in the courts of equity was an order. The common law was often characterized as more formalistic and rule bound, even rigid; equity prided itself on doing justice. The distinction between law and equity was imported into the early United States, but has been largely abolished in both England and the United States. The substantive law has been unified—or is at any rate organized along different lines—and most courts understand themselves to be administering both law and equity. The old distinction, however, may still be traced, in prayers "for equitable relief" as opposed to "money judgment," in understanding bankruptcy court as a court of equity, and elsewhere, especially in the general sense that courts are supposed to provide "equity"—to do the right thing, even if that means bending the rules a bit.[10]

Therefore, because he had no formal standing to sue, the shareholder who had been injured by corporate skullduggery turns to equity. As U.S. Supreme Court Justice (and chief U.S. Prosecutor at the Nuremburg trials) Robert Jackson put it, equity

> allowed [the stockholder] to step into the corporation's shoes and to seek in its right the restitution he could not demand in his own. It required him first to demand that the corporation vindicate its own rights, but when, as was usual, those who perpetrated the wrongs also were able to obstruct any remedy, equity would hear and adjudge the corporation's cause through its stockholder with the corporation as a defendant, albeit a rather nominal one.[11]

Thus the shareholder derivative suit was born: shareholders nominally claimed to sue their corporations, but were really suing boards of directors on behalf of their corporations. Many of the fiduciary duty and other cases in the basic corporation law course were brought as shareholder derivative suits.

As noted, if a shareholder wins his derivative suit, then any recovery goes to the corporation. So, in the present example, if the shareholder won, and then the corporation sued its CEO for taking a corporate opportunity and received damages, then the damages would go to the company. The shareholder would be only fractionally better off, because the company in which he owned shares was better off. In contrast, if the corporation did something to harm the shareholder individually, perhaps by not paying a dividend paid to the other holders of the same class of stock, then the shareholder would have standing to sue on his own behalf. This would be a direct suit, and any recovery would be paid to the shareholder.

Confronted with a shareholder derivative suit, a company may choose to fight it in court. In addition to the risks and costs of litigation, this is likely to be embarrassing. On the other hand, the shareholder and the board may settle the suit. Settlement can be very advantageous for both sides. Traditionally, settlements were paid directly to the shareholder and his lawyers, and them alone. In contrast, a judgment was and is paid to the corporation, and so the value of the judgment must be shared with all the other shareholders (although the plaintiff shareholder may recover legal costs). Legal doctrine has shifted, however, so that settlements generally must be approved by the court and are paid, like judgments, to the corporation. The plaintiff's lawyers still, however, generally receive their costs and fees, which many observers believe is more than an adequate incentive to bring frivolous suits.[12]

For the corporation (i.e., management including directors), a settlement removes the certain costs of extended litigation and the less certain risks of an adverse judgment and embarrassment. Moreover, a judicially approved settlement resolves the suit as a matter of law for the world (has *res judicata* effect), that is, other shareholders cannot sue on the same matter. Finally, and the law here is quite complicated, the bottom line is that the actual costs of settlement are almost always born by the company, either directly or more commonly through the intermediary of its directors and officers insurer—at any rate, directors rarely pay.[13]

Settlement of a shareholder derivative suit can thus be seen as a transfer of wealth from the shareholders as a whole to the plaintiff's lawyers. The structure of the shareholder derivative suit positions (tempts?) shareholders to file suits and settle them. Shareholders are often led into temptation. Lawyers alert to an opportunity to file a plausible derivative suit may search out potential shareholder plaintiffs, who need only agree to be plaintiffs. The lawyers then file suit alleging mismanagement of the corporation and commence settlement negotiations. If negotiations are successful, at least the lawyers—and one suspects the plaintiff—receive something.[14]

As suggested by the foregoing paragraphs, shareholder derivative suits have been widely perceived to be, in practice if not in policy, forms of extortion. Shareholder derivative suits may be filed for the purpose of settling (i.e., with no intention of vindicating the claims made in the suit). Such suits are called strike suits, and they have been bemoaned as an abuse of litigation and a form of extortion for most of the twentieth century. Again Justice Jackson:

> the remedy [of the shareholder derivative suit] itself provided opportunity for abuse, which was not neglected. Suits sometimes were brought not to redress real wrongs, but to realize upon their nuisance value. They were bought off by secret settlements in which any wrongs to the general body of share owners were compounded by the suing stockholder, who was mollified by payments from corporate assets. These litigations were aptly characterized in professional slang as "strike suits."[15]

At the same time, and without denying the existence of abuses, both shareholder derivative suits and securities class action litigation are widely believed to be necessary for the protection of important shareholder rights. Therefore, courts and legislatures, on the state and federal levels, have spent a great deal of energy trying to distinguish meritorious from frivolous cases. There is a great deal of law here, but the basic policy question is fairly easy to state: can legal procedures, filters, be devised that allow good cases to go forward and that discourage bad cases? Examples of such filters, frequently taught in the basic course, include requirements that plaintiffs in shareholder derivative suits post a bond for litigation costs;[16] make a demand upon the board of directors (or argue that the demand requirement is excused);[17] and/or may have their suit dismissed in court on the recommendation of a litigation committee.[18]

* * *

The shareholder derivative cases feel somehow more public than the cases we have considered in earlier chapters. This is largely because the plots are broader in scope, and more self-evidently so. In earlier chapters, the conflicts took place among the triumvirate of shareholders, managers, and directors. Legal institutions—legislatures and courts—set the stage and adjudged right and wrong after the fact. With the strategic understanding of shareholder litigation, however, the institutions of the law are directly involved in the conflict itself. In this chapter's cases, legal institutions and actors are not simple solutions, they are tools of domination, weapons. The remaining chapter in this part is also concerned with cases in which the conflict is defined outside the triumvirate of corporate governance, and law is as much a weapon as it is an articulation of peaceful relations. Law is complicitous in most forms of strategic behavior. Corporation law is a legal regime through which individuals exercise considerable power; society accepts and even approves of certain exercises of power. But a degree of ambivalence is to be expected.

Chapter 9

Struggles for Control of the Corporation

Law and Domination

THE IMAGES OF WAR THAT PERVADE DISCUSSIONS OF STRUGGLES FOR COR-porate control, especially "hostile takeovers," are not to be taken seriously—ac-tually comparing bidding on common stock with shooting a person is rather offensive. But apart from being fun in a juvenile sort of way, the violent language of control struggles teaches a valuable lesson introduced in the last chapter: law articulates the relationships that a society countenances, and not all those relationships are nice. A great deal of commercial life is about people dominating one another, and as we shall see in this chapter, a great deal of ingenuity goes into using legal devices for that purpose. But it would be overly pious to assert that domination is bad per se; at any rate, law does not offer any evidence for this righteous proposition. Indeed, law is the language in which winnings are consolidated. Rephrased, no winning could be consolidated un-less its legitimacy were recognized, that is, unless it were in some sense legal.

Professional apologists for "the law" like to point out that commercial law, including corporation law, is the language through which an economy is built and milk gets put on the table. True enough, but corporations—and specifically the law pertaining to the control of corporations—is also the language through which industries get restructured, businesses are shuttered, people lose their jobs, and social life generally becomes different (no doubt, getting better every day, and in every way). Oftentimes, in the all-too-human mix familiar from the rest of life, the good and the bad travel together. And with that for a prelude, let's go to the opera.

Hostilities and Modes of Retaining Control

Return, for the moment, to the managerial imagination of the corporation offered in chapter 7: the founding entrepreneur sells equity (ownership) interests in the company in order to raise the money necessary "to grow" the company. Shareholders have the right to vote for directors; directors have the right to fire management and hire new management. Thus, once he has sold a majority of the company's voting stock, our founding entrepreneur has offered himself as a hostage to the company's fortune. If he does not satisfy his constituency, he can be fired.

A shareholder who is discontented with the return on her investment has several options. First, as already noted and in general, a shareholder has the right to sell her stock. The right to sell may have been restricted upon issuance, or by other agreement, but the presumption is that common stock is "freely transferable." Whether or not a market (willing buyers) exists for her stock is quite another matter. If she sells her stock, however, our shareholder ceases to own shares and acquires instead cash, thereby exiting corporation law stage right. In that event, the corporation proceeds unchanged; only the owner of certain shares has changed.

Second, as discussed in the previous chapter, if directors have made decisions that she believes breach their fiduciary obligations to the company and to her, our exemplary shareholder may sue. As we have seen, however, it is difficult to win such suits. But if the first remedy available to our discontented shareholder is exit, the second is a lawsuit.

Third, our shareholder may come to believe that management is simply not very competent. With different management, she may reason, her shares would be worth more. Therefore, rather than sell, she should try and get new managers for what is, after all, her company. A shareholder cannot fire management or hire new management—the shareholder has no right to make such decisions. Directors do, however, so the directors must be convinced to fire the chief executive officer (CEO) and his team. The CEO and his team, however, usually *are* directors and play substantial roles in choosing the other directors. As a practical matter, therefore, our shareholder usually needs to replace most or all of the board of directors, that is, needs to elect new directors. Our shareholder in this case is called an *insurgent*.

At this point in the analysis, it is important to remember that, while not required by law, in practice managers are almost always shareholders. In a young company, the CEO may well be the founder. And in a company no longer led by its founder, the CEO by definition had the support of the board of directors who hired him, and thus presumably the support of a majority of the shareholders. The shareholders or even the board of directors may lose confidence in management; managers are fired from time to time. But the CEO starts out with a base of shareholder support; the confidence of the board is the CEO's to lose. Our insurgent's criticism of the existing management thus occasions management's feelings of betrayal and calls for loyalty. Rephrased, our insurgent's revolution against entrenched management is also a civil war among shareholders.

The strategic objective of both sets of shareholders is to control a majority of the votes at the next shareholders' meeting, either the regularly scheduled annual meeting or, if the occasion demands, a special meeting. There are several ways to secure a majority of the votes beforehand, including *voting agreements*,[1] *voting trusts*,[2] and *special stock*,[3] often discussed in the basic law course. Such mechanisms require agreement and, therefore, tend to be less useful for large groups of voters. Moreover, such mechanisms have traditionally been used to retain control of the company, and in some cases (such as issuing special stock) may require control of the company. Therefore, voting agreements, trusts, special stock, and the like tend to be instruments of those supportive of existing management.

Shareholder voting in large companies presents its own problems. There are corporations of all sizes and circumstance. However, the sort of corporation that concerned Berle and Means and most scholarship since and that dominates the U.S. imagination is a medium to very large corporation, in which most shares are held by a large number of relatively small shareholders, and shares are publicly traded on an exchange—the sort of company one would expect to see in the financial news.[4] Shareholders who control small amounts of stock often do not attend meetings, which is rational enough, as they could do little to influence the outcome. But like other meetings held for the purpose of voting, a shareholder meeting requires a quorum (usually defined as a simple majority of the shares outstanding[5]) in order for votes to be authoritative. If not enough people come to the meeting, then necessary business cannot be done.

Corporation law resolves this problem with the device of the *proxy,* which is essentially an agency agreement through which a shareholder authorizes someone else (called the *proxy holder*) to vote the shareholder's shares. By using proxies, a majority of shares outstanding may be represented at a shareholder meeting, even though most of the owners are not actually present. As a matter of course, management solicits the proxies of the shareholders prior to the annual meeting. Unsurprisingly, most shareholders—who have no intention of attending the meeting—give their proxies to management. And equally unsurprisingly, management's proposals are usually adopted. Thus, ordinarily, proxies provide a mechanism through which management gets the shareholders to elect management's slate of directors and to approve other relatively major decisions.

Proxy Fights

If the company has been doing poorly, however, our insurgent may be able to get proxies for her proposal to replace the board of directors and consequently management. This is called a *proxy fight* (i.e., a fight for the control of the corporation waged by the solicitation of proxies). One might consider a proxy fight as a sort of political campaign in which the insurgent's effort to elect a new board (and hence management) is pitted against the incumbent officers' and directors' efforts to retain their positions. Proxy fights are extensively regulated by both state corporation law and federal securities law, the so-called *proxy rules.* For present purposes, however, four facts are salient:

1. The incumbents may use company funds (ultimately, shareholder money) to wage a campaign to persuade major shareholders that the insurgent is crazy and that existing management should continue to run the company.
2. Management must tell the insurgent who the shareholders are (provide the shareholder list) or agree to mail the insurgent's materials to the other shareholders (the insurgent must pay the cost of the mailing). The second option inhibits the shareholder from contacting more important shareholders directly and campaigning.

3. The insurgent must finance her side of the proxy fight, although if she is successful she can be reimbursed.

4. A proxy does not change title to the shares. Thus, while a successful proxy fight might effectuate a change in management and make the insurgent's shares more valuable, her potential gain is limited. Most of the gains from improved management of the company will go to the other shareholders.

Thus, it is very difficult to wage a proxy fight, and the returns on even successful efforts are limited.[6]

"Buying" the Company

Instead of proceeding via a proxy fight, our discontented shareholder could simply offer to buy the company, that is, buy a controlling block of shares, which are, after all, ownership interests in the company. Shares carry with them the right to vote for directors; buying shares is therefore buying votes. Thus, if our insurgent can buy a sufficient number of shares, she will have also bought control over the board of directors and, therefore, control over management. To summarize, our discontented shareholder has four basic options, apart from lumping it: sell and exit; litigate (through a direct or derivative suit); campaign for better management; or buy the company.

There are numerous ways to structure an acquisition, but it is perhaps easiest to begin by thinking about the transaction strategically. There is a conceptual division between "friendly" and "hostile" deals. In a "friendly" acquisition, the directors and management of the company to be purchased cooperate with the buyer. In a hostile deal, the directors and management of the sought-after company resist the efforts of the would-be buyer.

Why, one might ask, do friendly deals exist? Why would management ever cooperate with a discontented shareholder who will presumably fire management? One way to approach this question is to reframe it; recall that any buyer of a company is, or will soon be, a shareholder. Thus, the question might be reasked, why would management ever recommend the sale of the company? And who buys companies? Usually other companies, often competitors. Companies often combine forces for reasons that have to do with the marketplace in which the company is doing business. That is, companies purchase other companies for strategic reasons: to increase market share, acquire a technology, eliminate a competitor, and so forth. Such reasons are particular to a given company and hence beyond the scope of this book, which is about the general and formal structure of corporation law. But even corporate lawyers should remember that companies do not actually make "widgets." Actual businesses are always in some situation, and their strategy must address their situation. Sometimes the wisest course is to exit gracefully, preferably with significant compensation—a merger may make much more sense than a bankruptcy.

It is an oversimplification to think in terms of discrete competitors who either compete successfully or who go out of business and disappear. Corporations, like metal objects, are somewhat malleable. They can be beaten into new shapes, reformed. So, suppose that company A is doing better than company B, and both compete with a third company, C. Why should company A necessarily try to take company B's customers one by one, as B slides toward bankruptcy? Why not buy company B? Especially if C might buy the company? Or suppose that company A has a great distribution network, but B has a great new product. Won't both companies make more money if they work together? Or note that both companies A and B must run many duplicative departments: accounting, accounts receivable, whatever. If the companies combine, costs can be cut. The marketplace reasons for companies to combine are endless.[7]

There are also reasons internal to the corporation, as opposed to in the marketplace, why management may cooperate with a bidder. First, managers usually have complicated employment contracts that contain clauses providing that, in the event the manager is terminated on account of the acquisition of the company, the manager is to be paid some massive sum. Such clauses are called *golden parachutes*, because the manager parachutes to safety in Palm Springs or some similar haven. Second, existing management may feel obliged to the shareholders (including, never forget, themselves) to sell the company for a high price. Third, and following from the second, courts may agree that selling the company, under these circumstances, is the fiduciary duty of management, as discussed in the *Revlon* case below.

Fourth, suppose management of the sought-after company attempts to resist the acquisition. Our bidder may then become "hostile" and approach the shareholders directly and simply offer to buy their stock. Because shareholders, not management, own the company, in principle and in the abstract, shareholders can sell the company even if the managers and directors disagree. By the same token, control of a publicly held company (and the attendant perquisites, including management positions) is always potentially for sale. Once a majority of the voting equity of the company has been sold to the public (once the company has been *floated*), then control over the company, and so top management jobs, depends on the continued satisfaction of shareholders with how the company is doing, which they perceive as how their investment is doing. Knowing that the potential for a hostile takeover exists, management may be more inclined to negotiate and to recommend that the board accept an appropriate merger proposal (not incidentally, often triggering a fine severance package).[8]

Combinations can take many forms. So competitors A and B can agree to *consolidate,* forming a third company, Newco. Alternatively, the corporation laws of Delaware and other states provide a process through which A and B can agree to operate as one company; affirmative votes of the shareholders of both companies are required. This is called a *statutory merger.* Or A can buy B's assets, leaving B an empty shell. Or A can make a *tender offer* (i.e., offer the shareholders of B the chance to sell ["tender"] their shares to A). Assuming that A thereby gains control, A can either operate B as a subsidiary or wind it up, folding its business into A, which is sometimes called a *de facto merger,* to indicate that the statutory process was not used. Such deals often require financing, of course, so in theory either A or B can convince the capital markets of the worthiness of their business plan and raise the money to acquire the shares of the other. Sometimes A and B pursue financing, for antithetical business plans, simultaneously, and the companies offer to buy each other. And more than one device can be used at once; a tender offer is often followed, for example, by a statutory merger. The combinations are nearly endless and great fun for a lawyer so inclined. This is law and finance at their puzzle-solving, structure-constructing, tinker-toys for grown-ups best.

Conflicts

Ordinarily, the board is supposed to make decisions in the best interest of the corporation and all of its shareholders. Suppose, however, that the best decision for the shareholders is to sell their company. A company may be worth more to a bidder—for whatever reason, including perhaps a mistaken valuation by the bidder—than it is to the present owners. The bidder, however, may choose to merge the acquired company into an existing company or simply sell off all the assets and dissolve the company.[9] In that case, the board's decision to facilitate the acquisition is, at the same time, implicitly a decision to dissolve the corporation. The board's duty, at this point, is to decide in the best interest of the shareholders and not the corporation per se.[10] To put the matter in a slightly different light: the board may, in the case of a failing company, recommend to shareholders that they dissolve the company.[11] Shareholders own the company and have the right to wind it up (i.e., destroy it).

To say that the board must make decisions in the interest of the shareholders does not, however, make matters completely clear. Recall the basic situation with which we began this chapter: a shareholder is discontented. She believes that the corporation is being badly managed, and if the company were better managed, her shares would be more valuable. She may make it her goal, then, to replace existing management by buying the shares necessary to control the board of directors. In order to buy the shares from sleepy shareholders, however, our bidder is going to have to offer a premium to the trading price of the shares. So, to take *Smith v. Van Gorkom,* discussed in chapter 8, as an example, the shares were trading at $38 per share when Pritzker offered $55 per share. The bidder seeks control of the entire firm, which must be worth something (and knowing that, the existing shareholders may hold out for a higher price). The premium above the pretakeover trading price is called the *control premium.*[12]

To complicate the example, but make it a bit more realistic, our unhappy shareholder need not have been a long-term shareholder. She might have simply noticed that the company was not performing as well as one might expect and began analyzing how it might be run better. Competitors do this all the time, and so do financiers variously called *buyout firms, private equity firms* (often organized as funds), and even *raiders.* All work by changing the structure of corporations through buying out existing shareholders. More to the point still, our discontent shareholder will almost certainly finance her acquisition of the company and will therefore have to convince a lender or, most commonly, the bond market, that her management team can make the business more profitable, even though she is going to have to pay a premium to acquire it and will thereby saddle the business with debt.

For their part, managers and directors almost invariably argue that the premium offered is too low (i.e., that the company is really worth more), and, therefore, this offer should be rejected. Managers tend to speak of the long-term interests of the shareholders. Let us assume a case in which the managers' argument, although self-serving, is nonetheless correct: the company is worth more than its market price suggests, even with existing management. Indeed, let us assume that the company is worth more than the bidder has offered. Yet in the short term, of course, if one had to choose between selling at the current market price and selling the share to the bidder, then the bid, with its control premium, is a better deal ($55 per share is more than $38 per share). Thus, what is best for "the shareholders" cannot be discerned: for shareholders who can afford to wait, by hypothesis, resisting the takeover is the right thing to do. For shareholders who are less patient, tendering the shares is the right thing to do. Shareholders are not homogenous. Indeed the bidder, too, is a shareholder. This problem remains rather open as a matter of theory, but in practice, courts have allowed directors to gloss over this uncomfortable reality and make decisions in "the long-term interest" of shareholders, decisions that are also in the interest of current management.

A Few Famous Battles

A financier with the delightfully improbable name of T. Boone Pickens owned some 13 percent of Unocal Corporation. Through Mesa Petroleum Company, which he controlled, Pickens made a "two-tiered front-end loaded" tender offer. The gist of the offer was that Pickens would pay $54 in cash for 37 percent of the shares of Unocal, which would give him absolute control of the company. Any remaining publicly held shares were to be exchanged for *junk bonds* nominally worth $54 per share, but likely to be worth significantly less. The offer was widely perceived as coercive and inadequate because it compelled shareholders to tender their shares at the first tier in order to avoid receiving the junk bonds comprising the "back-end" of the merger.[13]

Junk bonds, more politely called *high-yield debt*, are bonds that are issued by relatively risky companies, which might not be around to pay the bond. In order to compensate investors for the risk of default, issuers of high-yield debt offer higher interest rates. In contrast, *investment-grade debt* is issued by companies whose continued existence over the term of the bond is thought to be highly likely. There is nothing *in theory* wrong with the claim that Pickens was offering a package of junk bonds worth $54 per share—the value of the package depends on the diversification, interest rates, and actual risks of the bonds in the bundle. Therefore, there is nothing in principle ridiculous about Pickens's claim that the front end and the back of the tender offer were equivalent.[14] However, if the bonds were in fact worth $54 per share and were readily marketable, then why did not Pickens sell the bonds and use cash (i.e., why structure the offer in two tiers)? People who believed the valuation of the back end of the tender offer were immediately offered the chance to buy bridges.[15]

Confronted with this coercive offer, the Unocal board immediately began constructing defensive measures. (By this point, the military imagery becomes almost unavoidable.) Actually, the defense did not begin *immediately*: the investment banks Goldman, Sachs & Co. and Dillon, Read & Co. made a presentation to Unocal's board suggesting that Pickens's offer was wholly inadequate, and *then* the board and its advisors began erecting defenses. To begin, Unocal made a tender offer for its own stock: if Mesa gained a majority, then Unocal would buy the remaining outstanding shares with debt securities allegedly worth $72 per share (i.e., the remaining shareholders would be converted into creditors). Thus, if Pickens gained a majority stake in Unocal, he would have gained control of a debt-ridden company. The more likely result of Unocal's self-tender, of course, was that nobody would tender to Pickens for $54, because they would hold out for $72, and Pickens's effort to take over Unocal would fail. For obvious reasons, Unocal's offer was extended to all Unocal shareholders *except* Pickens.

Pickens sued, arguing that by excluding him from its tender offer for its own shares, Unocal had violated the fundamental principle of corporation law that all shares of a like class must be treated alike. In *Unocal Corporation Co. v. Mesa Petroleum Co.*, the Delaware Supreme Court disagreed with Pickens, and held that "[u]nder the circumstances the [Unocal] board had both the power and duty to oppose a bid it perceived to be harmful to the corporate enterprise."[16] The Unocal board believed (or it was in the business judgment of the board) that the offer was too low and hence not in the interest of shareholders. The board was therefore free to adopt defensive measures, including a self-tender offer.[17]

With regard to Pickens's argument that he had been discriminated against, the court pointed out that Pickens was renowned as a *greenmailer* (sounds like "blackmailer"). A greenmailer buys shares posing as (or perhaps with the option of becoming) a raider, and threatens to take over a corporation *unless* the corporation buy back his stock, naturally at a considerable premium to what he paid for it. Because Pickens could make a credible threat to take over a company, he had been quite successful as a greenmailer, that is, the managers of several companies had bought him out, sparing Pickens the bother of actually acquiring a company—an even more dramatic instance of strategic behavior by shareholders than those discussed in the previous chapter. Although recognizing the practice as problematic, the Delaware Court previously had upheld the authority of boards to use corporate funds to pay greenmailers, thereby discriminating against other shareholders *in favor* of the greenmailer.[18] So now that Pickens was the shareholder being discriminated *against*, the court was not inclined to listen to him complain of unfairness.

The *Unocal* decision hinged on the court's acceptance of the board's contention that Pickens's offer was too low. But suppose a bid is high? What is the duty of the board when a bidder offers shareholders a fair price, or a more than fair price, for their shares? *Revlon Inc. v. MacAndrews & Forbes Holdings, Inc.*, decided in the same court just a few months after *Unocal*, involved a struggle for the control of Revlon reminiscent of Florentine politics circa 1500. Ron Perelman, CEO of a company with the most un-chic name of Pantry Pride, sought to buy the storied cosmetics giant Revlon, headed by the very French Michel Bergerac (really). For its part, Revlon adopted various defenses, including a self-tender offer much like that found in the *Unocal* case, and a so-called *shareholder rights plan*, usually known as a *poison pill*. Under this plan, existing shareholders received, as a dividend from Revlon, additional rights against the company, contingent on the happening of a specific "trigger" event. In this case, upon the acquisition of 20 percent of the stock by any one person (who probably would be named Perelman), Revlon shareholders would receive the right to exchange each of their shares for a note with $65 principal, 12 percent interest, and maturity of one year. The pill could be "redeemed" (recalled) by the board of directors. Perelman made a counter offer, contingent upon the redemption of the poison pill. Revlon countered this offensive by acquiring some debt and, well, those interested can catch all the action from the sources in the notes.[19] This is a highlight film, however, so let us skip to the closing minutes!

As the struggle between Pantry Pride and Revlon wore on, Revlon began to seek an outside financier, a so-called *white knight* who could rescue them from the "raider" Perelman. Revlon and Forstmann Little agreed to conduct a management buy out (MBO). Under the agreement, Revlon would borrow a great deal of money, and use that money to tender for its own shares. The highly indebted company would be privately owned by its existing management and by Forstmann Little. Since management would own the shares, they no longer would have to worry about Perelman making tender offers.[20] By this point, Revlon's board had effectively decided that the company would be sold; the question was to whom.

Conflict continued, and eventually Forstmann Little and Revlon agreed that, if certain conditions were met, Forstmann would buy Revlon out, without the participation of Revlon's existing management. For its part, Forstmann protected itself through several legal devices, including (1) a cancellation fee and (2) a "lock up" option on two of Revlon's "crown jewels" (i.e., the right to buy two highly profitable Revlon divisions for less money than they were worth). It was also agreed (3) that the value of certain notes, which had been issued by Revlon earlier in this affair, would be supported, thereby protecting Revlon's board from a lawsuit by the note holders. Pantry Pride sued, arguing that the Revlon board, by favoring Forstmann over Pantry Pride, and protecting its own members from a lawsuit, was not fulfilling its duties to its shareholders. (Recall that Perelman, after all, was also a major shareholder *in* Revlon, not just some *outside* raider.)

The Delaware Supreme Court agreed with Perelman and Pantry Pride. Once the Revlon board had decided that the company would be sold, the board's duty was to get the best price it could for shareholders. To this end, many of the "defenses," such as the poison pill, were quite useful: they could be used as bargaining chips in order to obtain a higher price. But the defenses could not be used to favor one buyer over another at the expense of shareholders.

Perceived Consequences

Struggles for corporate control can be highly dramatic, and corporation law not only referees the contest, but supplies many of the weapons. But assuming we are not directly involved in one of these struggles, do we care? Or is this merely an amusement for the wealthy, sort of like yacht racing, thrilling but inconsequential?[21]

Struggles for corporate control do matter, at least in the aggregate. First, as has been suggested, corporate combinations, most dramatically hostile takeovers, are forceful ways to restructure companies, and even liquidate them. Many companies are badly organized and badly managed, and some companies should be liquidated. In this context, corporate combinations may be thought of as a sort of legal reconstruction. The shape of companies, the forms in which businesses are housed and through which they operate, are continually being built and rebuilt. And reconstruction, particularly on old stock, involves a certain amount of demolition.

Second, the threat of a struggle for corporate control may serve to discipline corporate behavior. In a series of articles beginning in the 1960s, Henry Manne argued that corporate managers knew they could be replaced by hostile takeover (or, more probably, by directors who themselves were worried about the possibility of a hostile takeover), and that this threat of replacement served to discipline corporate management.[22] The point remains a good one, although the dramatic rise in management compensation over the past generation, and the copious evidence of undisciplined management epitomized by the $6,000 shower curtain that Tyco bought for its CEO Dennis Kozlowski, may make an observer less than sanguine.[23]

Third, despite the enthusiasm of any number of tenured law professors for hostile takeovers, it is difficult to deny that the restructuring of corporations can occasion great dislocations—unemployment—and so great pain. On the other hand and as suggested above, mergers may be relatively sensible ways to liquidate companies headed for insolvency, a perhaps messier form of closure. In many cases, perhaps most, the closing of parts of a business, discharges in the name of redundancy, and the like that are brought about by the merger would have come sooner or later. Yet few if any human actions are inevitable in their details: it is almost always the case that a given transaction could have been played out otherwise. In the United States, it is often a merger or some other business combination through which a business is transformed and the lives of the people involved in that business are thereby upended. And so mergers or takeovers are emotional and resisted. Heightening the drama (and useful for popular entertainment) is the fact that business combinations almost always make some people much wealthier, or at least appear to, otherwise the deals would not get done. The contrast between the fortunate and the unlucky can be, shall we say, picturesque, and as with death, it is more than a bit silly to deny the emotion aroused by the process in the name of an abstract inevitability.

Fourth and finally, business combinations, including even hostile takeovers, not only restructure companies, but in the aggregate may restructure an entire economy. The shift from the economy of the 1950s to what is widely understood to be a new economy, different in important ways, was accomplished in large measure through the transformation of corporate structures and concomitant revolutions in the management suites of the nation. Economies that have made it very difficult to restructure companies—one thinks immediately of both Japan and Germany—also have had difficulties in reconfiguring their economies as a whole. This is not the place to argue in detail the connection between the microeconomic concerns of corporation laws and the transformation of a given economy; that can be left for comparativists and economic historians. And yet if every house in a city is renovated, or severed from its former neighbor, and perhaps joined in some way with another neighbor, one might expect the city to look different.

Part III

External Relations

Chapter 10

Agency, Responsibility, and Limited Liability

Agency and the Scope of Business

Most corporation law textbooks contain an introduction to general principles of agency law, which, as mentioned in chapter 3, governs situations in which one person (the *agent*) acts on behalf of another (the *principal*).[1] Agency law is worth understanding because agency relations are not only central to the corporation, but are to be found everywhere in business. All employees, including managers, may be the agents of their employers. Therefore, the responsibility that businesses bear to third parties for the actions and words of employees is a matter for agency law. (Of particular interest to lawyers, the attorney/client relationship is an agency relationship.) Although understanding the business world generally requires some knowledge of how relations between principal and agent ought to be conducted, agency law is especially worth teaching in the basic course on business associations because agency helps define the boundaries of the business association.

Companies (let's use "company" or "business" as a reminder that the enterprise may or may not be organized as a corporation) are responsible for the actions of their agents. So, if an employee of a company, acting on behalf of the firm, makes a contract, then the company is likely to be bound by the contract. Similarly, if an employee doing her job injures somebody, then the company is generally responsible for the damages. There are, of course, many complications (this is what lawyers are for), but the general ideas are familiar enough from daily life. Thus, in taking responsibility for many, if not all, actions of their agents, companies establish a role in society. Agency law thus clarifies the relationships between the business and the people affected by the business, the "citizens" of this book's title.

On the other side of the coin, in deciding what companies are responsible for, and to whom, courts at the same time decide what legally counts as "the business." If a manager is legally responsible for some action of the company's agent, then that action *is* the company's business, not least in the literal sense of "minding the business." The company needs to pay attention, needs to devote resources to making sure the agent performs properly. So, for obvious example, companies have to care what their sales personnel say, because the company profits or loses money based on the contracts the personnel make. Sales personnel are part of the company's business, whether "business" is understood in terms of legal liability, management, or finance. Addressing agency problems, problems of group responsibility, thus subtly requires courts (and so law students) to understand what the group is, that is, the scope and shape of the business association in question.

Understanding what the scope of the business is, knowing where the line between "inside" and "outside" the business is, can be difficult. In *A. Gay Jensen Farms, Co., v. Cargill, Inc.*,[2] Warren Grain and Seed Co. sold seed and other farm supplies to farmers around Warren, Minnesota, and Warren stored and purchased the grain that the farmers produced. The grain that Warren purchased from the farmers was sold on the Minneapolis Grain Exchange, or directly to companies such as Cargill. In 1964, Warren sought and received financing from Cargill, pursuant to a security agreement that gave Cargill substantial rights, including rights as a grain agent, and a right of first refusal on Warren's supply of grain. With the passage of time, Cargill's lending to Warren and Cargill's powers to oversee Warren's operations both increased. The relationship between the two companies thickened in other ways. Eventually, Warren shipped 90 percent of its grain to Cargill, only shipping to other buyers when Cargill had no capacity. And Warren became the contracting agent for delivery of proprietary wheat and sunflower seeds sold by Cargill.

During the 1970s, it became increasingly clear that Warren's business was in trouble. Cargill increased its supervision of Warren's operations. In 1977, an audit revealed that Warren was millions of dollars in debt to Cargill and to local farmers, and that Warren had falsified its records. Cargill refused further financing and sent an official to control the flow of funds in the last few days of Warren's operation. The farmers sued Cargill, arguing that Warren was an agent of Cargill, and that Cargill, as principal, was liable for Warren's debts. Cargill argued that it merely lent money to Warren, that Cargill was in effect just a bank, not a principal. The farmers won.

In this case, an investor, Cargill, in effect became a business owner without meaning to, and for completely understandable reasons. Cargill was a manufacturer and an international trader. Cargill was not a farming operation, nor even a local distribution operation. Cargill's business model required seed dealers and grain elevator operators such as Warren to serve sales, distribution, and warehouse functions, to be middlemen, between Cargill and the local farmers. So Cargill lent money to Warren, in order that such a middleman would exist in its part of the country. Like any lender, Cargill took a risk that the loan would not be repaid. Under the original agreement, Cargill took security interests in Warren's property, including a second mortgage on Warren's real estate, and a chattel mortgage on inventory and merchandise, that is, under certain circumstances, Cargill had rights to take Warren's property. But one might ask how much security these rights provided Cargill, in comparison with the amount of money that Cargill would ultimately lend to Warren? After all, the second mortgage meant that the holder of the first mortgage would in all likelihood get the value of the real estate; and how much would the value of the inventory and merchandise in Warren's possession come to? At any rate, Cargill itself was unwilling to rely on its security interests, and therefore took an increasingly active part in overseeing the running of Warren's business. Toward the end of the relationship, Cargill simply ran Warren's business. But even though Cargill took effective control, Cargill could not keep Warren from going bankrupt.

The question for the court was who was to bear the losses caused by Warren's bankruptcy? The court discusses this in terms of agency law, but the decision can be clarified if we put aside the legal jargon for a moment. To be childishly simple: if a bad thing happens, the party in control is to blame. Why? Because if a party was in control, it could have changed the situation, and then the bad thing would not have happened. So, as a very general matter, the party in control should be the party held responsible, which in court means, legally liable for damages. Cargill took control of Warren; Cargill should pay the farmers that Warren hurt. To bring the doctrinal language back into play, the person who works under the control of and for the benefit of another is called an agent. So the court has little difficulty labeling Cargill the principal, Warren the agent, and holding the principal liable for the actions of the agent. Cargill had unintentionally made Warren part of its business.

It would be easy enough to understand this case as the result of a series of bad business and legal decisions by Cargill; or even to dismiss this case as a bit of prairie populism, in which a deep pocketed corporation is forced to bail out a bunch of local farmers. Perhaps, but it is more important for present purposes to sympathize with Cargill and to understand the logic of its decisions. A company

> makes an investment;
> seeks to minimize risk;
> takes control of the situation;
> fails to prevent harm;
> is deemed responsible;
> is held legally liable.

This basic structure—investment/control/responsibility/liability—can be found everywhere. The conflict (How much control makes someone responsible for failure?) structures many of the agency, partnership and limited partnership, franchise, and "piercing the corporate veil" cases taught in the basic course on business associations.

The issue may be rephrased in terms of what counts as "within" the business. Cargill made itself "bigger" than it intended to. Along the same lines, consider the great jazz age case of *Martin v. Peyton*, which could easily provide the plot for a film about the foibles of high society.[3] Very rich men in New York, Peyton, Perkins, and Freeman, lend securities to a socially connected friend, John Hall, whose brokerage and banking firm, Knauth, Nachod & Kuhne, has run into substantial difficulties. In exchange, Peyton, Perkins, and Freeman receive substantial rights to oversee and perhaps even control Hall's company. The loan is squandered, largely on foreign exchange markets, and Knauth, Nachod & Kuhne fails. A creditor sues Peyton, Perkins, and Freeman, arguing that they are partners of Hall, and hence personally liable for Hall's debts (recall that partners do not have limited liability). Peyton, Perkins, and Freeman argue that they are creditors, not partners. In an elegant and very close opinion, Judge Andrews holds that the loan did not create a partnership, and Peyton and friends escape financial ruin.[4]

In cases like *Gay Jensen Farms* or *Martin & Peyton*, the legal role of the parties is not clear. As discussed in chapter 4, people do not come with legal labels: principal, agent, partner, creditor, and the like. Worse, the legal status of the parties is not something completely within their control. Certainly Cargill did not intend to become a principal in the grain elevator business in Warren, Minnesota, but it did. And certainly Peyton and friends did not wish to join Knauth, Nachod & Kuhne, as the documents memorializing their transaction made clear, but Judge Andrews nonetheless came within a whisker of holding them partners, and hence personally liable for the insolvency of the brokerage. In such cases, the parties do not control their own legal status. That is ultimately a question for the courts.

Limited Liability

In both *Gay Jensen Farms* and *Martin v. Peyton*, the businesspeople who invested their money in troubled businesses, Cargill and Peyton et al., had no intention of making themselves responsible for the business. In fact, they went to considerable, if ultimately futile, efforts to ensure that they were not responsible (i.e., not legally liable) for the obligations of the businesses in which they invested. Had they known they could be held liable, despite their efforts, they presumably would not have invested. Conversely, had they been willing to take responsibility for the businesses' obligations, presumably they would have insisted on buying the businesses outright. More generally, investment decisions are always made with an eye not only to the upside, the hoped-for return on investment, but also to the downside, the chance of unfortunate events like being held liable to the creditors of the failed business in which one has invested. Both of these cases raise the question of whether the law can afford more certainty to investors that they can avoid such responsibility than can be achieved through carefully drafted contracts disclaiming the responsibility. The answer is yes—investors can avoid being responsible for business failures through the institution of the corporation and similar limited liability entities established by statute.

As mentioned in part I, shareholders in corporations have "limited liability" for the actions of the corporation. Broadly stated, corporations—not their owners, the shareholders—are responsible for the actions of the corporation, which as a practical matter, means the actions of the corporation's agents. Thus, if the actions of a corporation's employee obligates the corporation (perhaps because the employee has broken a contract, or maybe somebody's leg), then the injured party may bring a lawsuit against the corporation, but not its shareholders. This sounds more complicated than it is. Imagine an ordinary citizen who, as a retirement investment, buys shares in a company with retail stores across the nation. Imagine that somebody falls in one of the stores, and sues, alleging that the floor was unsafe. Would we expect the citizen to be named as a defendant? Of course not.

Now imagine the investment is in a drug company, a product causes numerous deaths, and the company goes bankrupt. Would we expect the shareholders of the drug company, who are, after all, the owners, to be named as defendants? In fact, would we expect people to invest in a drug company at all if there is a risk that they might be personally liable for any disasters that might befall the company? Perhaps, at least if investors were in a position to make sure that the company were very, very well run, that is, if investors could afford the costs of monitoring the company. But keeping tabs on even one company is difficult, especially if the company operates in many countries. Thus it might be expected (the institution of limited liability is usually justified in terms of the expectation) that investors who might otherwise invest broadly would choose to invest in only a few businesses, and perhaps local ones at that, and many investors would be scared off altogether by the threat of personal liability for the manufacture of drugs. In short, the amount of investment in drug production would fall. Thus there is a deeply embedded public policy that shareholders are, as a general matter, only liable for corporate actions to the extent of their investment.

At the same time, the limited liability of shareholders is unsettling. After all, we usually speak of shareholders as "owners." If the business in question is a neighborhood furniture store, owned as a sole proprietorship, we in fact do expect the owner to be responsible (liable) for mishaps that are the fault of the business.[5] And it must be emphasized that limited liability claims arise in situations that are indeed the fault of the business. Limited liability questions arise when plaintiffs have good claims that the corporation cannot pay. If the plaintiff has a bad claim, then the corporation wins or settles the case, and the plaintiff does not seek money from the corporation's shareholders. If the plaintiff has a good claim and wins the suit, and the corporation has the resources to pay the judgment, then there is no question of asking a shareholder, in his or her personal capacity, to pay for harm done to the plaintiff by the corporation. Only if the plaintiff has a good claim, and the corporation cannot pay the judgment, does the plaintiff seek damages from the shareholder. In such cases, for a court to use doctrines of limited liability to shield the shareholder from paying the judgment is also saying that the plaintiff should pay.

One response to this difficulty is to ensure that people who do business with corporations know that they are doing business with a limited liability entity, and, therefore, know that the real owners of the entity, the shareholders, will not be liable for the obligations of the corporation in the event of some mishap. With such notice, third parties may then decide for themselves whether or not they wish to do business with a limited liability entity, presumably after a check of the company's capitalization, other assets, and especially insurance policies. Oftentimes, to protect themselves and as a condition of doing business, third parties insist that the owners of the business, or some other party, provide indemnification or other insurance for the transaction.

Obviously, notice that an enterprise is using a limited liability form of association is generally irrelevant to third parties in the context of noncontractual harms (torts)—one is rarely given the chance to pick between being hit by a truck owned by a sole proprietorship or a limited liability company (LLC). Notice of limited liability status may not be effective in the contractual context either. An officer of a corporation signing on behalf of the corporation must make it clear that it is the corporation, not the officer in his or her personal capacity, who is undertaking the obligations of the contract. Because, as mentioned, officers frequently sign as principals or guarantors, confusion is quite possible—and the mere fact that the third party is on notice that he or she is doing business with a limited liability entity is not enough to shield the officer from liability. Nonetheless, as noted in chapter 1, corporation statutes universally require corporations to signify that they are doing business in the corporate form by including "incorporated" or "corporation" or some variant in the company name, so that people doing business with the company are on notice that the owners of the enterprise enjoy limited liability.[6]

So what is the solution for the injured party, the plaintiff? Throughout the nineteenth and into the twentieth century, states attempted to ensure that corporations had resources adequate to meet their liabilities. After all, if the corporation can pay the injured third party, then limited liability raises no problem. There were a number of legal devices for accomplishing this objective. State statutes could simply require incorporators to raise a certain amount of money (*capital* or *stated capital*) as a condition for establishing the corporation, often $1,000. Sometimes capital was raised through the requirement that stock be sold at or above a minimum (*par*) value. Going forward, the corporation was required to keep such capital on hand, and in particular, could not issue dividends from the capital account.

Over the years, such devices to protect third parties from undercapitalized corporations have largely fallen from favor. With inflation, statutory minimum capital requirements such as $1,000 came to seem insignificant. Along the same lines, corporations began issuing stock with nominal or even no par value, so that the amount of capital (in this technical sense) generated through the sale of stock offered no real protection to third parties. More generally, a sensible capital requirement would have to take account of the business the corporation did. Businesses likely to cause larger losses to third parties should hold more money in reserve (in modern jargon, such businesses would require more assets in order to be able to self-insure). As we have seen, however, the entire thrust of corporation law has been to create a formal structure without reference to the particulars of this or that business. Concerns for third parties came to be addressed, if they were addressed, by different kinds of regulation. Thus, as a matter of corporation law, the problem of corporations incurring liabilities they cannot pay remains.

Limited liability may also be understood as a problem of corporate governance: if the shareholders do not have to pay, and the company as such has few assets, then it does not matter what legal liabilities the company incurs. The company is judgment proof. Knowing this, businesspeople may set up a company to operate a business in risky fashion, without taking the time and expense to be careful, and consequently making higher profits than they would if they operated the business in a prudent fashion. If something goes wrong, then the company will be liable, but not its owners. In such cases, limited liability can create an incentive for recklessness. Surely, in such cases, it must be wrong to shield shareholders from being held responsible for their businesses?

There is thus a fundamental tension between two "good"—broadly supported—policies: (1) society wants people to invest in companies without having to monitor every detail about how the business is conducted, and therefore gives shareholders limited liability; at the same time, (2) society wants companies to be operated carefully, and wants people with good claims to be paid, but limited liability creates incentives for companies to operate in a reckless fashion, without being able to pay for the damages they cause.

Piercing the Corporate Veil

This would seem to be a good lawyer's problem: Can a rule be articulated that distinguishes the cases in which the corporate form ought to be respected, that is, shareholders should enjoy limited liability (and plaintiffs should pay), from the cases in which courts "pierce the corporate veil" and hold shareholders liable for the actions of the corporation? The short answer is no, not really. The long answer is we can talk a lot about the problem. There are many of these "piercing the corporate veil" cases, from many jurisdictions, arising from many kinds of conflict, which have generated a great deal of commentary.[7] To simplify and generalize, however, courts have required plaintiffs who wish to hold shareholders liable for corporate actions to show two things: respect for the corporate form and some wrongdoing.

First, with regard to institutional form, courts have generally insisted that in order for shareholders to enjoy limited liability, the corporation must be run like a corporation. It is often said that "the corporate form must be respected." In order to make this determination, courts look to see if the corporation actually does business or is just a shell; does it take formal decisions; keep books and records; file taxes; and the like? Directors should act like directors and managers should run the company in the best interest of the corporation and its shareholders. The corporation should not be the "alter ego" of its owners, that is, the business of the corporation must be kept distinct from the business of its owners. In other words, the shareholders should not so utterly dominate the operation of the corporation that the interests of the corporation are indistinguishable from those of its owners, presumably because parties who are in complete control should be liable, as discussed with regard to *A. Gay Jensen Farms* and *Martin v. Peyton* above. So courts, for common example, look to see if the shareholders use company funds for personal affairs, especially without authorization from the board.

If one imagines a big company, a vast and well-established institution, then keeping the corporation's business distinct from the shareholder's business does not seem too difficult. As a result, distinguishing the corporation from its owners does not seem too hard, and it is not hard to imagine situations in which the corporation incurs legal liability. Whether or not the shareholder should be held vicariously liable for the actions of the company, it is clear that the liability would be vicarious. If, however, one imagines a small corporation, with very few shareholders, in which the same people fill all the corporate roles, it becomes far harder to talk about the "corporation" as an entity with business distinct from the business of its owners. Of course the owners "dominate" their business, and courts are left in the uncomfortable position of drawing lines.[8]

Second, courts have usually required plaintiffs who wish to pierce the corporate veil and hold shareholders vicariously liable for corporate activity to show that honoring the corporate form would result in fraud or some other injustice. In *Sea Land Services, Inc. v. Pepper Source*[9] the court pointed out that all veil-piercing cases involved some wrong. Plaintiffs seeking to recover from shareholders have a judgment in their favor and have been harmed by a corporation that is judgment proof. This is wrong, but it does nothing to distinguish cases in which shareholders should be held vicariously liable from cases in which shareholders should enjoy limited liability. Thus, the court required some wrong in addition to unpaid judgments for the underlying harm.

Most all of these issues are presented by the facts of the classic case *Walkovszky v. Carlton*.[10] Carlton ran a cab business in New York City. He established numerous small companies, each of which owned two cabs. As required by law, each cab company carried insurance, but the amount required was not very high. One of the cabs in Carlton's fleet seriously injured Walkovszky, a pedestrian. Walkovszky sought to recover against Carlton, arguing under a number of different theories that the corporate form should not be respected (i.e., that Carlton should not enjoy limited liability).

The case is usually taught for its facts, which so nicely illustrate how the corporate form can be abused that it is easy to misremember what the court actually decided. In a doctrinally technical (yet unconvincing) decision and over a blistering dissent, the court found fault with each of Walkovszky's theories. The court's decision appears to have been driven by policy considerations. The New York legislature had passed a law requiring cab companies to carry insurance. The court reasoned that holding Carlton (and similarly situated cab owners) liable for losses in addition to those paid for by the required insurance would, in effect, be to require cab companies to carry more insurance. The additional expense would be likely to drive certain small companies from business. The court reasoned that the legislature had already struck the balance between encouraging investment in cabs and ensuring the responsible operation of cab businesses. In setting an insurance requirement for cab companies to carry a relatively small amount of insurance, the legislature had decided that it wanted to keep small cab companies in business, even at the cost of having companies operate without the resources to pay for damages. The court declined to disturb the legislature's decision, so Walkovszky paid.

Now suppose that the shareholders are not natural persons, but other corporations. If corporation X has some of its capital invested in some unrelated other company Y, then it would seem that X should be treated as any other investor (i.e., not be held liable for the unmet obligations of Y). However, it is common practice for a corporation ("the parent") to establish another corporation and retain all, or substantially all, of the shares in the new company ("the subsidiary"). Although large enterprises are somewhat loosely referred to by the name of the controlling corporation, such enterprises actually are comprised of multiple, separately chartered, corporations. It is difficult to see why parent corporations should be shielded from liability for the actions of their subsidiaries. Indeed, if the company chooses to structure its business in divisions, without separately incorporating the businesses, then there is no presumption of limited liability. Nonetheless, the policy in favor of limited shareholder liability is so deeply entrenched that the liability of parent corporations for their subsidiaries is often analyzed as if the parents were ordinary shareholders.

In the silicone gel breast implants products liability litigation, the court found that Bristol-Meyers Squibb exhibited "substantial domination" over its wholly owned subsidiary Medical Engineering Corporation (MEC).[11] (Indeed, the domination was so substantial that the plaintiffs also sued Bristol-Meyers directly.) In a motion for summary judgment, Bristol-Meyers argued that, in order to succeed in their efforts to pierce the corporate veil and hold Bristol-Meyers liable as MECs shareholder, the plaintiffs also had to show fraud. The plaintiffs had presented no evidence that went to show fraud and therefore should lose. The court found that a showing of fraud was not necessary in all states (this class action multidistrict litigation consolidated individual claims made under the laws of several states), and therefore denied the motion for summary judgment.

To summarize: in most states, courts require a showing that the corporation was completely dominated by its shareholder, sometimes characterizing such a corporation as an "alter ego" of its shareholder. In addition, many courts require that respecting the corporate form—treating the corporation seriously as a responsible legal person—leads to fraud or some other injustice over and above the fact that the plaintiff's claims against the corporation go unsatisfied.

Hybrid Forms of Business Association

Obviously, doing business in a limited liability form of business association like the corporation has substantial advantages for investors. But the corporation has one major drawback, taxation, which is discussed in more detail in chapter 12. For present purposes, it is important to know that corporations are, like natural persons, taxed by the federal government on their income. In addition, dividend payments from the business to shareholders are taxed to the shareholders as income. This is often called double taxation. In contrast, partnerships are not taxed as entities, but as we saw earlier in this chapter, partners do not enjoy limited liability. Thus, traditionally and in general, in order to gain the limited liability offered by the corporation, businesses have had to submit to double taxation. It was and is a hard bargain.

In a few circumstances, however, it has long been possible to establish limited liability business entities that were not taxed, although any money distributed to the owners was taxed as individual income, such as the limited partnership and the S Corp. In the past few decades, however, states have established new forms of limited liability business association, notably the limited liability company (LLC), the limited liability partnership (LLP), and the closely related professional corporation (PC). For tax purposes, the federal government treats such entities as partnerships, that is, they are not taxed. The use of such entities has grown exponentially over the past few years; the creation of LLCs has outstripped the establishment of corporations. Such forms of association informally may be thought of as hybrids because, as already suggested, they combine key advantages of the partnership, on the one hand, and the business corporation, on the other.

- In general, like the corporation, hybrids offer limited liability for its owners (unlike the partnership).
- And unlike the corporation, but like partnerships, hybrid entities are not taxed on their profits (instead, profits made by the owners of the hybrid are taxed).
- With regard to management, hybrids may be managed by their owners (like a partnership), or may be run by professional managers hired by the company (like a corporation).

Doing business through a hybrid form, like doing business through a corporation, poses issues of responsibility. As with corporations, businesses using a limited liability form must put third parties on notice that they are doing business as a limited liability enterprise by including some such signifier in the name of the company (e.g., LLC or PC as part of the company name). In addition, limited liability has been increasingly extended to members of highly regulated professions (doctors and lawyers), whose businesses have traditionally been run as partnerships, presumably in the hope that professional standards ensure against reckless operation, and insurance will cover mishaps.

Chapter 11

Views of the Institution

Evolution (and Extinction)

CONSIDER THE FOLLOWING RATHER COMMONSENSE STORY OF A BUSINESS, which not incidentally places the basic forms of business associations in logical order. In corporation law casebooks, this progressive sequence is usually implicit, visible in the table of contents, but often set forth without much comment.

1. *Sole proprietorship.* Imagine an individual who opens and runs, all by herself, a small business as a "sole proprietor." At least with regard to business activity, the owner is pretty much indistinguishable from her business.[1] She is responsible for the business actions because they are her own actions, too. Thus the scope of the owner's legal responsibility and the scope of the owner's activity are the same.

2. *Agency relationship.* Imagine that our sole proprietor hires an employee. The owner is a principal, and the employee is an agent. The owner is liable for many actions taken by her employee. That is, the owner is now legally responsible for some things she did *not* do. Thus, due to the

operation of the employment contract, the legal scope of the proprietor's responsibility—the owner's business—is larger than the scope of the owner's activity.

3. *Partnership.* Imagine that our sole proprietor goes into business with someone else. The two people agree to run the business together, share in the profits, and be responsible for the liabilities of the business. They agree, in short, to form a partnership. Partners are simultaneously principals and agents of each other. As agent, each partner can bind the other partner(s) (make the other partner(s) responsible, liable). By the same token, as principal, each partner is responsible for the actions of her agents.

Partnerships, for many purposes, are legal persons. Thus, through an agency agreement, the law has created an entity that is not only distinct from its individual owners, but which is able to take on certain legal responsibilities. The partnership as such may be liable in contract or tort. The owners, however, manage the partnership. And for tax purposes, as we saw in the previous chapter, the profits of the business are taxed to the owners, rather than the partnership.

4. *Limited liability company or other hybrid.* Imagine that the partners begin to worry about liability. In compliance with state statute, they establish the business as an LLC, limited partnership, or other hybrid entity.

5. *Business corporation.* Assume that the business outgrows the LLC form and is structured in compliance with state statute as a corporation.[2] The owners invest their money in exchange for certain rights represented by a share. The owners have no rights, however, to operate the business. Instead, the corporation hires managers (e.g., employees, agents) to run the business. Legal affairs of the corporation are carried out by the corporation's managers, not its owners. The fact that operation of the business is almost completely independent of its ownership creates the agency problem, which is the traditional concern of corporation law, first discussed in chapter 3.

Like the famous image of a line of ancient primates, early hominids, prehistoric members of the genus *Homo,* and modern man (usually depicted as a thirty-something white guy who clearly has an office job but who is strangely both thin and nearly naked), this is a story of evolution.[3] A founding entrepreneur has a commercial idea and starts a small business. In order to expand, she needs to raise capital. She needs investors, who receive interests in the business, and so the capital structure—the form of business association—reflects the capital needs of the growing business. As described above, a sole proprietorship evolves into a general partnership, perhaps undergoes a stage as a limited partnership or an LLC, and finally becomes a corporation, perhaps even a publicly traded one. Whether or not explicitly, the idea of the evolution of forms of business association taps into widely told stories of men who follow their individualistic dreams and build corporate empires, from Henry Ford to Bill Gates.[4] The evolution of the forms of business association is thus presented not only as a reflection of the adventurous side of American capitalism, but also as a progressive narrative, in which business evolves toward the large publicly traded corporation.

In this "bottom up" account of the corporation, entrepreneurs trying to expand their businesses must both seek capital (raising problems of "finance") and expand their operations, in particular, hire people (raising issues considered under the heading of "agency").[5] Finance and operations are simply flip sides of the same coin, different perspectives on what is, after all, one business. The underlying point is that increases in the size of the business engender changes in the form of the business; changes in quantity entail changes in quality. In this story, the growth of businesses leads to ever more complicated forms of business organization, culminating in the business corporation.

As suggested in chapter 1, much the same story can be told, but from the opposite perspective, as the emergence of the corporation as a social institution distinct from its owners, indeed distinct from its personnel altogether. Consider the forms of business associations again, but this time in terms of (a) title to assets and right to contract; (b) management; (c) share in profits; (d) responsibility for losses (liabilities); (e) duration. If we reexamine the progression laid out above, we will see that the attributes of ownership shift from the owner to the entity.

1. *Sole proprietorship (with or without an agent)*:
   (a) the owner has title to the assets and makes contracts
   (b) the owner makes all decisions regarding the business
   (c) the owner makes all profits from the business
   (d) the owner is directly liable for the obligations of the business
   (e) the business lasts as long as its owner does business (i.e., has limited life)
2. *Partnership*:
   (a) the partnership, not the owner, has title to the assets and makes contracts

(b) subject to the rights of the other partners, and to agreement if any, each owner (partner) has an equal right to participate in management

(c) subject to the rights of the other partners, and to agreement if any, each partner has an equal right to share in the profits of the business

(d) the partnership is liable for its obligations, but partners may be held liable for the unmet obligations of the business

(e) the partnership lasts as long as the partnership agreement is ongoing; new partners may be added by agreement

3. *Limited liability company or other hybrid:*
    (a) the company has title to the assets and makes contracts
    (b) pursuant to the founding document (usually the operating agreement) the owners (members) have more, or fewer, rights to participate in the management of the business
    (c) pursuant to the founding document, members have more, or fewer, rights to participate in the profits of the business
    (d) the LLC is liable for the obligations of the business; if the LLC cannot pay, and absent special circumstances, the members are not liable
    (e) duration is variable; although some statutes require the operating agreement to define the entity's term, the trend is to allow for perpetual duration

4. *Business corporation:*
    (a) the corporation has title to the assets and makes contracts
    (b) pursuant to statute, the articles of incorporation, and the bylaws, the corporation is managed by professional managers overseen by a board of directors; owners ("shareholders") do not participate in management
    (c) shareholders have a right to a dividend only if declared, a decision in the business discretion of the board of directors; shareholders do not have a right to a payout of the profits of the company
    (d) the corporation is liable for the obligations of the business; if the company cannot pay, and absent special circumstances, the shareholders are not liable
    (e) duration is generally perpetual

To summarize the end points of this progression: the sole proprietorship is a mode of doing business, but it is not a legal entity distinct from its owner. The corporation is an entity, an institution, that exists independently of its owner. Thus, while the corporation might be understood as the product of ever more complicated arrangements made by businesspeople, such arrangements may also be seen to create an essentially autonomous institution, the emergence of which signifies the subordination of owners, which was after all the problem with which Berle and Means were concerned. Sometimes the same play may be watched as either a comedy or a tragedy.[6]

Academic Theories

For over a century, the business corporation in roughly its contemporary form has been recognized as important in American life. And for most of that time, it has been widely recognized that although we generally speak of a corporation's shareholders as its "owners," doing so strains ordinary conceptions of ownership. One owns a share in ways quite different from the ways in which one owns a house. It seems sensible to talk about a small business in terms of its proprietor, and a law partnership in terms of its partners, but we cannot really speak of a big corporation, as an institution, as if it were merely the business of shareholders. Recognition that the corporation is an institution, not just the business of the shareholders, gives rise to a venerable question in academic jurisprudence: what is the corporation? Can the institution be explained in terms of some "theory," that is, can the social phenomenon (the corporation) be explained in terms of something somehow less strange and more fundamental?

It should be emphasized that this question is primarily interesting to academics. Business life proceeds without much of a theoretically satisfying articulation of the corporation (or money or property or contract, for that matter). At the same time, there is an intuitive appeal to the question—it seems that one should be able to understand the corporation in some fundamental way. To indulge in taxonomy, here is a sketch of some of the approaches scholars have taken over the years.[7]

1. Under "concession" or "grant" theories, the corporation is a product of government action, the granting of permission to use the corporate form, and the corporation's life as a legal person is defined by its status vis-à-vis the state.[8]

2. Under "aggregation theories" the corporation is the sum of the interests of its individual participants. There are a number of different kinds of aggregation theories.

    (a) In the usually implicit "shareholder-centered" theory of most legal scholarship and teaching in the United States, the corporation is to be understood as a legal vehicle constructed for the benefit of share-holders.

(b) In the transaction cost model of the corporation, associated with Ronald Coase and mentioned in chapter 2, the corporation is a means of using long-term agreements to avoid the transaction costs of bargaining/contracting for every transaction involved in a business.

(c) In contractarian theories, often espoused by law and economics scholars, the corporation is a "nexus of contracts" among the shareholders, managers, directors, and sometimes other parties.[9]

(d) In "stakeholder" theories, the corporation is a set of relationships, some but not all of which are contractual, among not only shareholders, managers, and directors, but also other constituencies, such as employees, consumers, and neighbors.[10]

3. "Entity theories" treat the corporation itself as an actor. As discussed in chapter 1, the presumption that the corporation is an entity is deeply embedded in corporation law, and indeed in almost all legal discourse regarding the corporation. Debate has existed, however, from time to time since the late nineteenth century, over whether the corporation should be understood as the legal expression of a more fundamental social formation (i.e., whether the group is an appropriate unit of analysis).[11]

(a) In most social sciences, the corporation is understood to reflect social, economic, and especially institutional realities, including the tendency for people to form groups, and perhaps even more importantly, to think in terms of groups (this is common outside the legal academy; less common in law schools).

(b) In most contemporary economics, in which the corporation per se is not at issue, the corporation is usually treated as an actor, and often as a rational actor. In institutional economics, however, which seeks to analyze the corporation itself, the corporation is usually treated as a virtual market, along lines pioneered by Ronald Coase (see 2b above), or in more explicitly contractarian terms (see 2c above).

Such labels are only shorthand names, tags, for jurisprudential approaches to the corporation that have at one time or another been influential in various discourses in the United States. There are many variations on these themes, and the theories are not all mutually exclusive, and academics have come up with still others that may yet gain paradigmatic status.[12] Unsurprisingly, there is a considerable academic literature here, and this book makes no pretense of doing justice to what is at least a century of scholarship, much less presenting "the correct" theory of the corporation. (For the answers to these and other pressing questions, a rather extensive bibliography has been included.)

It is not at all clear how much one's theory of the corporation matters to one's policy positions, or vice versa. People on opposite sides of particularly long-standing political questions may use the same theory of the corporation; people on the same side may have different conceptions about the nature of the corporation. Description does not seem to determine prescription. Yet, in a given time and place, one's theory of the corporation tends to be associated with specific political perspectives.[13] Thus, although theories are not determinative, from time to time and in place to place, they tend to have certain specific associations. At present, for example, self-styled "progressives" tend to argue that the corporation should be understood as an entity, while economic conservatives tend to favor contractarian rhetoric. In the 1920s, however, progressives tended to be hostile to the entity notion of the corporation and stressed that companies were, after all, organizations of people. Then surveying the confusion, the pragmatist philosopher John Dewey argued that the question was not metaphysical, not "what is the corporation, really?" but instead what the conception "the corporation" was being used for—we think of things in different ways as the circumstances and purposes of our thinking change.[14] Especially in this case, I agree.

Social Purposes of the Corporation

The obvious place to look for the purpose of the corporation is in the articles of incorporation, or in the traditional language, the charter. As we have seen in chapter 2, however, the idea that a corporation must be established to accomplish a distinct purpose has faded over the past two centuries. Instead, the purpose of doing business as a corporation came to be seen as, essentially, doing whatever the business in question was, and so corporations are now routinely established for all legal purposes. Of course, the incorporators tend to have something much more specific in mind: businesses must have a plan for how they are going to make money. In particular, corporations often must be able to explain what they plan to do (must have a "business model") in order to convince shareholders and others to invest in the business. This idea of the purpose of the company, however, is not fixed and established beforehand in the charter, but instead, evolves over the life of the business. The business model—and hence the purpose of the business—is negotiated among the management, directors, and to a limited extent, the shareholders.

This is more than a little vague. Saying that the purpose of the business is to do business, as determined by the ongoing processes of corporate governance, says nothing about which businesses to leave, which to enter, how to conduct the company's affairs in a given business—all the internal struggles over governance of the corporation that were examined in part II of this book arise anew. At this juncture, it is often said that the corporation should do whatever is best for the shareholders. Indeed shareholder wealth maximization remains the dominant (and rather conservative) understanding of the central principle of corporate governance. But the principle that the corporation should be run for the benefit of its shareholders does not solve many practical problems. As we have seen, a short-term cost may be to the long-term benefit of the company (indeed, almost all investment imposes short-term costs). Thus, determining what is in the real interests of shareholders involves an imagination of the "shareholder" in question, a selection of time horizons, predictions of the future—rather contestable matters.

One way to understand this problem is in the context of corporate donations to charity, surely a common enough practice. On the surface, the decision of management (including directors) to have the corporation make a charitable gift conflicts with the desire of shareholders to receive the maximum return on their investment—money given to a charity neither is paid out to shareholders as a dividend, nor is it retained in the company, making the shares more valuable. But courts have consistently found charitable gifts, so long as they are reasonable in amount and in the interests of the company very broadly construed, to be legal. The classic teaching case is *A.P. Smith v. Barlow.*[15] A. P. Smith, a New Jersey company, made a charitable donation to Princeton University. The donation was challenged by a shareholder, who thought he had invested in a company, that is, given his money to people who would try to make money with it and return some of the proceeds to him.

In upholding the decision of the directors, the court stressed that corporations had to do business in a larger community, and that a degree of charity was both an aspect of doing business and in the long-term interest of the company. In essence, the court upheld the company's effort to do well by doing good, a stance that has become standard.[16] From this perspective, the corporation is a largely self-governing institution operating within society at large, and for such an institution, charitable gifts could be important. Courts and ultimately legislatures, therefore, have tended to allow the governance mechanisms of the corporation itself to resolve such questions.

If the classic problem of corporation law is the abuse of shareholders by management, however, then *A.P. Smith* may also be seen as an example of the failure of state corporation law to protect isolated shareholders. Why, if the general purpose of corporation law is to protect shareholders, would state law fail? One possibility is that while the ideal of state corporation law is the protection of shareholders, economic and political forces made states less likely to do so than one might hope. Running for governor of New Jersey (the Delaware, for corporation law purposes, of the turn of the century), Woodrow Wilson promised to rein in excesses of corporate power. Many corporations reincorporated in Delaware, where no such regulatory offensive was planned. Delaware's dominance as the site of incorporation stems from this time, and today, almost half of the large companies listed on the New York Stock Exchange are incorporated in Delaware.

In 1974, law professor William Cary argued that states had incentives to pass laws that would advantage managers and fail to protect shareholders.[17] In particular, Cary asserted, Delaware's corporation law was especially friendly to managers, and conversely unprotective of shareholders. Therefore, incorporators (who generally become managers once the company is established) were more likely to incorporate in Delaware, and existing companies were likely to reincorporate in Delaware. Delaware reaped a benefit by taxing the corporations incorporated there. Other states either had to lose tax revenue or modify their corporate laws to match Delaware, that is, to become more management friendly and less protective of shareholders, in what Cary called a "race to the bottom." Cary, therefore, recommended national legislation that would set minimum standards for corporations. (It is worth noting that the U.S. system of state business law is rather unusual; most countries have national "company" laws.)

A few years later, Judge Ralph Winter argued, in essence, that if Delaware's laws were disadvantageous to shareholders in fact, then the shares of companies incorporated in Delaware would trade at a discount.[18] Companies that reincorporated in Delaware should see a drop in the price of their stock. Shareholders would resist such reincorporations, or if necessary, sell their stock. In order to compete for incorporation, Delaware would have to change its laws. None of these things had been observed; therefore, Winter concluded, Cary's "race to the bottom" thesis was wrong.

A host of law review articles on all sides of the question issued forth.[19] The question sounded empirical and was generally treated as such, but unfortunately, proved very difficult to resolve empirically. It is far from clear what law counts as friendly to management, especially if one considers that the law on the books hardly predicts what a court will decide, and so comparing legal regimes—what would the management be able to do differently if incorporated in the following two or three (or fifty-one, including the District of Columbia) jurisdictions—becomes indefinite and impractical. Nor is it clear that state legislatures do much, if anything, to their corporate law codes (or that states do anything with regard to the selection of judges) in order to compete for incorporations. Nor is it possible to isolate the effect of "the law" on the price of stock with any degree of certainty, for the simple reason that many things affect the price of stock. Those things said, when the dust had settled, most law professors seem to think that Winter had the best of the exchange, and that corporation law was not getting worse. Perhaps this is unsurprising, especially during a bull market.

The Delaware debate, like the discussion of charitable gifts by corporations, turned on the question of the extent to which corporations could be trusted to govern themselves. Within corporation law discourse, the debate is usually presented starkly, but the question is one of degree. To say that the corporation is "largely self-governing" is not to say "entirely self-governing." As we have discussed, the actors within a corporation are not free to do whatever they please. As well as whatever social, economic, and indeed psychological constraints are imposed by doing business in a given time and place, corporate actors are legally and formally limited by the state statute, and by the articles of incorporation and bylaws of the corporation in question. At the same time—obviously—corporations do govern themselves, and neither courts nor legislatures want to have much to do with the overwhelming volume of often nitty-gritty decisions that the nation's businesses require.

Thus, there is a tension between the corporation understood as a creature of state corporation law, and the corporation understood as a self-governing institution. This question is often phrased as the extent to which state corporation law is understood to be "mandatory" or "enabling." Insofar as state corporation law is "mandatory," it creates a template that businesspeople must use in order to do business in the corporate form. Insofar as state corporation law is "enabling," then the law is understood as a set of "default" rules, which apply if the parties have not agreed otherwise.[20] The exact location of the line between mandatory and enabling is contested.[21] In times in which business appears to be running well, there is less pressure for governmental oversight. Businesspeople know how to run their own affairs, it is argued, and should be allowed to contract for the arrangements they prefer. In times of business crisis, such as the wave of accounting scandals in the first years of this decade, it is argued that business practices need to be regulated, and governments are likely to impose rules.

Chapter 12

Corporations and the State

Overview

Part III has been structured on the continuum between the citizen, through the civil institution of the corporation, to the state. So chapter 10 discussed the responsibility of business entities to third parties, the relationship between the business and citizens. Chapter 11 considered corporations on their own terms, by telling an evolutionary story, in which the form of business evolves from the sole proprietorship to the business corporation. The emergence of business institutions that were understood to be distinct from, even largely independent of, the people who own them or work for them raised an old question: can the corporation be defined on its own terms, or in terms of its own purposes? Chapter 11 declined (or failed!) to answer the question with the pragmatic excuse that the corporation requires different understandings in different circumstances. This chapter, predictably enough, considers the relationship between the corporation and the state.

In this chapter we assume that, regardless of the jurisprudential questions surrounding the nature of the corporation, the state has relatively few practical problems recognizing corporations. After all, corporations are established by filing papers with a state government, which keeps records of the corporations established in that state, and doing business in good standing. Also, governments routinely require corporations to register their existence: to file for taxes; to apply for permits, licenses, and otherwise to comply with regulatory requirements; or simply to inform a government that they are doing business in the jurisdiction. So, blithely assuming that "what is the corporation" and "what are corporations for" are not serious practical problems, this chapter examines a few of the relations between the corporation and the state, particularly the tax status of corporations. As we will see, taxation suggests how the typology of institutions set forth in chapter 11, extending from the individual to the corporation, may be extended to encompass agencies of the state itself.

Tax

As we have discussed, for legal purposes pertaining to the operation of a business, the corporation is almost indistinguishable from a natural person. So a corporation may own property, including real property and securities. A corporation may enter into contracts, may be the subject of regulation, and may carry on legal proceedings like lawsuits. A corporation may be responsible (liable), indeed so responsible that it seems natural not to hold the nominal owners of the corporation liable for harms done by the corporation. Creating a structure that organizes people so that they can be treated as a single thing, an entity, is perhaps the greatest success of corporation law.

Corporations resemble natural persons in another way: their income is taxed by the federal government and most state governments. "Corporate tax law" is a small but rather necessary part of the basic course in business associations, but it is also taught as a separate advanced course. Some basic discussion of corporate tax is necessary in the basic course because tax considerations often drive the business decision to adopt one or another form of association (e.g., to do business as a limited liability company or a corporation, as mentioned in the previous chapter). And tax considerations are also relevant to other issues that arise in the basic course, such as the dividend discussed in *Kamin v. American Express* in chapter 6.

More importantly for our present purposes, nothing expresses the legal status of the corporation, and the relationship between the corporation and the state, more clearly than tax law. Federal tax law, by taxing the "private interest" of the business corporation, positions the business corporation vis-à-vis the state much as if the corporation were a natural person. Business corporations themselves (not just their owners, the shareholders) are expected to act in their private interests and to pay taxes on their income. And business corporations act much as natural persons do when regulated—they tend to try and avoid, or at least minimize, the interference of the regulation.

Three basic ideas should get us started:

1. *A corporation and its shareholders are taxed separately.* The corporation is taxed on its income, according to the applicable corporate tax rate. If the corporation uses profits, after taxes, to issue a dividend to its shareholders, then the dividend is counted by the government as income taxable to the shareholders, according to the applicable individual income tax rate. As mentioned in the previous chapter, the money made by the corporation and distributed to shareholders is thus taxed twice, once at the corporate level and again at the shareholder level. This is often called *double taxation.*

2. *Tax rates are set through political processes.* Neither corporate nor individual tax rates are constant. Nor do they have any constant or principled relationship to one another. Although tax can be very important to a business, and technically difficult for its lawyers, much of tax law, starting with rates, must be assumed.

3. *The tax rates that apply to a certain transaction affect the economics of that business or transaction.* Someone (a tax lawyer) has to work out the tax consequences of structuring a business or a transaction in one way or another. A great deal of what corporations, and businesses more generally, do is motivated by the tax consequences of this or that course of action.

As with any tax, people would rather avoid paying corporate tax. Consequently, and increasingly, businesses avoid incorporating and choose to do business through another form of business association. As discussed in chapter 10, and to repeat, hybrid forms of business association allow enterprises to receive both the limited liability associated with the corporation and the "pass through" taxation associated with partnerships. To simplify: the federal government gives hybrid forms of business association the choice of being treated, for tax purposes, like a partnership or like a corporation. If the hybrid chooses to be treated like a partnership (as they virtually all do), then the government deems the hybrid to pay out its income to its owners, who are individually held liable for their shares of the hybrid's income. In effect, this forces hybrids to pay at least enough of their income out to the owners so that the owners can pay their individual federal tax bills. Thus the government still taxes the income made by the hybrid, but does so at the level of owners (usually individuals), not at the level of the business entity. Although the government receives tax revenue from the income of the business, because the income is taxed only once, the individual owners get to keep more of the profits of the business than they would under a double taxation regime.

Under these circumstances, why would the owners of any business choose to incorporate? The business planning considerations can get quite complex, but by way of introduction, consider an enterprise with relatively little profit in its early years and with owner/investors interested in long-term gain. Consider, for example, a high-tech start-up established as a corporation. Such a company is likely to pay no dividends in the early years. This company would pay relatively little corporate tax (because it has relatively little income), and the owners would pay no income tax on their shares (because the company pays no dividends). On the other hand, if such an enterprise is operated as an LLC or other hybrid, any profits that the company does make (perhaps unlikely in the high-tech start-up context) will be deemed by the Internal Revenue Service (IRS) to be distributed to the owner as income. This might hamper the ability of the company to retain capital for growth. Moreover, the LLC and other hybrid forms tend to be established through more contractual processes, which may hinder the free transferability, and hence the liquidity, of their equity securities. More generally, both the venture capital markets and the public equity markets (like NASDAQ) are institutionally structured around common stock in corporations, and the developed body of law and institutions is developed to deal with trade in corporate equity. Thus the start-up's need for financing may compel its use of the corporate form.[1]

As the business grows, from the perspective of owners—most obviously founding entrepreneurs, but also highly compensated managers, and indeed wealthy individuals generally—there are problematic tax consequences of operating a successful business as an LLC or other pass-through entity. As already noted, the LLC's annual income creates a taxable event for an individual. But the situation is different in a business structured as a corporation. Dividends are taxed, and if the share is sold at a profit, the profit is taxed.[2] But if the shareholder simply holds the shares, and the company grows and the shares become more valuable, the shareholder pays no tax on his or her increased wealth—Bill Gates and Warren Buffett could have never become so rich if every time Microsoft or Berkshire Hathaway increased in value they had to pay taxes. Moreover, many young businesses compensate employees with equity, because people may be willing to work for little cash pay if given some ownership in a company they believe will be valuable at some point. If that belief is correct and the company in fact does become valuable (for example, Google), then such employee/shareholders may require a chance to cash out some of their equity. In order to do that, they will require a market for their stock, and hence in all likelihood an *initial public offering* (IPO) of the stock, amusingly enough sometimes called a "liquidity event" in this context. Thus, especially as the company grows, financial market considerations may indicate use of the corporate, rather than a hybrid, form, in spite of the problem of double taxation. To summarize this sketch: for a business designed to throw off cash from operations to its owners, an LLC is more likely to be the right form of business association; for a business designed to grow over time, a corporation may well be a better choice.

The relationship between the corporation and the government established by tax law is unsurprisingly problematic. If a corporation is taxed on income, then the corporation has an incentive not to show taxable income. Perversely, income tax creates an incentive to keep the company's costs high. Indeed, many very big companies show, for tax purposes, little income. So, for example, salaries are a cost to the company (i.e., paying high salaries reduces the income taxable to the corporation). Thus there are tax advantages to paying major investors through salaries rather than dividends, but this might not be in the interest of all shareholders. For another example, interest payments on debt are a cost to the company, but dividends paid out to shareholders are not. Management, therefore, has an incentive to raise capital through debt rather than equity financing. Debt, however, tends to be a bit riskier than equity (because debt repayments presume adequate and stable cash flows), so the tax regime may be creating an incentive for management that is not in the best interest of the corporation and its shareholders.

More generally, taxes (all taxes) create "distortions," that is, encourage behaviors that would not exist in the absence of the tax.[3] Sometimes this is a good thing (consider, for example, a tax on cigarettes, designed to discourage smoking), but in the business context, tax policy generally seeks to raise revenue while minimizing its effect on behavior. Rephrased, it is thought to be inefficient if people are making business decisions in order to avoid taxes. Instead, a business decision should be made on the merits of the business at hand, not on the basis of the tax consequences of various options. Most other advanced economies, even those with very "social" governments, impose lower taxes on the corporation than the United States does. Consequently, a variety of proposals have been made to eliminate double taxation, or at least taxation on dividend payments.

To get some sense of the political difficulties surrounding such proposals (which have been made throughout the past century), imagine if corporations were not taxed, as was the case prior to 1913. In such a world, a titan of business such as Henry Ford could control a huge fortune, a concentration of economic power, by controlling the corporation. Although it may be doubted that the world of 1913 was very different from our own in this regard, legally accepting our own gilded age would require the public frustration, indeed humiliation, of a number of social commitments that run fairly deeply in U.S. society and so law. Americans tend to believe that citizens participate in (including pay for) their government, indeed that governments—from community barn raisings to constitutions—are formed by collective efforts. At least in the twentieth century, government has been seen as a vehicle for the provision of opportunity to the less fortunate and the modest redistribution of wealth (hence inheritance tax, latterly called the "death tax," as well as graduated income taxes, and of course the "confiscatory" capital gains tax). And from the very beginning of the republic, concentrations of power outside the government have been viewed with some suspicion. Sophisticated schemes for corporate tax reform attempt to address such concerns in various ways, but the government's reluctance to allow private wealth to accumulate within corporations without asserting tax authority is easy enough to understand.

So far, we have seen that the federal tax on business corporations creates an incentive to avoid incorporation altogether and affects (distorts) the behavior of corporations in probably undesirable ways. Corporation tax law thus establishes a classic regulator/regulated relationship, in which the public interest, represented by the government, opposes the individual interests of the private sector. But suppose the corporation is understood to be part of the public sector?

Imagine an enterprise that the government might itself wish to undertake. For administrative and financial reasons, a government might want to establish a public company in order to accomplish some particular governmental end. For example, the federal government chartered the Federal National Mortgage Association (Fannie Mae) in an effort to lower the cost of borrowing for home purchases, and hence to increase private home ownership among Americans.[4] The Peace Bridge linking the United States and Canada provides a more local and very concrete example. Government does not tax itself, nor does government tax such public companies, which are doing the government's work. Tax law distinguishes between the business and the public corporation, between private and public interests: the former is taxed, the latter is not.

More commonly, many public spirited activities are typically conducted through "not-for-profit" organizations, including religious institutions, universities and schools, hospitals, charities that help the less fortunate, theaters, orchestras, and other performing arts institutions, and any number of institutions designed to promote some cause or another, ranging from the preservation of old houses to the preservation of ducks for hunting. So long as not-for-profit enterprises are operated in furtherance of a recognized public purpose, they are not taxed.

The term "not-for-profit" is a bit misleading. Many such enterprises are immensely profitable in the simple sense of taking in revenues more than adequate to cover their costs, or the somewhat broader sense of earning a net positive return on their operations and investments—Harvard University springs to mind. What not-for-profits may *not* do is distribute profit to owners, for the simple reason that they have no owners. Not-for-profits may be legally organized in various ways, including corporations, trusts, foundations, or simple associations, but they share a defining characteristic: none of these forms of association have owners. There is nobody who is the "residual claimant" (i.e., if the business were to be liquidated, there is nobody with a claim to whatever assets are left over after all the liabilities have been paid off). By the same token, in none of these forms of organization is there a person who has an individual economic interest in maximizing the company's profit. Although revenue may exceed costs, since there are no owners, any profit cannot be distributed to the owners. Thus there cannot be a conflict between the public purpose for which the entity was established and the individual economic interest of the owners. The entity is therefore free to pursue what is often called its "charitable purpose."

To summarize: by taxing the income of the business corporation, tax law relates the government to the corporation in ways closely analogous to the way the government (at least the IRS) is related to the individual taxpayer. Tax law implicitly presumes that corporations themselves will act in their individual interests, that is, to make money, and therefore expects corporations to pay taxes on their income. In contrast, public companies and not-for-profits are clearly on the "public" side of the private/public divide; that is, they are not presumed to act in their own interests. Therefore, such institutions are not taxed.

The Same Relationship in Other Areas of the Law

Although it takes us some distance from the basic course, it is worth mentioning in passing that other areas of the law establish the same relationship between the state and the business corporation as does tax law, albeit not without a degree of controversy, also like tax law. Specifically, both criminal law and constitutional law treat the business corporation, to a surprising degree, as if it were a natural person.

Criminal law. Corporations can be held criminally liable for the acts of their employees. In general, if, but only if, an agent commits a criminal act within the scope of his or her employment and the act is intended, at least in part, to benefit the corporation, then the corporation may be liable. In that case, both the act and the intent (i.e., the basic prerequisites for criminal liability) may be imputed to the corporation.[5] The criminal liability of corporations is addressed by Chapter VIII of the Federal Sentencing Guidelines, the "Organizational Sentencing Guidelines."[6] The Sarbanes-Oxley Act of 2002 increased the penalties for corporations that violate the securities laws.[7] Rephrased, in the right circumstances, a corporation is treated as a person who can violate the criminal law, that is, the social order.

Constitutional law. Constitutionally, corporations are treated like people in many, but not all, circumstances. Over 100 years ago the U.S. Supreme Court held that the Fourteenth Amendment to the U.S. Constitution, which establishes in pertinent part that no state shall "deny to any person … the equal protection of its laws" includes corporations within its definition of "person."[8] And the Supreme Court has repeatedly held that corporations have "political" rights to free speech.[9] One should not take this too far: corporations are not treated exactly as if they were people, even by the Supreme Court. For example, at least as of this writing, corporations do not enjoy a constitutional right against self-incrimination.[10]

In general, however, both criminal and constitutional laws position the business corporation vis-à-vis the state as if the corporation were a natural person. Business corporations are expected to act in their private interests; are expected to abide by the rules, including the rules of criminal law; and they have certain rights, including certain constitutional rights, even the right to participate in political debate. The business corporation is treated by the law as a sort of citizen. Should this be very surprising? In a commercial society, we endow business organizations with personality all the time. The vast world of marketing and advertising, the media environment, indeed much of the built environment, create a sense of corporate personality in the minds of consumers and other economic actors, a sense on which people rely. Within companies, much of management and business relations would be impossible without a collective sense of what the organization is about. If this sense of corporate personality is entailed in our economy and our society, why would we expect the imagination of the law to be so different?

Chapter 13

The Mirror of Securities Law

Coporation (Private) Law and Securities (Public) Law

CORPORATION LAW HAS LONG BEEN UNDERSTOOD TO BE ESSENTIALLY private law.[1] The corporation has long been a way to own a business, albeit with certain privileges and obligations defined by the state. As discussed in chapter 2, however, over the course of the nineteenth century, the state became less involved in the creation of corporations. Acts of the legislature establishing corporations were superseded by laws of general incorporation, under which the creation of particular corporations was a ministerial (bureaucratic) act of some official, usually the secretary of state. Corporations, which used to be founded for some specific purpose, came to be established for "any legal purpose" (i.e., to make money for their investors' private enterprise). The title of the Berle and Means classic is *The Modern Corporation and Private Property.* Their understanding of the central problem of the corporation as an agency entails a conception of the corporation in terms of the private interests of the owners who have the agency problem, the shareholders. And the more recent elaboration of that conception of

147

the corporation, the corporation understood to be a nexus of contracts, similarly focuses attention on the private interests of the individuals who make such contracts.

In the course of the twentieth century, a related body of law sprang up that was explicitly public minded, securities law. Among other things, securities law governs the sale of a corporation's stock to the public and subsequent trading in the stock. Thus the share holding the base of the governance structure of a public company arises from transactions governed, not only by corporation law, but also by securities law. Moreover, securities law affects contests for corporate control in numerous ways, including the distribution of proxies and oftentimes the raising of capital. Truthful disclosure cases (e.g., *Basic v. Levinson*[2]), insider trading cases (e.g., *Chiarella*[3] or *O'Hagan*[4]), and the recent wave of accounting scandals (such as Enron or Worldcom) all turn on violations of the securities laws. Understandably, most corporation law classes include an introduction to, and most corporation law scholars also concern themselves with, securities law.

Although both corporation law and securities law are concerned with the governance of large corporations, the two bodies of law form something of an odd couple. Corporation law is overwhelmingly state law; securities law is primarily federal law. Although judges largely have made corporation law, securities law is the province of complicated statutes and regulation and much more complicated bureaucratic practice. And although corporation law has defined itself as a species of private law, securities law is explicitly public. Indeed, as a matter of intellectual history, it is worth considering whether state corporation law has been able to remain so private in character because public concerns have been addressed under the rubric of federal securities law. Securities law thus offers a competing, or at least complementary, view of the corporation as an institution.

Background

To begin understanding securities law, one must return to the stock market crash of 1929. The impact of the crash and the ensuing depression on U.S. law can hardly be exaggerated. It was an epochal time; that is, it changed the structure of thought. Out of any number of eye-catching statistics, consider the following: between September 3 and November 13, 1929, the market capitalization of the corporations listed on the New York Stock exchange, the core of U.S. industrial economy, lost $30 billion out of a total of $80 billion.

Banks failed. The savings of many very ordinary investors were destroyed.[5] Their confidence shaken, people stopped spending, and the real economy contracted—the Great Depression had begun. The causes of the stock market crash and the relationship between the collapse of the financial markets and the contraction of the real economy were contested at the time, and remain contested among academics today. There was and is widespread belief, however, that the financial markets of the late 1920s were not sound. Much investment was made on the basis of little more than salesmanship and hope. Prices, nonetheless, were bid up to levels never before seen. Outright fraud was widespread. Loss of confidence in equity markets, and then in finance more generally, led to the contraction of the real economy. In his successful campaign for president in 1932, Franklin Delano Roosevelt promised that the federal government would enact widespread financial reform.[6]

At the time, many people believed that capitalism itself was failing and that the crash of 1929 was the forerunner of a more complete collapse of the free enterprise system. Even many people who were not Marxists had no confidence in the financial system and, therefore, did not invest. People began to lose trust not only in other individuals, as fraud implies, but more importantly, in the system itself. Therefore, the challenge facing government was to restore confidence in the institutions of the financial system writ large and, hence, capitalism as a way of doing business, indeed, as a form of social life.

To present the problem confronting the Roosevelt administration in the most general and starkly ideological terms: how does a democratic government act to save belief in the free enterprise system (i.e., belief in the proposition that private individuals and institutions organized along nongovernmental, indeed, nondemocratic, lines can make a whole society work, can serve the public interest)? Why isn't the necessity of federal government action further proof of the failure of the free enterprise system? Many people at the time made precisely this argument; many others attacked Roosevelt for being a communist. (An old political adage has it that if you piss everybody off, you are doing something right.) The solution offered by the Roosevelt administration was to use a massive and newly established federal bureaucracy to reconfigure the initial conditions and, oftentimes, to referee the outcomes of market interactions. Thus, rather than nationalize key failing industries, as was done in much of Europe, and rather than let markets run themselves, Roosevelt placed the federal government in the position of self-consciously constructing markets. The structure and regulation of the financial markets in the United States to this day are the direct result of the federal government's response to the Great Depression; it was a New Deal indeed for America.

Roosevelt's promise to reform the financial markets was quite radical. Up until that point, there had been relatively little regulation of the financial markets, and much of the greater part of what regulation did exist was the province of the states. Kansas had passed the first state securities law in 1911.[7] Although other states passed similar laws, such laws had limited jurisdictional reach, multiple exceptions, and were spottily enforced. Suffice it to say that nobody believed that state laws had constrained the stock market bubble of the late 1920s. Within months of Roosevelt taking office, however, Congress enacted the Securities Act of 1933, which regulates the offering of securities to the public. Shortly thereafter, the Securities Exchange Act of 1934 established the Securities and Exchange Commission (SEC). The 1934 Act also governs the trading of securities and regulates many securities market participants, notably brokers, dealers, and to some extent, exchanges. Other laws regulating other aspects of the financial markets followed throughout the 1930s.

From Roosevelt's campaign to the present, securities law has been billed as a response to fraud. Numerous securities laws make fraud illegal, and so the statement is not untrue. Few people support fraud, and so the statement is good politics as well. However, fraud has been illegal under the common law since time immemorial. There was no need for the federal government to pass major legislation, establish massive bureaucracies, and transform the way America's leading companies raised capital and conducted ordinary business, if the government's only purpose was to prohibit people from defrauding one another.

Disclosure

Although the federal government regulates the financial markets in various ways, the central mechanism through which the securities law works is *disclosure*. Companies who sell their shares to the public, or whose shares are traded among the public, are legally required to disclose to the public vast quantities of information about the company, its business, its personnel, and its prospects. Investors may use that information in deciding whether or not to invest and, collectively, in pricing the security. Rephrased in the jargon: the public securities markets in the United States operate under a mandatory disclosure regime. The lawyers among you are already asking questions like: What is public? What is a security? What constitutes compliance with disclosure? What, practically, must be disclosed? This is the stuff of securities law and of many legal practices.

Federal securities regulation is not substantive, which means that the law does not guarantee the quality of investments. Securities laws do not prohibit companies from offering very risky securities to the public. Consider, in this regard, shares of stock in start-up high-technology companies, or high-yield (junk) debt offerings made by companies teetering on the verge of bankruptcy. Rather than prohibit the sale of such securities, the law requires only that the nature of the investments be made publicly available. Presumably, investors will assess the risk and price the securities accordingly. Thus, rather than guaranteeing the quality of an investment opportunity, the securities laws ensure that prospective investors have access to information about the investment. The federal securities laws then reflect the hope that, with the provision of good information, the security will be priced sensibly by people in the marketplace.[8] In theory, at least, securities should be well priced, that is, should cost about what they are worth.

By the same token, publicly available information should make fraud rare. In the words of Louis Brandeis (before he became a Justice of the Supreme Court), sunshine is the best disinfectant. Public scrutiny, information, causes people to behave appropriately. (Significantly, although the line has been used in many contexts, Brandeis had the financial markets in mind. The quote is from an influential book titled *Other People's Money, and How the Bankers Use It.*)[9] More importantly still, if the mispricing of individual stocks becomes rare, then the problem confronting the nation as a whole, great financial market bubbles like that preceding the 1929 crash, should not arise. Or that, at any rate, has been the theory and the hope. In practice, of course, matters are much more complicated, and much of the academic discipline of finance is an exploration of these complications.

In requiring the disclosure of company information, the regulation of the securities market is quite different from the regulation of most other markets. By way of comparison, under the common law, the basic rule for most sales is *caveat emptor,* let the buyer beware. The old rule has been complicated by the development of consumer protection laws, regulation of real estate transfers, and the like, but in general, in markets governed by the common law, the buyer has the basic responsibility of informing him- or herself of the qualities of an item, although fraud (lying about the item, to the detriment of the buyer) has always been illegal. For another comparison: in many modern markets for mass-produced consumer goods (consider foodstuffs, or household appliances) certain minimum standards are imposed on producers by state or federal regulation. It is simply illegal to sell food, for example, that does not meet Food and Drug Administration standards. And for certain goods (e.g., airline travel or many drugs), the goods themselves are controlled. In contrast, the primary role of government in the regulation of the securities markets is to ensure that the public has access to the information on which investment decisions may be made soundly.[10]

Insider Trading

This brings us to the glamorous and frustrating area of insider trading law. The securities laws establish that, as a general matter and absent a legally specified exception to the rule, a great deal of information on companies whose shares are publicly traded will be made publicly available. At the same time, even publicly traded companies are private enterprises. Businesses have secrets, proprietary information, at the very least, things they do not want their competitors to know. So the question arises how to balance (a) the investing public's interest in information about the business, and more generally, in disclosure and a well-informed market for securities, with (b) a legitimate business interest in proprietary information (and in the aggregate and more deeply, society's interest in robust competition among businesses, which presumes a degree of self-interest).

The SEC and the courts have determined that it is illegal for people employed by or otherwise inside a company, or who owe some other duty to the company (e.g., a lawyer), and who possess material nonpublic information, to trade on the basis of such information. Yes, the rule is hard to state correctly in plain English, but the basic idea is nicely illustrated by two cases with nearly identical facts, *Goodwin v. Agassiz*[11] and *SEC v. Texas Gulf Sulphur*,[12] separated by 35 years during which the Depression occurred and the great federal securities statutes were passed. In both cases, the officers of mining companies had news of successful explorations and, therefore, reason to believe that their companies were likely to become much more valuable. Both companies kept the discoveries secret while they bought land and/or mining rights. (Again, under the common law, there is no duty to disclose, and the mining company agents presumably did not tell the landowners what the mining company had learned about the minerals under their property and, therefore, about the value of the land.) Meanwhile, the officers and other insiders bought stock and stock options in their own companies. Eventually, the discoveries were announced and the stock prices shot upward. Shareholders who had sold stock and did not make money from the new discoveries sued.

And here the cases diverge. Working from Massachusetts corporation law, the court in *Goodwin v. Agassiz* was unwilling to extend the concept of fiduciary duty so far as to require a manager to disclose company secrets ('We've struck it rich, hold on to your stock!') to an existing shareholder. Since the company's shares were traded on an exchange, as a practical matter, informing all shareholders would have required public disclosure divulging the company's secrets. Such disclosure would have hurt the company and hence its shareholders, because the mining rights would become more expensive once landowners understood that they possessed valuable minerals.[13]

In contrast, working from Section 10b of the Securities Exchange Act of 1934, and SEC Rule 10b-5, both prohibiting fraud, the court in *Texas Gulf Sulphur* prohibited insiders from trading on undisclosed information: either the information could be divulged to the public, at which point insiders could trade on it, or the information could be kept secret, but insiders had to refrain from trading.[14]

As with much in the law, the devil is in the details. Endless amounts of litigation have surrounded questions such as who, exactly, counts as an insider. Suppose one has material nonpublic information, but on a different company? Does it matter how one got the information? What must be proven about why the insider traded? Does price count as information? And there are devils in the general idea, too: the Supreme Court has repeatedly refused to say that all participants in the marketplace must have effectively the same access to information, that all investors have equal access to information, or what might be called a level playing field.[15] A moment's reflection reveals how difficult it would be to achieve a level playing field: publicizing information is difficult, and many, perhaps most, trades are made on the basis of investor belief in having better information than the marketplace.[16] Yet despite all the troubles in providing an elegant formulation, insider trading remains illegal in the United States. As a society, evidently, we do not want the equity markets to be understood as a rigged game.

Pricing and Society

The concern for public information that runs through securities law is often straightforwardly expressed in terms of protecting investors from fraud. Obviously, it matters to individual investors that they be able to price their investments fairly accurately. And particularly today, when many of society's institutions (consider universities, hospitals, or nonprofit foundations), and especially savings for education, health, and retirement, are tied up in equity markets, investor protection is clearly a matter of great public concern.

More subtly, disclosure addresses what is perhaps the central problem of securities law, which is loss of faith in capitalism itself. How does mandatory disclosure of company information regarding equity securities help guard against loss of faith in capitalism? To begin thinking about this problem, consider a start-up company. In order to begin operations, the company needs to raise money. The company cannot borrow money from a bank, because it has no steady cash flow with which to service the loan and nothing to provide as collateral. So the company proposes its idea to potential investors, who demand, in return for their money, an ownership stake in the company (i.e., blocks of common stock). The price investors are willing to pay for the equity is, from the point of view of the start-up company, the amount of capital it can raise. Such early stage investors are often called venture capitalists. As the company grows, however, it may need more capital than it can obtain from private sales, and so the company may offer equity to the public, most famously in an initial public offering (IPO).[17] Companies that can raise more capital can weather storms, expand faster, even buy out their competitors. Access to capital is the lifeblood of any company, but especially a start-up. To put it in Darwinian fashion, access to capital is the terrain on which the selection of companies occurs.

The survival of a business is, obviously, a vital concern for the parties involved, but it is a matter of public concern, too. Society should want good companies with good ideas to receive ample funding and bad companies with bad ideas to receive none. Thus pricing is the mechanism by which this society chooses the components of the commercial environment, which, in a commercial society, is much of the social environment writ large. Rephrased, insofar as a society is capitalist, it is well governed only if the pricing is good. But to say that pricing is good is to say that investors are well informed. The securities laws are thus an effort to improve pricing and, hence, capitalism as a system of public ordering.[18]

A very important twist is that the stock market is largely comprised of investors trading shares among themselves. A typical situation: some A sells 1,000 shares of some long-established company, XYZ, to some party B. Neither A nor B have any relationship to XYZ company other than being shareholders, and XYZ company receives no money on the trade. Why must XYZ disclose information about itself to the market? Rephrased, why is there a public interest, in this situation, that XYZ be properly priced (aside from protecting

B from stock market bubbles)? To put the question in terms of the statutes, the preceding paragraph provides a rationale for the social importance of the '33 Act, which concerns the offering of shares by a company to the public, but says nothing to justify the '34 Act, which concerns the public trading of such shares, except of course for the durable issues of investor protection and wealth management.

The operating success of XYZ is linked to its share price in numerous, if often vague, ways. A company with a strong share price can, if it needs to, raise more money by offering more shares. A strong share price is also useful in negotiating with other sources of capital (e.g., banks). Moreover, companies compete through strategic acquisition of other companies; many such acquisitions are paid for with shares. High share prices make acquisitions less expensive and thus facilitate the growth of the buyer. High share prices (usually expressed as market capitalization, that is, share price times number of shares outstanding) provide the financial market's measure of the worth of a company, and bigger is better. Such prestige makes it easier to hire good employees, especially top management. Less ethereally, managerial pay has been shown to correlate with market capitalization—managers of bigger companies are paid more. And executives are often paid in equity (stock or stock options); high share prices make it cheaper for the company to pay executives a great deal.

On the other hand, a weak share price signals the company's overall weakness to the market. A company whose share price has fallen may be a target for a takeover, as discussed in chapter 9. Moreover, falling share prices may make it difficult for the company to raise capital to make improvements, or even to replace an aging plant or otherwise keep the business up to date. At the extreme, falling share prices affect other financial obligations. A company with a plummeting share price may be unable to raise funds in the short-term debt (commercial paper) market that many companies use to ensure they have operating capital on hand. Downward plunges in share price also can result in the downgrading of the company's credit rating.[19] Failure to maintain an adequate credit rating is a common event of default in debt financings, generally resulting in the entire loan becoming immediately due and payable, which may result in the insolvency of the company. Thus, on both the upside and the downside, the share price influences the health of companies, and ultimately, their survival.

The nomenclature is suggestive: once a company has offered and sold shares to the public, it is no longer a private business but is instead considered publicly held. Although such a company may still have trade secrets or other proprietary information, in general a publicly held company's business is, as the name implies, public. And a world of public companies should not be understood in terms of a simple bifurcation between private and public, between markets and government. Some institutions, obviously including publicly traded business corporations, are between the citizen and the state. Private enterprise is a very public matter.

Public and Private Understandings Encore

Understanding corporations to be *both* private (as emphasized by corporation law) and public (as emphasized by securities law) inevitably raises the question of which predominates in a given case. Most disputes within corporation and securities law can be understood as contests over whether to move the institution one way or the other, in a public or in a private direction. This lends a certain predictable (let us avoid the word boring) quality to policy discussions in the area. Unfortunate events are likely to occasion efforts to make the institution more public by requiring more individual liability, judicial oversight, and other involvement by government institutions. The parties who own or otherwise control corporations are likely to resist such involvement (who likes government involvement?), thereby tending to move the institution in a private direction. So, for example, Enron and other accounting scandals led to the hurried passage of the Sarbanes-Oxley Act of 2002, which among other things required enhanced disclosure.[20] And just as predictably, once the political furor over the accounting scandals had abated, the argument was advanced that the costs of compliance with Sarbanes-Oxley outweighed the benefits. More generally, specifying what companies must disclose and then doing so are the substance of several specialties in both legal and accounting practice. Sarbanes-Oxley is only a recent development in a professional practice that stretches back to the original securities laws. The SEC and its supporters perennially argue that more disclosure is necessary for confidence in the markets, and implicitly, for informational efficiency/price discovery. And on the other side, those who must pay the immediate costs of compliance, and their partisans among the press and in the academy, perennially argue that market participants will inform themselves. Thus the line between public and private, and in a sense, between the corporation considered to be private property of the shareholders and the corporation considered to be a public institution, is continually contested.

Chapter 14

Conclusion

Charting the Corporation's Place in Civil Society

To RECAPITULATE, INTEGRATE, AND EXTEND THE ARGUMENT OF THE PRECEDing chapters: business associations, indeed the institutions of civil society, can be organized along a spectrum from private to public, between citizen-owners and the state. Consider figure 14.1, which is organized around two perspectives—that of the owner of the institution and that of the public, associated with the state. Obviously, this is a simplification, but all maps are—the question is what can we learn?

The dashed line represents the legal attributes of ownership. Understanding property through the classic metaphor of "sticks in a bundle," with each stick representing a legal right, the sole proprietor has the largest possible bundle of sticks. The sole proprietor can do everything an owner can do. Consequently, the law does not even recognize the sole proprietorship as a separate legal entity, and the owner and the business are, for the purposes of business law, indistinguishable. If we move slightly to the right, however, to partnership, we see that a partner's right to profit, right to manage, and risk of loss are

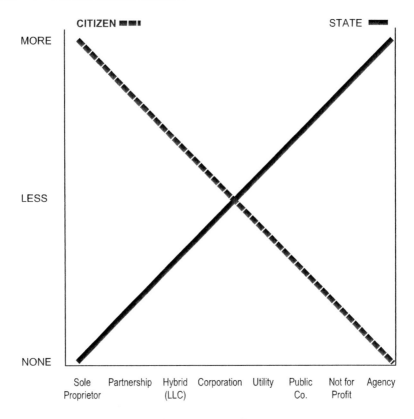

Figure 14.1 Between the Citizen and the State

all compromised by the existence of the partnership and the partners—the partnership exists in important ways distinct from its owner. Moving on in the same direction, members of a limited liability company (LLC) (or owners of other hybrids) have substantially fewer rights to manage the business. Nor may the owners establish an LLC without obtaining the permission of the state. Although members of an LLC have substantial flexibility in establishing their entity, their rights to manage the business and to take profit from the business are circumscribed by the operating agreement. Moreover, the downside of beneficial ownership—the risk of loss—is blunted by limited liability, that is, the institution rather than the owners is ultimately liable for the obligations of the business.

The scope of ownership in a business corporation is narrower still. Shareholders have less flexibility in establishing a corporation—the parameters of the entity are largely established by state law. Moreover, in corporations, shareholders have no right to manage the business and no direct claim on the profits of the business—they are entitled to a dividend if and only if it is declared by the board of directors. (Similar arrangements are possible in an LLC, if the members so contract.) Shareholders are thus the "owners" of a business corporation in only a nominal sense. Nonetheless, a great deal of law insists that shareholders are the beneficial owners of the company, that is, that corporations are to be operated on behalf of shareholders. And in the event that the company is dissolved, shareholders are the residual claimants, whose claim to whatever assets may remain is based merely on the fact that they are shareholders.

Corporations may be more or less "public," which means, conversely, that the owner, or the business on behalf of the owner, may have more or less freedom to function autonomously, in what we would recognize as a "private" fashion. As discussed in chapter 13, once a company offers securities to the public, it is responsible for making a great deal of information publicly available. Many things that had once been "the company's business" must be disclosed; the heretofore private must be made public. Moreover, in order to comply with securities laws, the business must be run, and accounted for, in ways and according to schedules that make public disclosure possible. As discussed in chapter 6, the Sarbanes-Oxley Act even restricts how publicly traded companies may be governed (e.g., by requiring that audit and compensation committees be comprised of independent directors). Thus, as we move from the ordinary business corporation, organized by incorporators in accordance with state statute and custom, to the publicly traded corporation, we find that the organizational role of the law, relative to the initiative of the owners, increases.

This trend—less ownership, more law—continues as we move farther to the right across the chart. Although not discussed in this book because it is beyond the basic class of corporations, highly regulated companies such as utilities and banks have owners, but they are not wholly free to set prices. At the same time, the markets in which such entities operate are, to varying extents, protected from competition. Thus the risks and returns of competition in the marketplace are to a significant degree shifted to the state. Public companies like Fannie Mae, discussed in chapter 12, are in much the same situation as banks and utilities, only more so. Public companies have nominal owners (shareholders), but their owners do not establish them. Instead, public companies are established via legislation for some economic purpose important to the government. Public companies are also highly regulated in how they do business. Governmental, rather than institutional, processes often choose those who will direct public companies (by political appointment rather than by shareholder vote). In short, the owner of a public company is an almost completely passive investor.

As also discussed in chapter 12, not-for-profit corporations have no owners. Not-for-profits are, however, established by private individuals for the public good. Thus the only role of an individual, operating in his or her private capacity, is to establish the entity. To complete the chart, consider the government agency. Although government agencies may engage in economic activity, there is no role for the private individual as such within the organization. The owner has disappeared. Thus, as we move to the right on the chart, we see that the legal powers of the owner decrease. More generally, the private individual plays less and less of a role in the life of the entity, eventually disappearing altogether.

Inversely, still reading the chart from left to right, we see that the public interest in the entity, represented by the dashed line, increases. Beginning all the way to the left, the government is simply unaware of the sole proprietorship as such, and the proprietor's business is virtually indistinguishable from its owner. The proprietor can do whatever he or she wants with the business.

Partnerships, however, have legal interests distinguishable from the interests of any one owner. Partnerships are legal entities, if weak ones, and so part of society. Moreover, partners must take the interests of their fellow partners into account according to community standards (recall *Meinhard v. Salmon*).

If partnership introduces the idea of the social, then moving slightly to the right on the chart, to hybrid entities such as LLCs, introduces the idea of the official. Most basically, forming a limited liability enterprise such as an LLC, or indeed a corporation, requires a filing with the government in accordance with an enabling statute, and the public disclosure of constitutive documents. For tax purposes, however, the LLC and other "pass-through" entities are merely accounting entities.

In taxing the business corporation, however, the government takes a direct monetary interest in the entity. Moreover, and still moving to the right, as the corporation grows and seeks finance in the public markets, it must regularly disclose to the public—and to government regulators—details of its business. Corporations in certain highly regulated industries, especially those deemed necessary for the operation of society as a whole (e.g., utilities, finance) are operated as much through regulatory, as through commercial, mechanisms. The government may even set prices. Although public companies have owners, they are founded by governments for a statutorily defined public interest.

Not-for-profit entities are established and operated in furtherance of a named public interest, and because they have no owners, they represent no private interest at all. Not-for-profits do represent an individual interest, however, the charitable (eleemosynary) interest for which the institution was founded.

Finally, while the government agency engages in commercial activity, agencies are definitively public institutions. Agencies are established by public action (legislation) in the public interest, rather than being established by private initiative. Agencies function by operation of law rather than through the market (most simply, agencies are funded through tax revenues rather than sales). As parts of government, agencies are respected by coordinate parts of government. Agencies are not only not taxed, they are generally speaking immune from suit under doctrines of sovereign immunity. Thus, as we move from left to right across this institutional spectrum, the public interest in the association increases, until the association becomes simply an organ of the state.

As we see from looking at the chart, the lines cross at the business corporation, perhaps, at the publicly traded business corporation. To the left of that point, their owners dominate the entities, and it makes sense to associate the association with individual owners, to think of these entities in "private" terms. To the right of that point, the entities are dominated by the state, and it makes sense to think of the entities in "public" terms. At the midpoint, however, both the influence of individual owners and the influence of government are relatively low. Conversely, because it is dominated neither by its owners nor by the state, the business corporation has a relatively high degree of institutional autonomy.

As we move from left to right across the chart (one more time, with feeling), the owners' legal rights and privileges (sticks in the bundle of ownership) are given up by owners and are picked up by the entity. The legal capacity of the owner is inversely correlated with the personality of the entity. So, as we have seen, the owner of a sole proprietorship can do whatever he or she wants with the business, which is the same thing as saying that the sole proprietorship has virtually no legal personality. Partners are constrained in what they may do vis-à-vis the partnership, and a partnership, however, has certain legal capacities, notably to own property and to make contracts. In contrast to partnerships, a hybrid entity is considered the legally responsible (liable) entity, and may enjoy perpetual life. In most hybrids and all corporations, managers hired by the entity manage the business. Rephrased, a core attribute of ownership—the authority to make decisions—is done by the institution, not by the owners, the members, or the shareholders. The corporate entity is understood to be a person for tax purposes and even for some of the purposes of criminal and constitutional law.

If we keep going to the right, however, at some point, perhaps with the publicly traded corporation, or maybe with the bank, utility, or public corporation, the state asserts a public interest, and, conversely, both the autonomy and the private character of the institution's decline. Once the corporation offers securities to the public, not only is most of its information no longer private, but securities law dictates much of how the entity is run. And if we move from publicly traded corporations to banks and utilities, we see that their ability to set prices—perhaps the core function of any business—is controlled by law. Consonantly, the state shields such entities from competition. Such "business" entities are largely protected and removed from the marketplace by the state. Moving farther to the right, public corporations are founded by governments, via acts of the legislature, for governmental purposes, albeit in markets. Although public corporations nominally have owners, their shareholders are entirely passive investors.

To play the game out, not-for-profits are founded by individuals, but for a recognizable public purpose, and they may continue to do business as a not-for-profit entity only so long as they continue to operate in furtherance of a public purpose. Not-for-profits have no owners, and are therefore largely free of market constraints altogether (many not-for-profits subsist on gifts and perhaps endowment income, not revenue from operations). Thus not-for-profits may be understood as part of the social order defined in opposition to the private interests that comprise markets, as in an essential sense public rather than private. Since not-for-profits are already "public" in character, they are not taxed—taxes are levied on the "private" sector in order to pay for the public order. By the same token, government agencies enjoy all of the foregoing attributes of legal personality and, in addition, are generally immune from suit under doctrines of sovereign immunity, unless they waive their immunity. Thus, as we move to the right, the legal personality of the entity converges on that of the state, just as the left end of the spectrum represented the convergence of the legal personality of the business with that of its owner.

* * *

We are now in a position to rearticulate the sense of unease raised in the preface and with which chapter 2 ended. The categories of U.S. legal thought, and particularly private law, are profoundly individualistic. The social world imagined by the law is inhabited by individuals who may come together to "establish a more perfect union," as the Constitution's preamble has it. One manifestation of this imagination is the first year of law school, the unifying experience of U.S. legal education, in which students are taught what rights individuals have against one another (the common law courses), and against the state (constitutional law and criminal law), along with a bit of procedure.

It should be obvious that this imagination is ill-suited for thinking about civil institutions, including the business corporation. Forced to accommodate civil institutions conceptually, however, the legal community has tended to treat such institutions in three rather inconsistent ways, all three of which have been illustrated in this book. Either (a) the association is understood in terms of its owners, who are tacitly assumed to be individuals; (b) the association is treated as public; or (c) the association is itself treated as an individual, an "entity." These accommodations work well enough at the poles—surely the individual is an adequate proxy for the sole proprietorship, and surely agencies are organs of the state.

As we approach the middle of the spectrum, however, comprised of "private" institutions of enormous social significance, such characterizations come to seem implausible, at best partial. Surely there is more to the corporation then the owners, the shareholders. Nor is it plausible to understand corporations as organs of the state; corporations simply have too much autonomy that is not legitimated by democracy or even the operation of public law. So we are left attempting to understand the corporation on its own terms, which often seems awkward. None of which is to argue that the sky is falling (it may be, but that is not the argument here). To say that the corporation cannot be reduced to its owners or the state, and to be dissatisfied with understanding it as an entity is to report a weakness of our political thought. Our legal tradition is more comfortable with individuals and the state, and therefore has difficulties conceptualizing groups.

At the same time, and while intellectually inelegant, such partial conceptualizations often work well enough. One must also recall that corporations are comprised of individuals, that corporate governance often works, and that public law is important. The logic of these plays should feel familiar, even when the interplay among what the U.S. law recognizes as legitimate ownership interests, the ill-defined autonomy of civil institutions, and the public interest is complicated in detail (and this book is only an introduction). Academic corporation law is a deeply traditional U.S. effort to articulate vague and contested senses of what might be good arrangements for a society imagined to be comprised of individuals trying to survive, civil institutions that matter, and limited government.

Notes

Notes to the Introduction

1. Digests (often called hornbooks) are quite traditional in legal education. For example, Robert W. Hamilton's *The Law of Corporations in a Nutshell* (2000), published in the West Group's "Nutshell" series of "succinct explanations" of the law, runs to 635 pages, exclusive of front and back matter. "Succinct" has a special meaning among law professors. Treatises tend to be as long and presume an authority that this book eschews. Study guides are much shorter and generally mapped to specific, widely taught casebooks.

2. See Henry Hansmann and Reinier Kraakman, "The End of History for Corporate Law," *Georgetown L. J.* 89 (2001); Reinier R. Kraakman, et al., *The Anatomy of Corporate Law* (2004).

3. Jack B. Jacobs, Justice of the Supreme Court of Delaware, has written that corporate law disputes "generated more human drama than any TV soap opera ever could." Justice Jack B. Jacobs, "The Uneasy Truce Between Law and Equity in Modern Business Enterprise Jurisprudence," UCLA School of Law, Program in Business Law and Policy Occasional Paper Series, January 2006, at 9.

4. This point—the main pedagogical thesis of this book—could easily be overdone. Mae Kuykendall argues that corporation law is impoverished precisely because we as a society do not tell many nuanced stories of business life. In many ways I agree. Three points will have to suffice for present purposes. (1) Clearly the "narratives" discussed in this book are thin and feature stock characters who do not convey the richness we expect from great art. *Smith v. Van Gorkom* is no *Anna Karenina*. (2) Characters or institutions that are somewhat abstractly or formally defined, that is, without nuance, may be employed in a range of situations. The "hero" or "the shareholder" does not tell us much, but sometimes tells us something useful. (3) A serious response—and our conversation on this matter is ongoing—requires conception of the law's

(especially corporation law's) relationship to bureaucracy, and the place of the arts, especially the novel, in contemporary society. Such matters are far beyond the scope of the basic class in corporations and, therefore, of this book.

5. Bayless Manning, "Shareholders Appraisal Remedy: An Essay for Frank Coker," *Yale L. J.* 72 (1962): 223, 245.

6. The efficient capital markets hypothesis (ECMH) is a very influential and rather contested set of ideas that claim that in an efficient market, price quickly incorporates all available information. As a result, prices reflect news and are therefore unpredictable. For a popular introduction see generally Burton Makiel, *A Random Walk Down Main Street* (8th ed., 2003). For an influential statement in the context of the corporation, see Ronald Gilson and Reinier H. Kraakman, "The Mechanisms of Market Efficiency," *Virginia L. Rev.* 70 (1984): 549; "The Mechanisms of Market Efficiency Twenty Years Later: The Hindsight Bias," *J. Corp. L.* 28 (2003): 715.

7. Ronald J. Gilson, "Value Creation by Business Lawyers: Legal Skills and Asset Pricing," *Yale L. J.* 94 (1984): 239.

8. See, for example, Ralph Nader and Wesley J. Smith, *No Contest: Corporate Lawyers and the Perversion of Justice in the United States* (1996).

9. The character of legal scholarship, and corporation law scholarship in particular, has not been constant over the years. See Mae Kuykendall, "Reflections on a Corporate Law Draftsman: Ernest L. Folk's Lessons for Writing and Judging Corporate Law," *Rutgers L. J.* 35 (2004): 391.

Notes to Chapter 1

1. See *Security and Exchange Commission v. W. J. Howey Co.*, 328 U.S. 293, 301 (1946). "The test [for whether an investment contract is a security, and so like a share of common stock] is whether the scheme involves an investment of money in a common enterprise with profits to come solely from the efforts of others." There is a bit of slippage here; my quip depends on an analogy. The *Howey* court sought to define "investment contract," not "common share." However, the fundamental problem before the court was how to define "security," and hence the reach of the federal securities laws, a problem the court approached through the attributes of the paradigmatic security, the share of common stock.

2. William C. Powers, Jr. "Report of Investigation by the Special Investigative Committee of the Board of Directors of the Enron Corp. 2 (2002) ("Fastow ... received tens of millions of dollars [he] should not have received ... at Enron's expense"). See also David A. Westbrook, "Corporation Law after Enron: The Possibility of a Capitalist Reimagination," *Geo. L. J.* 92 (2003): 61 ("Individuals with duties to Enron ... made millions of dollars at Enron's expense, without informing other members of management or the Board of Directors"); Kurt Eichenwald, *Conspiracy of Fools: A True Story* (2005).

3. See Lucian A. Bebchuk, "Toward Undistorted Choice and Equal Treatment in Corporate Takeovers," *Harv. L. R.* 98 (1985): 1693, 1705 ("[Managers] might be concerned not only with shareholder interests but also with their own private interest"). See also *Revlon, Inc. v. MacAndrews & Forbes Holdings Inc.*, 506 A.2d 173 (Del. 1985) (the court held Revlon violated its duty to maximize shareholder value by accepting an offer for less money that included additional benefits to the directors).

4. See Lynn A. Stout, "The Mechanisms of Market Inefficiency: An Introduction to the New Finance," *J. Corp. L.* 28 (2003): 635; Kent Greenfield, "Using Behavioral Economics to Show the Power and Efficiency of Corporate Law as Regulatory Tool," *U.C. Davis L. Rev.* 35 (2002): 581; Donald C. Langevoort, "Behavioral Theories of Judgment and Decision Making in Legal Scholarship; A Literature Review," *Vand. L. Rev.* 51 (1998): 1499. For an economic rather than legal approach, see Robert J. Shiller, *Irrational Exuberance* (2000); Andrei Shleifer, *Inefficient Markets: An Introduction to Behavioral Finance* (2000).

5. The federal government has the power to create corporations, but rarely does so, and then for explicitly public purposes. Business corporations are usually creatures of state law.

6. Lawyerly questions abound: does the company opt in to the state law? Or opt out? And with regard to what aspects of governance? Quorum? Cumulative voting? And so forth—the laws of different states vary in such particulars, but share a conceptual structure. Practicing lawyers, of course, are responsible for the particulars.

7. States may deem the corporation to have been in existence from the date of filing of its articles of incorporation or the date of the state's acceptance. In addition, legal issues arise about the activities of the incorporator prior to incorporation, a topic beyond the scope of this book.

Notes to Chapter 2

1. President Nicholas Murray Butler of Columbia University, Remarks at the 143rd Annual Banquet of the Chamber of Commerce of the State of New York (Nov. 16, 1911), in James Willard Hurst, *The Legitimacy of the Business Corporation in the Laws of the United States 1780–1970* (1970): 9.

2. Recent books criticizing the corporate form on moral grounds include Ralph Estes, *Tyranny of The Bottom Line: Why Corporations Make Good People Do Bad Things* (1996); Marjorie Kelly, *The Divine Right of Capital: Dethroning the Corporate Aristocracy* (2001); Lawrence E. Mitchell, *Corporate Irresponsibility: America's Newest Export* (2001). The corporation, of course, has its contemporary ideological defenders. See, for example, John Micklethwait and Adrian Woolridge, *The Company: A Short History of a Revolutionary Idea* (2003).

3. In 1991 Ronald Coase was awarded the Bank of Sweden Prize in Economic Sciences in Memory of Alfred Nobel. See Ronald Coase, "The Nature of the Firm," *Economica* 4 (1937): 386–405.

4. See Robert Gordon, "Critical Legal Histories," *Stan. L. Rev.* 36 (1984): 57.

5. A few interesting pieces that have crossed my desk recently, all of which take issue with the triumphal narrative reproduced in the text, include Michel Aglietta and Robert Cobbaut, "The 'Financialization' of the Economy, Macroeconomic Regulation and Corporate Governance" (2003); Pierre Gervais, "What Is the "Industrial Revolution?" (2003) and "The Cotton Factory in a Pre-Industrial Political Economy: An Exploration of the Boston Manufacturing Company 1815–1820" (2003); Joshua Getzler and Mike Macnair, "The Firm as an Entity Before the Companies Acts" (2005); Jason Kaufman, "Origins of the Asymmetric Society: Political Autonomy, Legal Innovation, and Freedom of Incorporation in the Early United States" (2006); Mark Roe, "Legal Origins, Politics and Modern Stock Markets" (2006).

6. At the same time, certain activities that we understand to be collective have been conceived in rather more personal terms. Louis XIV's claim that "I am the state" is a fine statement of not only the ideal of absolute monarchy, but the older understanding that the king, personally, was the government, and whose word was therefore law. Similarly, the feudal code of allegiance was a personal code, as well as an ornament to a system of land tenure and military taxation. Finally, a great deal of what our society tends to see as corporate business, especially banking, was once carried on by families such as the Fuggers and Medicis, and a bit later, the Rothschilds.

7. C. E. Walker, "The History of the Joint Stock Company," *Acct. Rev.* 6 (1931): 97, 99; Franklin A. Gevurtz, "The Historical and Political Origins of the Corporate Board of Directors," *Hof. L. Rev.* 33 (2004): 89, 115–22.

8. See Gevurtz, "The Historical and Political Origins of the Corporate Board of Directors," *Hof. L. Rev.* 33 (2004): 89, 110, 117–20. Much hinges on definition. Some version of the corporation—doing business in groups—can be traced further back, at least to Rome. See, for example, Micklethwait and Woolridge, *The Company,* 12.

9. The relationship between the South Seas Bubble and the Bubble Act is complicated and often misunderstood. See Erik F. Gerding, "The Next Epidemic: Bubbles and the Growth and Decay of Securities Regulation," *Conn. L. Rev.* 38 (2006): 393, 408.

10. See Charles P. Kindleberger, *Manias, Panics, and Crashes* (1978): 97–99; Armand DuBois, *The English Company after the Bubble Act 1720–1800* (1938).

11. This is the conceptual beginning of what is known in finance as portfolio theory—how does one think about the risks and returns of a collection (often called a "basket") of investments? The contemporary academic discipline is often dated from the work of Harry Markowitz in the 1950s. For a highly readable introduction, see Peter L. Bernstein, *Against the Gods: The Remarkable Story of Risk* (1996).

12. See Joseph H. Sommer, "The Birth of the American Business Corporation: Of Banks, Corporate Governance, and Social Responsibility," *Buff. L. Rev.* 49 (2001): 1011.

13. Treasury of the Secretary William Crawford, writing of the second Bank of the United States to its president, Langdon Cheves: "The first duty of the Board [of Directors] is to the stockholders, the second is to the nation." Quoted in Richard E. Ellis, *Aggressive Nationalism: Law and Politics in the Early Republic* (forthcoming). Justice Marshall in *McCulloch v. Maryland,* 17 U.S. (4 Wheat.) (1819): 316, treated the Bank as essentially public.

14. These state laws were not uncontroversial. Here as elsewhere, the text provides the ideological view that prevailed. Certainly it was not obvious then, and is not obvious now, that increasing the share of U.S. social life organized through the corporate form makes U.S. social life more democratic. See "Incorporating the Republic: The Corporation in Antebellum Political Culture," *Harv. L. Rev.* 102 (1989): 1883, 1884–88.

15. A number of historians have argued that, while limited liability is not unimportant, it is not so pivotal as described by the traditional account of the development of modern corporations. James Willard Hurst put it: "Tradition assigns as a prime limited-commitment inducement the limited liability of shareholders to outsiders for debts of the enterprise. The tradition has substance and has gained more substance with time. But the record requires qualification." Hurst, *The Legitimacy of the Business Corporation,* 26. Morton J. Horwitz is in accord: "It is not usually appreciated that truly limited shareholder liability was far from the norm in America even as late as 1900. Though by the time of the Civil War the common law had evolved to the

point of presuming limited shareholder liability in the absence of any legislative rule, in fact most states had enacted constitutional or statutory provisions holding shareholders of an insolvent corporation liable for more than the value of their shares." Horwitz, *The Transformation of American Law, 1870–1960: The Crisis of Legal Orthodoxy* (1992/1994): 94.

16. See *Isaac Riddle v. the Proprietors of the Locke and Canals on the Merrimack River* (7 Mass. 169, 1810).

17. See Horwitz, *The Transformation of American Law*, 83–84.

18. Del. Code Ann. tit. 8, § 102(a)(3) (2001).

19. See Kent Greenfield, "Ultra Vires Lives! A Stakeholder Analysis of Corporate Illegality (with Notes on How Corporate Law Could Reinforce International Law Norms)," *Va. L. Rev.* 87 (2001): 1279.

20. Still, courts have held that promoters owe a fiduciary duty to corporations not yet formed. See, e.g., *Southern-Gulf Marine Co. No. 9, Inc. v. Camcraft, Inc.*, 410 So.2d 1181 (La. App. 3 Cir. 1982).

21. Bayless Manning, "The Shareholder's Appraisal Remedy: An Essay for Frank Coker," *Yale L. J.* 72 (1962): n. 5 and accompanying text.

22. See for example, Marc Galanter, "2005 James McCormick Mitchell Lecture, Planet of the APS: Reflections on the Scale of Law and Its Users," *Buff. L. Rev.* 53 (2006): 1369; David A. Westbrook, "*Galanter v. Weber*," *Buff. L. Rev.* 53 (2006): 1445; Douglas Litowitz, "The Corporation as God," *J. Corp. L.* 30 (2005): 501. In Jewish folklore, a golem is an artificial man made of clay that can be brought to life through Cabalistic incantations and magic. In some versions of the legend, golem is created to protect Jews but ends up spinning out of control and must be destroyed.

Notes to Chapter 3

1. This is overly dramatic, of course. Many operations, ranging from individuals to companies to governments, carry debt on an ongoing basis. Such debt would hardly seem to be transformative. On the other hand, in the absence of ready credit, such operations would presumably risk being technically insolvent, that is, unable to pay obligations when due. Thus what one might call operational credit, ranging from credit cards to commercial to government paper, might be thought to be transformative in another way: rather than changing the scale of the undertaking, they make the undertaking highly liquid, which comprises much of their modern character.

2. As suggested in this example, and as discussed in the next chapter, in the real world the conceptual distinctions between debt and equity may be hard to maintain; indeed legal relationships are often unclear, mixed, or contested.

3. The text relies on an imagination of relatively stable long positions. One of the functions of contemporary finance theory, both based on and operationalized by modern securities markets, is to obscure the temporal character of finance. In a net present value world, the future is discounted out of mind. And because people are willing to trade on their expectations, even an instrument as expressly temporal in character as a futures contract tends to be understood in the present tense (i.e., because X is expected to happen, instrument Y now has cash value

Z). In a similar vein, consider underwriting, venture capital in a bull market, or day trading, each of which obscures the temporal character of the relations established by finance.

4. In the financial markets, in some contrast, the institution of "clearing" allows investment without the establishment of a relationship between counterparties to the trade. Most trades are done over an intermediary, often the exchange itself, or sometimes a separate "clearing house," which bears the risk of default. Parties who wish to participate in such markets, however, must establish a relationship with the institution providing the clearing function.

5. See Henry Hansmann and Reinier Kraakman, "The Essential Role of Organizational Law," *Yale L. J.* 110 (2000): 387, 392–93.

6. In the institution known as a trust, discussed in chapter 5, these two aspects of ownership are held by different people: the economic benefits of ownership go to the beneficiary of the trust, while control over the trust is held by the trustee.

7. Except in certain well-defined situations (e.g., a takeover). See *Unocal Corp. v. Mesa Petroleum Co.,* 493 A.2d 946 (Del. 1985).

8. A testable law for how markets actually set the prices of stock is the Holy Grail of finance; my bet is the Grail will be found first.

9. Shareholders also have a number of miscellaneous rights, including the right to inspect the company's books and records; the right to be bought out in the case of a merger (appraisal rights); and the right to bring suit on behalf of a company (a so-called shareholder derivative suit). Shareholders also sometimes enjoy rights to buy shares (preemption rights).

10. Sometimes companies issue two classes of common, meaning voting, stock, often called Class A Common and Class B Common, with different voting rights.

11. The relatively modest cost of individual shares has widely been thought to encourage investment and make resale easier (promote liquidity), giving rise to the old Wall Street saying that shares prices "went to $100 and split." For example, a share selling at $110 might be "split" into two shares, so that an investor who started the day with 100 shares would end the day with 200. In a widely known anomaly, share prices tended to rise with a split. In our example, shares might trade at slightly more than $55, perhaps because the share split itself indicated management's confidence in the company.

12. Investment Company Institute and Security Industries Association, *Equity Ownership in America* (2002): 16.

13. It is interesting to note that modern business corporations and calculus, both based on the summing of infinitesimals, appeared in England around the same time. Isaac Newton lost money in the South Seas Company.

14. At the time, both were academics, but both men would spend much of their careers in the federal government.

15. Adolf A. Berle, Jr., and Gardiner C. Means, *The Modern Corporation and Private Property* (1932): 32.

16. It must be remembered that the situation is different if a shareholder owns a substantial percentage of a corporation's stock, either because the company is quite small or the shareholder is very large. But for obvious reasons, attention has been focused on the governance of medium to large companies, where shareholder passivity is the rule.

17. See, for example, *In Re the Walt Disney Co. Derivative Litigation,* 907 A.2d 693 (Del. Ch. 2005), affirmed, 906 A.2d 27 (Del. 2006) upholding the controversial payment of a severance package worth upward of $100 million to short-lived former Disney president Michael Ovitz

because then-CEO Michael Eisner and other members of the board of directors were found not to have breached their fiduciary duties in connection with Ovitz's hiring and subsequent termination. See also Lucian Bebchuk and Jesse Fried, *Pay without Performance: The Unfulfilled Promise of Executive Compensation* (2004): 47–48.

18. Agency law is discussed in more detail in chapter 10.

19. I have argued that the tension between shareholders and managers is a rather primitive way to understand what happened at Enron, and perhaps some of the other recent accounting scandals. See David A. Westbrook, "Corporation Law after Enron: The Possibility of a Capitalist Reimagination," *Geo. L. J.* 92 (2003): 61, 121. This is not to argue that the tension that Berle and Means identified so powerfully is not real, or even present at Enron. Certainly shareholders were hurt by the abuses of management.

20. As this is written, the merits of the Sarbanes-Oxley Act are publicly contested in precisely these terms: are the provisions of the act necessary to protect shareholders (usually "the equity markets") from another Enron? Or does the Act go "too far" and impose excessive requirements on companies? *Plus ca change, plus c'est la meme chose* (the more things change, the more they stay the same). Once again, intellectual history raises uncomfortable questions about just what it is that scholars do. On the intractability of this debate, see David A. Westbrook, "Telling All: The Sarbanes-Oxley Act and the Ideal of Transparency," *Mich. St. L. R.* (2004): 441, 446–48. Roberta Romano, however, views corporation law as having been fundamentally transformed, "in the eighties," although she traces the transformation to Manne's writing in 1965. See Roberta Romano, "After the Revolution in Corporation Law," *J. Legal Ed.* 55 (2005): 342. Romano, needless to add, sees herself as a revolutionary.

Notes to Chapter 4

1. This makes a limited amount of perverse sense: litigation suggests failed negotiation and badly handled transactions. Such negative object lessons, however, are usually too subtle for students trying to learn the basic law being argued, not what was wrong with a relationship established in prior years and now contested.

2. *Lochner v. New York,* 198 U.S. 45 (1905); Grant Gilmore, *The Ages of American Law* (1977).

3. John Henry Schlegel, "Walt Was Right," *J. Legal Ed.* 51 (2001): 599, 599–600.

4. See Pierre Schlag, *The Enchantment of Reason* (1998).

5. The literature on American Legal Realism is vast. Introductions include Gilmore, *The Ages of American Law*; Morton J. Horowitz, *The Transformation of American Law 1870–1960: The Crisis of Legal Orthodoxy* (1992); John Henry Schlegel, *American Legal Realism and Empirical Social Science* (1995); and William Twining, *Karl Llewellyn and the Realist Movement* (1973).

6. See Twining, *Karl Llewellyn and the Realist Movement*, 382, commenting on the general acceptance of legal realism and the now commonplace phrase: "Realism is dead; we are all realists now."

7. And, at least in an Article III court, it would be difficult to imagine such an abstract proceeding satisfying the "case or controversy" requirement of the U.S. Constitution.

8. See O. W. Holmes, *The Common Law* (1881): 1.

9. In an ordinary employment contract, in which a business hires an employee, the business assumes liability for the agent's actions within the scope of employment fairly broadly construed.

10. Holmes, *The Common Law* (1881): 1.

Notes to Chapter 5

1. *S.E.C. v. Chenery Corp.*, 318 U.S. 80, 85-86 (1943) (Frankfurter, J.; citations omitted).

2. There are, of course, far more sober things to say about the history of the trust. A classic place to start is J. H. Baker, *An Introduction to English Legal History* (1979): 243–44.

3. "Infidelity" literally means unfaithful, from Latin *fide*, faith, a nice turn on "good faith."

4. Harold Marsh, Jr., "Are Directors Trustees?" *Bus. Law.* 22 (1966–67): 35, 36.

5. See Adolf A. Berle, Jr., and Gardiner C. Means, *The Modern Corporation and Private Property* (1932); William W. Bratton, Jr., "Berle and Means Reconsidered at the Century's Turn," *J. Corp. L.* 26 (2001): 737.

6. Such suits are called shareholder derivative suits and are discussed in chapter 8.

7. Outside directors almost never pay. Bernard Black, Brian Cheffins, and Michael Klausner, "Outside Director Liability," *Stan. L. Rev.* 58 (2006): 1055. When directors do pay, the sums may not be that much. In the much ballyhooed Enron settlement, ten former Enron directors paid some $13 million, a drop in the $60 billion lost shareholder value bucket of Enron's collapse. But the same ten directors sold more than $250 million worth of Enron shares. The settlement was reportedly structured to represent some 10 percent of pretax profits on the Enron stock sales. See Lucian Bebchuk, "What's 13 Million among Friends?" *New York Times*, January 17, 2005.

8. See, for example, Lucien A. Bebchuk and Jesse M. Fried, *Pay without Performance* (2004); Michael B. Dorff, "Softening Pharaoh's Heart: Harnessing Altruistic Theory and Behavioral Law and Economics to Rein in Executive Salaries," *Buff. L. Rev.* 51 (2003): 811.

9. Sarbanes-Oxley Act of 2002 § 301, 15 U.S.C.A. § 78j-1 (2002).

10. Sometimes taught through *Regenstein v. J. Regenstein Co.*, 97 S.E.2d 693 (Ga. 1957).

11. Sometimes taught through *Broz v. Cellular Info. Sys., Inc.*, 673 A.2d 148 (Del. 1996).

12. *Meinhard v. Salmon,* 164 N.E. 545 (N.Y. 1928).

13. See *Meinhard*, at 547.

14. See generally Richard A. Posner, *Cardozo: A Study in Reputation* (1990); Andrew L. Kaufman, *Cardozo* (1998).

15. See *Meinhard*, at 546.

16. See *Meinhard*, at 547.

17. *Meinhard*, at 547.

18. *Meinhard*.

19. "The judgment should be modified by providing that at the option of the defendant Salmon there may be substituted for a trust attaching to the lease a trust attaching to the shares of stock [of Midpoint Realty Company], with the result that one half of such shares together with one additional share will in that event be allotted to the defendant Salmon and the other shares to the plaintiff." *Meinhard*, at 549.

20. *Meinhard*, at 547.

Notes to Chapter 6

1. *Kamin v. American Express Co.*, 383 N.Y.S.2d 807 (N.Y. Sup. Ct. 1976).

2. Note that Amex shareholders might receive the value of the DLJ stock under either course of action. Under the first course of action, Amex sells the DLJ stock at fair value and retains cash equal to the value of the stock. The price of Amex stock should be unchanged by the sale of the DLJ stock and should reflect the present (discounted) value of Amex's investment in DLJ. Under the second course of action, Amex distributes an asset, the DLJ stock, as a dividend to its existing shareholders. Presumably, Amex stock goes down in price (because DLJ was worth something), but however much the DLJ stock was worth, the shareholders would receive it.

3. For the exception that proves the rule, see *Dodge v. Ford Motor Co.*, 170 N.W. 668 (Mich. 1919) (requiring a dividend), discussed in the next chapter.

4. See Gretchen Morgenson, Obituary, "Barber B. Conable, 81, Dies; Congressman and Bank Chief," *N.Y. Times*, Dec. 2, 2003, at B8.

5. See "American International Group: Hank Yanked," *The Economist*, Mar. 19, 2005; Gretchen Morgenson, "A.I.G. Board Said to Weigh Chief's Future Amid Inquiry," *N.Y. Times*, Mar. 14, 2005, at C1.

6. See Bayless Manning, "The Business Judgment Rule and the Director's Duty of Attention: Time for Reality," *Bus. Law.* 39, (1984): 1477. My discussion owes quite a lot to Manning's prescient text.

7. Manning, "The Business Judgment Rule," 1498.

8. Melvin A. Eisenberg, *The Structure of the Corporation* (1976), 164–72.

9. See Melvin A. Eisenberg, "The Architecture of American Corporate Law: Facilitation and Regulation," *Berkeley Bus. L. J.* 2 (2005): 167.

10. The association is imperfect, however: directors of corporations are not expected to insist on the degree of prudence, even caution, from managers running companies that trustees are supposed to exercise in managing the corpus of trust. Shareholders are not beneficiaries of trusts; corporations are constructed and operated as riskier ventures.

11. Sarbanes-Oxley Act of 2002 § 301, 15 U.S.C.A. § 78j-1 (2002).

12. See David A. Westbrook, "Telling All: The Sarbanes-Oxley Act and the Ideal of Transparency," *2004 Mich. St. L. Rev.* (2004): 441.

13. *Smith v. Van Gorkom*, 488 A.2d 858 (Del. 1985).

14. The issues for directors become more complicated still when the buyers are also shareholders and managers, as in a "going private" transaction. The classic case is *Weinberger v. UOP*, 457 A.2d. 701 (Del. Supp. 1983) (en banc).

15. Del. General Corp. Law Sec. 102(b)(7).

16. Rumor has it that at least one agreement was signed, unread, at the opera.

17. See Symposium, "Theory Informs Business Practice, Roundtable Discussion: Corporate Governance," *Chi.-Kent L. Rev.* 77 (2001): 235, 238.

18. See, for example, Robert M. Lloyd, "*Pennzoil v. Texaco*, Twenty Years After: Lessons for Business Lawyers," *Tenn. J. Bus. L.* 6 (2005): 321, 328–30. One is reminded of the old joke about accountants: CEO interviews prospective accountant, says "I have only one question. What is 2 + 3?" Candidate says "Five." The CEO says, "Thank you for your time, that will be all," and has his secretary set up the next interview. The next candidate is asked the same question and is similarly dismissed. This pattern continues for weeks,

until one day, when the CEO asks his standard question and the intense young man in his office doesn't say anything. Instead, he thinks hard for a minute, and then asks the CEO, "Well, sir, what sort of number did you have in mind?" "You're hired," answers the CEO.

Notes to Chapter 7

1. *Dodge v. Ford Motor Co.,* 170 N.W. 668 (Mich. 1919).

2. See Anne Jardim, *The First Henry Ford: A Study in Personality and Business Leadership* (1970), 95–104.

3. The surplus would have been even larger had Ford not raised wages in his factories to a level considerably above the going rate. See Allan Nevins and Frank Ernest Hill, *Ford: Expansion and Challenge: 1915–1932* (1957), 325–27.

4. *Dodge v. Ford,* at 685. The court said, "There should be no confusion (of which there is evidence) of the duties which Mr. Ford conceives that he and the stockholders owe to the general public and the duties which in law he and his codirectors owe to protesting, minority stockholders. A business corporation is organized and carried on primarily for the profit of the stockholders."

5. *In re Walt Disney Co. Derivative Litigation,* 907 A.2d 693, 698 (Del. Ch. 2005), affirmed *In re Walt Disney Co. Derivative Litigation,* 906 A.2nd 27 (Del. 2006).

6. *In re Walt Disney Co. Derivative Litigation,* at 698.

7. See Dalia Tsuk Mitchell, "Shareholders as Proxies: The Contours of Shareholder Democracy," *Washington & Lee L. Rev.* 63 (2006): 1503–78.

8. These are admittedly questions of degree. In extreme cases, as in Enron or Worldcom, managerial misconduct can result in catastrophic losses to shareholders who, in light of the plummeting market, may not be able to sell their shares. To make matters worse, Enron and many other companies use shares as a way to increase employee commitment to the company. There are various mechanisms for helping workers become owners, including compensating employees with stock or options, employee share ownership plans (ESOPs), or encouraging employees to use their 401(k) funds (retirement funds) to buy company stock. Such mechanisms, however, may have the unintended result of concentrating, rather than diversifying, an employee's holdings. Rephrased, one of the largest "assets" most people own is their job; further investment in their employer hardly protects employees from the failure of the company.

9. See Cynthia A. Williams, "The Securities and Exchange Commission and Corporate Social Transparency," *Harv. L. Rev.* 112 (1999): 1197, 1246–47 (describing a 1968 shareholder proposal to amend the Dow Chemical Company's certificate of incorporation in order to stop the sale of napalm for use in Vietnam).

10. In smaller corporations, and in the case of very significant shareholders in larger corporations, major shareholders generally are represented on the board. In the venture capital context, sometimes a board seat or two is a condition of the financing. There have been proposals to allow widespread shareholder participation in the nomination of directors of large corporations. This may be a good idea, but there is little reason to believe that the institutional investors who control large blocks of stock will nominate a different sort of person to the board;

presumably they will be represented by sophisticated businesspeople with substantial experience on corporate boards.

11. See Margaret M. Blair and Lynn A. Stout, "Trust, Trustworthiness, and the Behavioral Foundations of Corporate Law," *Univ. Pennsyl. L. Rev.* 149 (2001): 1735–810, "Team Production in Business Organizations: An Introduction," *J. Corp. L.* 24 (1999): 743–50, "A Team Production Theory of Corporate Law," *Va. L. Rev.* 85 (1999): 247.

12. See David A. Westbrook, "Corporation Law After Enron," *Georgetown L. Rev. 92* (2003): 61–127.

13. See Margaret Jane Radin, *Reinterpreting Property* (1993), 2–3.

Notes to Chapter 8

1. This issue is sometimes taught through *Villar v. Kernan,* 695 A.2d 1221 (Maine 1997), on which the text is based.

2. See Douglas K. Moll, "Shareholder Oppression and 'Fair Value': Of Discounts, Dates, and Dastardly Deeds in the Close Corporation," *Duke L. J.* 54 (2004): 293.

3. 328 N.E.2d 505 (Mass. 1975).

4. 621 P.2d 270 (Alaska 1980).

5. 353 N.E.2d 657 (Mass. 1976).

6. See, for example, Minn. Stat. Ann. 302A. 751 (2000); N.J. Stat. Ann. 14A: 12–7 (1999). See Moll, "Shareholder Oppression and 'Fair Value'."

7. See, for example, *Donahue v. Rodd Electrotype,* 328 N.E.2d 505 (Mass. 1975); *Jones v. H.F. Ahamanson & Co.,* 460 P.2d 464 (Cal. 1969) (acknowledging a duty of the majority shareholders to act within the interests of other shareholders); *Comolli v. Comolli,* 246 S.E.2d 278 (Ga. 1978) (finding that a majority shareholder's actions "must be consistent with good faith to the minority stockholder"); *Fought v. Morris,* 543 So.2d 167 (Miss. 1989) (requiring "the majority's action [to] be 'intrinsically fair' to the minority interest"); and *Crosby v. Beam,* 548 N.E.2d 217 (Ohio 1989) (applying a heightened fiduciary duty between majority and minority shareholders).

8. See, for example, *Weinberger v. UOP, Inc.,* 457 A.2d 701 (Del. 1983) (examining fair dealing and price as a whole to evaluate fairness); *Rosenstein v. CMC Real Estate Corp.,* 522 N.E.2d 221 (Ill. App. Ct. 1988) (finding a majority shareholder may eliminate a minority shareholder as part of a merger); and *Yeager v. Paul Semonin Co.,* 691 S.W.2d 227 (Ky. Ct. of App. 1985) (balanced the interests of the minority shareholder against the majority's and holding that "freezing out" is not prohibited).

9. Recent work and bibliography on closely held enterprises is available at Symposium: "The Future of Closely Held Business Entities," *Wake Forest L. Rev.* 40 (2005): 751.

10. The common law courts once employed trial by battle, and the culture to this day tends to understand justice in terms of rather full-blooded combat between diametrically opposed adversaries. Even today, "pit-bull" litigators pride themselves on a "take no prisoners" approach. See Edward L. Rubin, "Trial by Battle, Trial by Jury," *Ark. L. Rev.* 56 (2003): 261 (maintaining that on a second look, trial by battle has a lot to teach us about our own adversarial trials). From this perspective, equity is not a remedy at law at all, but serves to ameliorate law's harshness. The "prayer for equitable relief" was a prayer for relief *from* the law. So today, when debts are

restructured in bankruptcy, the harshness of the creditors' legal claims—which are legal—are ameliorated by the equitable action of the bankruptcy judge.

11. *Cohen v. Beneficial Industrial Loan Corp.*, 337 U.S. 541, 548 (1949).

12. See Roberta Romano, "The Shareholder Derivative Suit: Litigation without Foundation?" *J. Law, Economics, and Organization* 7 (1991): 55.

13. Indeed, outside directors almost never pay. Bernard Black, Brian Cheffins, and Michael Klausner, "Outside Director Liability," *Stan. L. Rev.* 58 (2006): 1055. Moreover, shareholder litigation is far less common than all the fuss would indicate. See Romano, "The Shareholder Derivative Suit," n. 12. That said, the settlement of both shareholder derivative suits and securities class action cases, which are structurally rather similar, is particularly dynamic, quite interesting, and has spawned a scholarly literature. See, for example, Black et al., "Outside Director Liability"; Sean J. Griffith, "Uncovering a Gatekeeper: Why the SEC Should Mandate Disclosure of Details Concerning Directors' and Officers' Liability Insurance Policies," *U. Pa. L. Rev.* 154 (2006): 1147; Elliot J. Weiss and John S. Beckerman, "Let the Money Do the Monitoring: How Institutional Investors Can Reduce Agency Costs in Securities Class Actions," *Yale L. J.* 104 (1995): 2053; Romano, "The Shareholder Derivative Suit," n. 12; Janet Cooper Alexander, "Do the Merits Matter? A Study of Settlements in Securities Class Actions," *Stan. L. Rev.* 43 (1991): 497.

14. A similar situation exists with securities class actions. The securities laws create numerous causes of action for various violations of law or regulation. In many cases, the damages suffered by individuals will not be enough to justify litigation. Individual claims can be aggregated, however, and addressed in a single massive litigation by certifying a class of claims. The pressures to settle, using company money, and with generous provision for the lawyers' efforts, are much the same as those in the shareholder derivative suit. In an effort to curb what it saw as excessive numbers of securities class actions, Congress passed the Private Securities Litigation Act, Pub. L. No. 104-67, 109 Stat. 737 (1995). Courts immediately began to disagree on what the new law required. See also Weiss and Beckerman, "Let the Money Do the Monitoring," 2053.

15. *Cohen v. Beneficial Industrial Loan Corp.*, at 541, 548.

16. *Eisenberg v. Flying Tiger Line, Inc.*, 451 F.2d 267 (2d Cir. 1971).

17. *Grimes v. Donald*, 673 A.2d 1207 (Del. Sup. Ct. 1996).

18. *Zapata Corp. v. Maldonado*, 430 A.2d 779 (Del. 1981).

Notes to Chapter 9

1. See, for example, *Ringling Bros. Barnum & Bailey Combined Shows, Inc. v. Ringling*, 53 A.2d 441 (Del. 1947).

2. See, e.g., *Abercrombie v. Davies*, 130 A.2d 338 (Del. 1957).

3. Del. Code Ann. tit. 8, § 151 (2005).

4. Mark Roe, *Strong Managers, Weak Owners: The Political Roots of American Corporate Finance* (1994), 223. In many other industrialized countries, even very large corporations are controlled by large financial institutions. This may increasingly be true in the United States. See John C. Bogle, *The Battle for the Soul of Capitalism* (2005), 60–61.

5. Del. Code Ann. tit. 8, § 216 (2005).

6. Proxy fights were more prevalent in the 1960s and 1970s, but were almost completely replaced as a mechanism for struggles for corporate control in the 1980s and 1990s by the hostile takeover. Since then, however, proxy fights appear to have made a modest comeback. See generally Paul H. Edelman and Randall S. Thomas, "Corporate Voting and the Takeover Debate," *Vand. L. Rev.* 58 (2005): 453, 458–61.

7. For a personal perspective on a host of mergers, some quite significant, and spanning decades, see Bruce Wasserstein, *Big Deal: Mergers and Acquisitions in the Digital Age* (1998). Wasserstein is an investment banker, and the strength of the book is the intimacy and length of his experience.

8. *Smith v. Van Gorkom*, 488 A.2d 858 (Del. 1985), discussed in chapter 8, involved a friendly merger, as does a very famous securities law case widely taught in the basic corporations class, *Basic Inc. v. Levinson*, 485 U.S. 224 (1988).

9. Such "bust up" mergers were relatively common, and they received a great deal of negative publicity, in the 1980s.

10. See *Revlon, Inc. v. MacAndrews & Forbes Holdings, Inc.*, 506 A.2d 173 (Del. 1986), discussed below.

11. Bankruptcy mavens on occasion suggest that, once the corporation has entered "the zone of insolvency," then the board of directors owes its duty to the creditors of the company, not to the shareholders. The creditors of a company, after all, receive assets from the dissolution of the company before the shareholders, who are residual claimants. I think this is a bit of an overstatement. Bankruptcy law clearly prohibits directors of an insolvent company from granting a dividend to shareholders; that would be a fraudulent conveyance and a bad thing. But directors cannot cause the corporation to do any number of bad things; the necessity of ensuring that a corporation makes a good faith effort to fulfill its obligations does not somehow transform the character of the corporation. In the terms of this book, the specter of insolvency does not make creditors into central figures in the corporate drama.

12. But see William J. Carney, "Appraising the Nonexistent: The Delaware Courts' Struggle with Control Premiums," *U. Penn. L. Rev.* 152 (2003): 845, 860.

13. *Unocal Corp. v. Mesa Petroleum Co.*, 493 A.2d 946 (Del. 1985). See also Note, "Protecting Shareholders against Partial and Two-Tiered Takeovers: The Poison Pill Preferred," *Harv. L. Rev.* 97 (1984): 1964, 1966. One may also defend the two-tiered tender offer as a device to discourage hold-out problems and thereby make acquisition, and hence restructuring, more likely. See Michael C. Jensen, "The Takeover Controversy, Analysis and Evidence" (1988), 320.

14. Even risky debt securities can be bundled into valuable, and not very risky, packages. Michael Milken has been widely credited with making this basic idea of finance actually work in the bond markets. See generally Daniel Fischel, *Payback: The Conspiracy to Destroy Michael Milken and His Financial Revolution* (1996); James B. Stewart, *Den of Thieves* (1991); Connie Bruck, *The Predators' Ball: The Junk-Bond Raiders and the Man Who Staked Them* (1988).

15. According to the Unocal directors, the value of Unocal was "substantially above the $54 per share offered in cash at the front end." Meanwhile, the "junk bonds" comprising the "back end" merger were determined to be worth "far less than $54." Accordingly, the back end of the offer was ostensibly much worse than what Unocal directors claimed the fair price was. See *Unocal* at 955.

16. See *Unocal* at 949.

17. See *Unocal* at 957–59. The Securities and Exchange Commission subsequently prohibited discriminatory self-tender offers for publicly traded companies. Other defensive measures, most notably poison pills, remain permissible.

18. See *Cheff v. Mathes*, 199 A.2d 548 (Del. 1964).

19. See *Revlon Inc. v. MacAndrews & Forbes Holdings, Inc.*, 506 A.2d 173 (Del. 1985). See also William J. Carney and Leonard A. Silverstein, "The Illusory Protections of the Poison Pill," *Notre Dame L. Rev.* 79 (2003): 179.

20. This transaction is often called a *leveraged buy out* (LBO). Whether called an LBO or MBO or sometimes LMBO, the basic idea is the same. Management causes the company to borrow money, which is used to buy the stock. If all of the stock is purchased and the company is no longer publicly traded, this is called a *going private* transaction. Some so-called *private equity funds* specialize in taking companies private. This may make sense particularly in depressed stock markets, when it is plausible that the market capitalization does not reflect the company's actual value.

21. The legal and financial machinations of hostile takeovers are sufficiently exciting to have been the stuff of fairly popular books, including Connie Bruck, *Predator's Ball*, *Barbarians at the Gate* (1988), and Bryan Burrough and John Helyar, *Barbarians at the Gate: The Fall of RJR Nabisco* (1991); and the movie *Wall Street* (Twentieth Century Fox, 1987).

22. Henry G. Manne, "Mergers and the Market for Corporate Control," *J. Pol. Econ.* 73 (1965): 110, 113.

23. See Andrew Ross Sorkin, "Ex-Tyco Officers Get 8 to 25 Years," *N.Y. Times,* Sept. 20, 2005, p. A1.

Notes to Chapter 10

1. Agency law is a conceptual mess that generations of learned discussants have not succeeded in clarifying much. From time to time the American Law Institute, an organization of academics, judges, and practitioners, "restates" the law as best practiced in U.S. jurisdictions. See Restatement (First) of Agency (1933); Restatement (Second) of Agency (1958). A Restatement (Third) of Agency is on its way.

2. 309 N.W.2d 285 (Minn. 1981).

3. 158 N.E. 77 (N.Y. 1927).

4. As an aside, New York has a great tradition of commercial dispute resolution. New York is named in "choice of law clauses" in contracts written worldwide, even for business with no particular connection to New York. (A choice of law clause provides that, in the event of a dispute between the parties with regard to matters governed by this contract, the dispute shall be resolved in accordance with the law of a particular jurisdiction.) In addition, a great many such contracts choose New York courts as a forum, relying on the depth and sophistication of the judges, the practicing bar, and the substantive law the state offers. This jurisprudential tradition has produced (and been produced by) a number of great judges. William Andrews was one such judge. His colleague Benjamin Cardozo, discussed in chapter 5, and for whom a law school is named, is probably the most famous.

5. This is a stylization, of course. It may be argued that we actually expect insurance companies to bear the risk, which is not untrue, so long as one keeps in mind that owners must pay for insurance; many operations are underinsured; insurance companies often deny coverage; and many small businesses cannot survive the increase in rates subsequent to the payment of a claim.

6. In the early 1990s, Professors Hansmann and Kraackman suggested that limited liability might be abolished, thereby setting off a very heated academic debate. See Henry Hansmann & Reinier Kraakman, "Toward Unlimited Shareholder Liability for Corporate Torts," *Yale L. J.* 100 (1991): 1897; Joseph A. Grundfest, "The Limited Future of Unlimited Liability: A Capital Markets Perspective," *Yale L. J.* 102 (1992): 387; and Henry Hansmann and Reinier Kraakman, "Do the Capital Markets Compel Liability? A Response to Professor Grundfest," *Yale L. J.* 102 (1992): 427.

7. For an introduction to contemporary scholarship, see "Symposium: The Changing Face of Parent and Subsidiary Corporation: Enterprise vs. Entity Liability," *Conn. L. Rev.* 37 (2005): 605 et seq.

8. In some cases in which shareholders truly dominate the business, plaintiffs may be able to sue shareholders on a theory of direct liability, rather than vicarious liability.

9. 941 F.2d 510 (7th Cir. 1991).

10. 23 N.Y. 2d 714 (1968).

11. *In re Silicone Gel Breast Implants Products Liability Litigation,* 887 F. Supp. 1447 (N.D. Ala. 1995). The court found, inter alia, that Bristol was the sole shareholder of MEC; two-thirds of MEC directors were Bristol employees; Bristol did due diligence on risks at issue; MEC presidents reported to Bristol officers, many of whom did not realize they were members of MEC's board; MEC's products were distributed by another Bristol subsidiary for free; MEC submitted its budgets to Bristol for approval; Bristol prepared consolidated federal tax forms (Bristol declared MEC's revenue, and so forth); Bristol advertised its name on MEC products; Bristol said MEC's products were safe.

Notes to Chapter 11

1. There are ways, of course, in which the law applies to the owner but not the business per se. Consider marriage or voting.

2. As LLCs have become more established, quite large enterprises use the form. There are, however, tax and financial market advantages to using the corporation, as opposed to the LLC, for larger businesses. Therefore, and for historical reasons, really large businesses in the United States are at least presently conducted as corporations.

3. Although this evolutionary tale is usually told in the abstract, the sequence can be personified so that it becomes the story of a particular business, the creation of an individual person. See David G. Epstein, Richard D. Freer, and Michael J. Roberts, *Business Structures* (2002).

4. See David Skeel, *Icarus in the Boardroom: The Fundamental Flaws in Corporate America and Where They Came From* (2005).

5. Discussed most directly in chapters 3 and 10, respectively.

6. "Corporations, the control group, and managers are no less in control today than they were a century ago.... But we see things differently. Instead of the need to protect minority shareholders by allowing them to organize or by protecting their individual right to participate, we see shareholders as sufficiently able to protect themselves (mostly by investing in mutual funds). Instead of shareholder organization or the shareholder proposal rule, our discussions focus on the ability of shareholders, typically institutional investors, to vote and exit. In short, having destroyed all other alternatives, we are back where we began. Yet the phenomenon we described at the turn of the twentieth century as a menace to the individual investor and American democracy more broadly, we describe today as democracy's sustaining and legitimating force." Dalia Tsuk Mitchell, "Shareholders as Proxies: The Center of Shareholder Democracy," *Washington Lee L. Rev.* 63 (2006): 1575–76.

7. For overviews of the jurisprudence see David Millon, "Frontiers of Legal Thought: Theories of the Corporation," 1990 *Duke L. J.* (1990): 201; Morton J. Horwitz, *The Transformation of American Law, 1870–1960* (1992), chap. 3.

8. Although the language of concession is not used, perhaps the most interesting contemporary theorizing about the corporation insists on the necessity of the state. Henry Hansmann and Reinier Kraakman, "Law and the Rise of the Firm," *Harv. L. Rev.* 119 (2006): 1333; "The Essential Role of Organizational Law," *Yale L. J.* 110 (2000): 387.

9. Classic citations include Michael C. Jensen and William H. Meckling, "Theory of the Firm: Managerial Behavior, Agency Costs and Ownership Structure," 3 *J. Fin. Econ.* 305 (1976); Harold Demsetz, "The Stucture of Ownership and the Theory of the Firm," 26 *J. L. Econ.* 375 (1983); Frank H. Easterbrook and Daniel R. Fischel, *The Economic Structure of Corporate Law* (1991).

10. For a sampling, see Lawrence E. Mitchell, ed., *Progressive Corporate Law* (1995).

11. In what might be termed contemporary economic philosophy, entity theories are often attacked as violating "methodological individualism" (i.e., the precept that the individual is the proper unit of economic analysis). Interestingly, noting the seeming inevitable rise of the concentration of business around the turn of the twentieth century, economists at the time generally argued that the corporation, trust, or some other legal expression of collectivity was a corollary to economic development. See generally Horwitz, *The Transformation of American Law, 1870–1960*, especially at pp. 80–85.

12. Margaret M. Blair and Lynn A. Stout, "A Team Production Theory of Corporate Law," *Va. L. Rev.* 85 (1999): 247; Stephen M. Bainbridge, "Director Primacy: The Means and Ends of Corporate Governance," *Nw. U. L. Rev.* 97 (2003): 547; "The Board of Directors as Nexus of Contracts," *Iowa L. Rev.* 88 (2002): 1.

13. Horwitz, *The Transformation of American Law, 1870–1960*, at p. 68: "But their [the jurist Oliver Wendell Holmes, Jr., the philosopher John Dewey, and the law professor Felix Cohen] attempt to discredit the then orthodox claim to a non-political, non-discretionary mode of legal reasoning led them to ignore the obvious fact that when abstract conceptions are used in specific historical contexts, they do acquire more limited meanings and more specific argumentative functions. In particular contexts, the choice of one theory over another may not be random or accidental because history and usage have limited their deepest meanings and applications."

14. John Dewey, "The Historic Background of Corporate Legal Personality," *Yale L. J.* 35 (1926): 655.

15. 98 A.2d 581 (N.J. 1953).

16. 8 Del. C. sec. 122(9).

17. William L. Cary, "Federalism and Corporate Law: Reflections upon Delaware," *Yale L. J.* 83 (1974): 663.

18. Ralph K. Winter, "State Law, Shareholder Protection, and the Theory of the Corporation," *J Leg. Stud.* 6 (1977): 251, *Government and the Corporation* (1978).

19. Classic citations include, in chronological order: Cary, "Federalism and Corporate Law"; Winter, "State Law, Shareholder Protection"; Daniel R. Fischel, "'The Race to the Bottom' Revisited: Reflections on Recent Developments in Delaware's Corporation Law," *Nw. U. L. Rev.* 76 (1982): 913; Frank H. Easterbrook, "Antitrust and the Economics of Federalism," *J. L. Econ.* 26 (1983): 23; Roberta Romano, "Law as Product: Some Pieces of the Incorporation Puzzle," *J. L. Econ. Org.* 1 (1985): 179; Elliot J. Weiss and Lawrence J. White, "Of Econometrics and Indeterminacy: A Study of Investors' Reactions to 'Changes' in Corporate Law," *Cal. L. Rev.* 75 (1987): 551 ; and Lucian A. Bebchuk, "Federalism and the Corporation: The Desirable Limits on State Competition in Corporate Law," *Harv. L. Rev.* 105 (1992): 1435.

20. This debate can be jurisprudentially understood as a conflict between concessionary and entity theories of the corporation, on the one hand, and contractual theories, on the other.

21. A current version of the question: does Delaware law permit shareholders to amend the articles of incorporation to require that a shareholder rights plan (popularly known as a "poison pill") be adopted only by a unanimous vote of the board of directors, and in any event, be valid only for one year? Poison pills are intended to make hostile takeovers difficult and, therefore, have the effect of entrenching management; at the same time, poison pills may give directors bargaining power in a takeover fight, which could be used to help shareholders. The question is thus whether Delaware law is at this point "enabling" (and allows shareholders to agree to limit the power of directors, for good or ill), or whether the statute is "mandatory," and requires that directors have certain powers, including the power to adopt poison pills. As of this writing, the question is unanswered. See *Bebchuck v. CA, Inc.*, 902 A.2d 737 (Del. Ch. 206) (Memorandum Opinion and Order dismissing motion for declaratory judgment on the question as unripe).

Notes to Chapter 12

1. Those things said, the choice of business form is often quite contestable, and the reasons why high-tech start-ups have been established as corporations are hardly obvious. In particular, the start-ups' almost certain early stage losses could be passed through to the owners to offset tax owed on income from other sources—so it is not clear that more start-ups should not be established as LLCs. For analysis and citations to the literature, see Richard A. Mann, Michael O'Sullivan, Larry Robbins, and Barry S. Roberts, "Starting from Scratch: A Lawyer's Guide to Representing a Start-Up Company," *Ark. L. Rev.* 56 (2004): 773.

2. In recent years the capital gains tax rate (payable on sales of stock) has usually been lower than the income tax rate (payable on dividends). This disparity has provided an additional incentive for companies to retain profits rather than distribute them as dividends. At the same time, retention of profits has been thought to magnify the importance of accounting to stock valuation, and hence to increase the temptation for fraudulent accounting. The tax cuts of 2003 temporarily lowered the tax rate on dividend income, thereby effectively removing this

disparity. The question of relative tax rates remains politically contested. For an overview, see John W. Lee, "Class Warfare 1988–2005 Over Top Individual Tax Rates: Teeter-Totter from Soak-the-Rich to Robin-Hood-in-Reverse," *Hastings Bus. L. J.* 2 (2006): 47.

Another way around the problem: a publicly traded corporation may use excess cash to repurchase shares in the open market, thereby increasing the value of the shares left outstanding (which, after the repurchase, represent a larger percentage of the company). Open market repurchases have largely replaced the dividend for such companies. For a critical view, see Jesse M. Fried, "Informed Trading and False Signaling with Open Market Repurchases," *Cal. L. Rev.* 93 (2005): 1323.

3. The concept of distortion presumes the political imaginary of liberal economics, a state of nature that government may distort.

4. Note how close this notion of the public company comes to the early nineteenth-century (pre-Jacksonian) idea of the corporation, as discussed in chapter 2.

5. See generally Michael Viano and Jenny R. Arnold, "Corporate Criminal Liability," *Am. Crim. L. Rev.* 43 (2006): 311.

6. U.S.S.G. Manual, sec. 8C2.1-2.7 (2005).

7. Sarbanes-Oxley Act, Pub. L. No. 107-204, sec. 805(a)(5), 116 Stat. 745 (2002) (USCA).

8. *Santa Clara County v. Southern Pacific R.R Co.,* 118 U.S. 395 (1886). There is considerable controversy regarding what *Santa Clara* meant when it was decided, but it has passed into the lore standing for the proposition that corporations are "persons." See Horwitz, *The Transformation of American Law, 1836–1937* (1994), chap. 3

9. See *Pac. Gas & Elec. Co. v. Pub. Utils. Comm'n,* 475 U.S. 1 (1986); see also *First Nat'l Bank v. Bellotti,* 435 U.S. 765 (1978) (holding unconstitutional a law prohibiting a corporation from participating in a debate over a referendum).

10. *Braswell v. United States,* 487 U.S. 99 (1988).

Notes to Chapter 13

1. See, for example, Robert B. Ahdieh, "In Praise of Mixed Governance: Federalization, Nationalization, and the Sarbanes-Oxley Act," *Buff. L. Rev.* 54 (2005): 721, 731–32.

2. *Basic Inc. v. Levinson,* 485 U.S. 224 (1988).

3. *Chiarella v. United States,* 445 U.S. 222 (1980).

4. *O'Hagan v. United States,* 521 U.S. 642 (1997).

5. William K. Klingman, *1929: The Year of the Great Crash* (1989), 301. For perhaps a profound brief evocation of what the Depression did to the American psyche, see James Buchan, *Frozen Desire: The Meaning of Money* (1997), chap. 10.

6. See Steven Neal, *Happy Days Are Here Again: The 1932 Democratic Convention, the Emergence of FDR, and How America Was Changed Forever* (2004), 6.

7. State securities laws are called "blue sky" laws, because they were designed to prevent unscrupulous promoters from selling shares in speculative schemes which have no more basis than so many feet of "blue sky." See *Hall v. Geiger-Jones Co.,* 242 U.S. 539, 550 (1919).

8. Some blue sky regulations are substantive, that is, they endeavor to ensure that only investments of a certain quality are offered to the public.

9. Louis Brandeis, *Other People's Money and How the Bankers Use It* (1914), 92.

10. It is of course true that even in the equity markets, there are other forms of federal regulation. Broker-dealer regulation springs to mind. Even here, however, I would argue that the licensing and other requirements imposed by government on industry participants can be conceptually understood as an effort to create an informationally efficient market, more truly so today than in 1933.

11. 186 N.E. 659 (Mass. 1933).

12. 401 F.2d 833 (2d Cir. 1968), cert. denied sub nom. *Coates v. S.E.C.*, 394 U.S. 976 (1969).

13. See *Goodwin v. Agassiz*, at 659.

14. *SEC v. Texas Gulf Sulphur*, at 848.

15. See *Dirks v. SEC*, 463 U.S. 646, 655–58 (1983).

16. See Sanford J. Grossman and Joseph E. Stiglitz, "On the Impossibility of Informationally Efficient Markets," *Am. Econ. Rev.* 70 (1980): 393.

17. In addition, venture capitalists and other early-stage investors may need to realize some cash from their investments.

18. Three points somewhat beyond the scope of this book. First, the squeamishness about the word *capitalism* in U.S. policy discourse is rather remarkable. See John Kenneth Galbraith, *Economics of Innocent Fraud* (2004), 3–9. Second, I have serious doubts about whether one should take claims to informational efficiency, and hence the possibility of true pricing, seriously. See David A. Westbrook, "Telling All: The Sarbanes-Oxley Act and the Ideal of Transparency," 2004 *Mich. St. L. Rev.* (2004): 1441, *City of Gold: An Apology for Global Capitalism in a Time of Discontent* (2003). Third, Henry Manne famously argued that insider trading improves the efficiency (i.e., the accuracy of prices) because insiders have good information, and for this and other reasons, insider trading ought to be legal. See Henry G. Manne, "Insider Trading: Hayek, Virtual Markets, and the Dog that Did Not Bark," *J. Corp. L.* 31 (2005): 167 (reviewing almost 40 years' of argument).

19. Various independent "credit agencies," such as Moody's or Standard and Poor's, rate the debt issued by major corporations.

20. Sarbanes-Oxley Act of 2002, Pub. L. No. 107-204, 116 Stat. 745 (codified in sections 11, 15, 18, 28, and 29 U.S.C.).

Glossary

This glossary is intended to help the reader unfamiliar with certain terms to understand the text. Many of the words listed have multiple and overlapping meanings and associations, some of which are quite technical, amorphous, or both. Not all of these meanings are expressed by these definitions. This glossary errs on the side of simplicity and clarity.

Certain words with which the text is concerned throughout, and for which the simplification of definition is likely to cause substantial misunderstanding, e.g., "corporation," are not defined here.

accounting scandals. During the first decade of the twenty-first century, a number of prominent publicly traded companies, beginning with Enron, revealed that their accounting had been inaccurate. Confidence in Enron and several other companies, notably Worldcom, evaporated, and spectacular bankruptcies ensued.

agency. Legal relationship in which one party, the "agent," agrees to work for the benefit and under the control of another party, the "principal." The law of agency also includes other relationships somewhat different from, but understood to be similar to, agency. Common examples of agency include an employee working for a company, and a lawyer working for a client.

agent. See "agency."

aggregation theory. Understanding of the corporation as the combination of interests of various participants in the business.

appellate opinion. A written explanation of the legal authority and judicial reasoning upon which a decision in a court of appeals (a court reviewing a prior decision, of a "lower" court) is based.

articles of incorporation. Basic constitutive document of the corporation. The articles are filed with the state in which the company is incorporated and may be changed only by a shareholder vote. A political analogy would be a nation's constitution. Compare "bylaws."

audit committee. Committee of the board of directors of the corporation, charged with ensuring that the company has proper accounting. (VI-11)

balance sheet. A fundamental accounting document, which presents the company's assets, liabilities, and their difference, the equity in the company, at a particular time.

bankrupt. Unable to pay obligations when due; sometimes called "insolvent."

bankruptcy. The condition of being bankrupt. The law, largely federal, pertaining to the rights of debtors and their creditors in the event of a bankruptcy.

beneficial ownership. Rights to the economic benefits of property, e.g., profits produced thereby. Beneficial ownership does not include the legal rights to manage or otherwise control property. For common example, in a trust, the "beneficiary" of the trust receives the economic benefits of the property, but the "trustee" is the legal owner, i.e., makes decisions regarding the disposition of the property.

blackletter. Clear, unequivocal, and uncontested legal rules or doctrines, easily written down (and studied).

blue sky law. State securities law.

board of directors. Group charged with oversight of the corporation's affairs and especially its management, on behalf of the corporation and its shareholders.

bond. A type of debt obligation. Bonds are securities, and may be traded on exchanges. Markets in bonds are regulated by federal law. Bond obligations are secured, i.e., the obligation is backed by a right to take property. In contrast, "debentures" are similar debt obligations, but are unsecured. The word "bond" is often used to refer to both bonds and debentures. The person who owns a bond is called the "bondholder."

breach. To violate, or a violation of, a contractual or other obligation, or the state of being in violation of such obligation.

business judgment rule. Judicial doctrine according to which courts will not disturb the judgment of the board of directors absent a breach of fiduciary duty.

business model. Informal term for the idea that animates an enterprise. The answer to the question, "What does this business do?" The business model may affect the choice of legal form the business takes, e.g., whether it is structured as a partnership or a corporation. The business model is also important in financing negotiations.

buyout firm. A company that takes control of a corporation by "buying out" the shares of existing shareholders, thereby acquiring voting control over the company, and hence control of the board and management. The term "buyout" thus reflects corporate governance concerns. Recently, there has been emphasis on "private equity firms" or "private equity funds," which often engage in substantially the same business, but the terms reflect the investors' interests in the acquiring entity, and the fact that the buyout often results in a publicly traded company becoming privately held, and therefore substantially less regulated under the securities laws. From the perspective of corporate management, the would-be acquiring firm—especially if headed by a colorful leader, as is often the case—may be referred to as a "raider."

bylaws. Rules by which the corporation governs itself. Bylaws may be changed by a vote of the board of directors. A political analogy would be statutes. Compare "articles of incorporation."

canon law. System of law developed by the Church, especially in Europe during the Middle Ages, both for the regulation of the Church's affairs, and for lay matters under the jurisdiction of the Church.

capital gains tax. Tax on the profits from the sale of investment assets, which are taxed at a rate lower than that of ordinary income.

capital structure. The structure of legal rights among the parties within, and hence control over, a business entity that results from the financing of the entity.

capitalization. The monetary value of the company as determined by the sum of the value of the ownership interests. For example, if a company has a million shares outstanding, and each share is traded for $10 each, the company is capitalized at $10,000,000.

caveat emptor. Latin, "let the buyer beware." The idea is that a buyer is responsible for informing himself of the qualities and defects of a contemplated purchase; the buyer cannot subsequently complain that he was ignorant of some defect in the purchase.

centralized management. Hierarchically organized group of people employed to run a company, as in a business corporation. In contrast, partnerships are traditionally managed by the partners, who are also owners, i.e., management is decentralized.

certificate of incorporation. See "articles of incorporation."

charter. See "articles of incorporation."

chattel mortgage. A contingent right to take possession of and title to moveable property.

class action. Judicial procedure through which substantially identical claims brought by similarly situated parties are litigated in one process. For example, various consumers of a widely sold defective product may bring their claims through a single class action.

close corporation. Sometimes called a "closely held" corporation. Corporation with small number of owners, and oftentimes, a dominant owner. Close corporations may present opportunities for abuse of shareholders without substantial voting control. Some states have judicial doctrines or statutes designed to curb such abuse.

common law. Originally, the system of law established by the English crown, and hence "common" to all of England. Term is now used to refer to legal systems derived from this system and featuring a prominent role for the judge.

common stock. Ordinary voting stock. Traditionally, common stock holds a single vote per share and receives a dividend in the event and the amount declared by the board of directors acting in their discretion. In the event of the company's dissolution, common stockholders receive proceeds from the company's assets only after all the other claims have been satisfied, i.e., the common stockholders are the residual claimants.

compensation committee. Committee of the board of directors charged with determining what compensation will be paid to management.

concession or grant theory. Understanding of the corporation as a gift, or at least a creature, of the state.

conglomerates. Corporations comprised of operationally unrelated businesses.

continuity of existence. Idea that a corporation continues to function independently of the participation of any particular person, i.e., the departure (or death) of a participant will not cause the dissolution of the enterprise. Therefore, and at least in principle, the corporation has "perpetual duration."

contractarian theory. Understanding of the corporation as a set, or "nexus," of contracts, explicit or implicit, among the participants in the business.

control premium. Shares within a controlling block of shares (representing control of the company) are usually sold at a premium compared to the price of shares sold in ordinary trading, when control questions are not at issue. The difference between the price of a share within the controlling block and the ordinary price of a share is called the "control premium." In the same vein, tender offers are routinely made at a substantial premium to the current trading price.

convertible preferred stock. Nonvoting preferred stock which may be converted into common stock and voted.

corporate form. The corporation as a form of business association, an institutional template, as opposed to another form of business association, such as the partnership or LLC.

corpus. The body of assets managed by a trust.

creditor. A lender. In bankruptcy, anyone with a claim against the company, e.g., unpaid suppliers or employees.

death tax. Polemical name for an inheritance tax.

debt. An obligation to pay. Debt sounds in contract (a owes b), as opposed to equity, which sounds in property (a owns an interest in b), but the distinction can be hard to draw in practice.

debt financing. Financing in which capital is obtained in exchange for debt obligations of the company. A typical example would be a commercial loan from a bank, or perhaps a bond offering. Contrast "equity financing."

disclosure. The securities laws establish a mandatory disclosure regime, under which companies that seek financing from the investing public must make certain information readily available to the investing public.

diversify. Principle of risk management and investment strategy in which investments are made in unrelated enterprises. The idea is colloquially expressed as "do not put all your eggs in one basket."

dividend. A payment, in cash, securities or other asset, from a corporation to its owners. Generally, dividends represent a distribution of profits, and are sometimes called "distributions."

due care. Legal requirement that persons be sufficiently careful. Varies with type of person and situation, and therefore impossible to define in the abstract.

duty of care. Fiduciary duty of directors to be careful in fulfilling their duties as directors. Notoriously difficult to define in the abstract.

duty of loyalty. Fiduciary duty of directors to be loyal in fulfilling their duties as directors. Principally concerned with avoiding various sorts of conflict of interest, or if an action involving a conflict of interest is unavoidable, making sure the action does not result in harm to the corporation and its shareholders.

eleemosynary. Fancy word for charitable.

entity theories. Understanding of the corporation as a thing or person.

equity. A word with many meanings, pertinently including (i) ownership interests in a corporation, i.e., its shares; (ii) the value of such interests, understood as the balance between the assets of the firm and its liabilities; (iii) a lawsuit asking a court, in the interest of fairness, to issue an order.

equity financing. Financing in which capital is obtained in exchange for equity interests in the company. The typical example is an offering of shares. Contrast "debt financing."

fiduciary. Pertaining to any of numerous legal relationships, in which one party is obliged to act in furtherance of the welfare of another, as in a trust. The person so obliged to act is often called "a fiduciary," who has "fiduciary duties." For example, directors have fiduciary duties to the corporation and its shareholders.

floated. To sell shares in a company to the public, so that the monetary value of the company "floats" with changes in the price of shares.

freely transferable interests. Able to be traded without restriction. An important characteristic of shares in a corporation is that, in general, they are "freely transferable" ownership interests, that is, an owner of shares of common stock may sell her stock without obtaining the permission of the company or other parties. In contrast, partnership interests are not freely transferable.

freeze out. See "squeeze out."

friendly acquisition. Acquisition of control over a company accomplished with the cooperation of the acquired company's management. Compare "hostile takeover."

golden parachute. Large payment made to executives on the termination of their services.

graduated income tax. Income tax with a rate that increases with the amount of income taxed, e.g., the federal income tax.

greenmailer. Informal and derogatory name for a person who buys a substantial share of a company's stock and threatens to take over the company. Management may use company funds to repurchase the shares, albeit at a premium, resulting in potentially huge profits to the greenmailer, and protecting management jobs.

gross revenue. The sum of revenues taken in, without deductions.

high yield debt. Debt instruments carrying a high interest rate.

hostile takeover. Informal name for the acquisition of a company accomplished despite the opposition of the management of the acquired company (the "target"). Compare "friendly acquisition."

hybrid. Informal name for numerous forms of business association that combine some characteristics of the partnership and some characteristics of the corporation. Examples include the LLC and the LLP.

incorporator. Person who files the papers with the state establishing the corporation. Insofar as the person is also lining up investment interest and otherwise establishing the business, she may also be called a "promoter."

indemnify. To restore a victim' a loss, especially a legal loss. Corporations often sign contracts indemnifying directors and executives from liability arising in conjunction with their duties.

independent director. A director of a company who is not employed by the company, in contrast to an "inside director," who is employed by the company, as well as serving on the board of directors.

inside director. See "independent director."

insider trading. Illegal trading in securities of publicly traded companies by management and other persons deemed "inside" the company and who are in possession of nonpublic information.

insurgent. A shareholder who seeks to take control of a company, or at least to effect a change in the board and top management.

interested director transaction. A transaction in which the corporation has an interest, and a director of the corporation has a noncorporate interest. The sale of a corporate asset to a director of the corporation would be an interested director transaction.

investment bank. A company which engages in underwriting, i.e., the initial purchase of securities from the issuer and resale to the public or other buyers.

investment grade debt. Relatively low-risk debt. The debt of companies is evaluated ("rated") by private companies called "ratings agencies," such as Moody's or Standard & Poor's.

IPO (Initial Public Offering). First offering of shares in a company to the public. IPOs are often highly lucrative and are heavily regulated by the SEC. Through an IPO, a privately held company becomes a public company.

issuer. Company that offers stock in itself.

joint-stock association. Unincorporated form of business association, in which ownership interests in a common pool are represented by shares of the company's stock. Sometimes called a joint stock company. To confuse matters, historically, joint stock companies are regarded as the precursors of the modern corporation, and some were chartered by the government.

joint venture. Form of business association in which different interests jointly undertake a specific enterprise; similar to a partnership, but generally bounded by the terms of the venture rather than a business.

junk bonds. Informal name for relatively risky bonds, presumably with a high interest rate. See "high yield debt."

Legal Classicism. Often somewhat derogatory name for late nineteenth and early twentieth century legal scholarship. See legal realism.

Legal Realism. Intellectual movement among law professors in the United States in the 1920s and '30s, understood at the time and since as a rebellion, on several levels, against prior generations of legal scholarship, which came to be called "Classical." Legal Realism attacked Classicism's pretensions to deductive certainty and to the status of law as an autonomous science. Politically, Legal Realism is associated with the rise of the regulatory state. While the contours of the rebellion and what it means are endlessly debated, within the academy, the revolution was successful, and how legal scholarship is done was transformed. Contemporary legal scholarship is clearly descended from the Realists, as the saying goes, "we are all realists now." Sometimes called "American Legal Realism" in distinction from various other "realist" movements in the law elsewhere.

leverage. Debt. As with a see-saw, both the lender and the borrower gain influence in the relationship.

LBO (Leveraged Buy Out). Transaction in which a company takes on debt, "leverage," in order to buy out existing owners. Result is a company with different owners (often management) and considerable debt obligations.

limited liability corporation. Ordinary business corporation, in which the shareholders enjoy limited liability, i.e., their shares may become worthless and they may lose their investment, but they will not lose other assets.

LLC (Limited Liability Company). Statutorily defined form of business association. As in a corporation, owner/investors (usually called "members") enjoy limited liability, but as in a partnership, the entity pays no income tax.

LLP (Limited Liability Partnership). Form of business association, commonly used by lawyers and other professionals, in which the owners enjoy limited liability, but the entity does not pay income tax.

liquid. Of an asset, easily convertible into cash; of an entity, with cash on hand or readily available.

management buyout. See "leveraged buy out."

managers. Hierarchically organized group of people who run an enterprise. Within a corporation, managers as such do not have an ownership interest in the corporation. They are hired by the corporation, and are agents of the corporation.

merger. Form of acquisition of a company in which one company acquires another, and one of the companies is dissolved.

minority shareholder. Shareholder holding less than 50%, or practically speaking, less than a controlling interest, in a corporation. NOT a reference to the race, ethnicity, or any other aspect of the shareholder as a person.

minutes. Records of a meeting, e.g., the meeting of a board of directors.

monopoly. A trade in which a seller has no competitors and therefore can set prices. Such a market is monopolistic.

mutual fund. An investment company in which shares are sold to the public, and the proceeds are used to invest in other companies. Widely used for retirement savings, mutual funds are regulated by federal law.

NASDAQ (originally, National Association of Securities Dealers Automated Quote System). An exchange, now independent of the National Association of Securities Dealers, which is a self-regulatory organization for securities market professionals.

nexus of contracts. See contractarian theory.

No-fault termination. In the United States, employment contracts are generally "at will," that is, they may be terminated for any reason, including simple change of mind, by either party. In response, some executive employment contracts include severance payments, often substantial, to be paid to the employee who is terminated for some reason other than the fault of the employee.

not-for-profit organization. A business association organized in any of several ways, but which does not have owners, and which therefore is not operated for the profit of the owners. Not-for-profits are organized for charitable, educational, religious, and other purposes. In general, not-for-profits are not taxed, and contributions to them may be tax-deductible. Common forms of not-for-profit enterprise include the unincorporated association, the charitable trust, and the statutorily defined corporation.

NYSE (New York Stock Exchange). A marketplace for the trading of securities, especially stock, in New York City.

par value. The minimum value for which a share of stock may be offered, stated in the articles of incorporation, which established a minimum capitalization for the company. Today, companies issue "low par" or "no par" stock, thereby frustrating the purpose of the requirement of a par value.

partners. See "partnership."

partnership. Form of business associations in which two or more persons (the partners) agree to carry on, as co-owners, a business for profit. Since the partners are co-owners, they all share in management, profits, and losses of the business, subject to agreement.

performance based compensation. Payment to corporate executives designed to ensure that the executives have incentives to perform well, by correlating the amount of compensation to the performance of the company or the executive. The traditional way to do this is by granting stock or stock options to the executives; if they manage the company well, such grants will be that much more valuable. Performance based compensation schemes have been widely criticized as having little to do with performance, and everything to do with increasing executive pay.

perpetual duration. See "continuity of existence."

piercing the corporate veil. Judicial practice of holding shareholders personally liable for the activity of the corporation or its agents, in certain egregious circumstances.

poison pill. Informal name for a legal instrument used as a defense against hostile takeovers, more technically called a "shareholder rights plan." The defense works like this: Poison pills are distributed to shareholders. Upon the occurrence of a specific triggering event, usually the acquisition of a certain percentage of voting control in the company by a would-be raider, the pill gives shareholders monetary rights against the company, thereby making the company less attractive.

preferred stock. Stock with a preference over common stock. Preferences may be for dividends, redemption rights, or distribution of assets upon dissolution of the company.

prima facie. Latin for "at first sight," or "on the face of it."

principal. See "agency."

private bill. A law passed for the particular benefit of an individual, discrete group, or locality. Before the mid-nineteenth century, the right to incorporate typically was granted via private bills.

private equity firm. See "buyout firm."

pro rata. Latin, according to a certain rate, proportionately. In the context of corporate governance, shareholder voting is *pro rata,* that is, the number of votes a person has to cast is proportionate to the number of shares held by that person. Contrast "per capita," by the heads, in which each participant gets an equal vote.

product liability. Law giving persons injured by defective products legal rights against parties who manufacture and distribute such products. A species of tort law.

promoter. See "incorporator."

proxy. Agency agreement through which one party votes the shares owned by another party. The person voting the shares is called the "proxy holder."

proxy fight. An effort to replace the board of directors, and thereby take control of the company, through the solicitation of proxies.

proxy holder. See "proxy."

publicly traded company. A company whose shares or other securities are traded amongst the public, and which is therefore subject to the federal securities laws governing such trade, and requiring regular disclosure of the company's business.

quorum. The number within a group, e.g., a board of directors or a shareholder meeting, required in order to take binding action.

raider. See "buy-out."

ratified. To approve an action after it has been accomplished.

redemption rights. Rights to repurchase shares from shareholders.

res judicata. Latin, a thing judicially acted upon or decided, and hence generally not subject to being contested again.

residual claimant. The party to whom, upon the dissolution of a business, and after all claims against the business have been satisfied, any remaining assets of a business are due. The owner.

resolution. Formal decision, taken by vote, of a board of directors.

respondeat superior. Latin, "let the master answer." Doctrine that the principal in certain kinds of principal/agent relationships (traditionally called master/servant relationships, notably including employer/employee relations) are legally responsible for the actions of the agent.

risk averse. Relative unwillingness of most people to invest if there is a chance of losing a significant portion of their assets, i.e., most people would hesitate to make very good investments (investments with a high expected return) if there was a chance that failure of the investment would leave them penniless.

Roman law. The law of the Romans at any of several periods in their history, combined with the successive "receptions" of such law in legal systems and academic thought throughout European history, and with legal systems (many outside Europe) derived therefrom or influenced thereby. Contrast "common law."

Sarbanes-Oxley Act of 2002. Law passed in response to accounting scandals which, among other things, required enhanced disclosure; required compensation and audit committees be comprised of independent directors; reorganized the regulation of the accounting profession; and increased penalties for violations of the securities laws.

SEC (Securities and Exchange Commission). Federal agency charged with regulating the securities markets. Established by the Securities Exchange Act of 1934.

securities. Stocks, bonds, and similar instruments.

Securities Act of 1933. Federal law passed in response to the Depression and as part of Roosevelt's New Deal. Regulates the offering of securities to the public.

Securities Exchange Act of 1934. Federal law passed in response to the Depression and as part of Roosevelt's New Deal. Regulates the exchange of securities on the markets, various actors within the financial industries, the disclosure of corporate information, and establishes the SEC.

shareholder-centered theory. Understanding of the corporation to exist to make money for shareholders understood as owners.

shareholder derivative suit. A suit brought by a shareholder, on behalf of the corporation (hence "derived" from the legal claim of the corporation), because management is unwilling to bring suit, usually in situations in which it is claimed that the directors and/or management have legally harmed the corporation.

shareholder rights plan. See "poison pill."

shareholders. Group of people who contribute money to the corporation in exchange for the ownership interests in the corporation represented by their "shares."

shares. Ownership interests in a corporation.

sole proprietorship. A business enterprise owned by a single person.

special stock. A class of stock with special characteristics vis-à-vis the common stock, usually quite limited in number, and usually carrying substantial voting power.

squeeze out. In a close corporation, the denial of a meaningful return on the investment of a minority shareholder (generally by diverting the firm's profits), thereby inducing the minority shareholder to sell stock to the company or dominant investor(s) at an unfairly low price, hence "freezing out" or "squeezing out" the shareholder. See also "close corporation."

standing. Having a sufficient stake in a legal controversy to bring a lawsuit (standing to sue).

statutory merger. A merger done according to the process set out in the state corporation law statute. Substantially the same economic results can usually be achieved in other ways, so there are strategic and legal questions regarding how to structure the transaction.

stock. See shares.

stock certificates. Paper representing shares, and ownership thereof. Most stock in large corporations today is not certificated.

stock options. The right, but not the obligation, to buy (a call) or sell (a put) stock at a predetermined price (the strike price).

strike suits. Derogatory name for shareholder derivative suits.

summary judgment. A judicial decision based upon the pleadings of the parties to a litigation, without a trial of the facts. A "motion for summary judgment" is an argument, to the court, that even if the facts are as stated by the opposing party, the moving party should win. Because the facts are not in dispute, summary judgments often give rise to clear statements of the law, and hence appear in textbooks.

takeover. See "hostile takeover."

tender offer. An offer to buy shares.

trust. Legal institution in which the control over a body of assets, the "corpus," is given to one party, the "trustee," who is obligated to manage the assets for a third party, the "beneficiary" of the trust.

underwriting. See "investment bank."

ultra vires. Latin, "beyond the powers," i.e., acts which are not within the scope of the corporation's power to act, as defined by its charter and state law.

voting agreement. An agreement among shareholders to vote shares in a certain way; a device for maintaining voting control over a company.

voting trust. An arrangement in which shares are placed in a trust, and voted by the trustee; a device for maintaining voting control over a company.

white knight. Informal. Financier who offers to buy a substantial share of stock or otherwise help a target company's management prevent a hostile takeover.

Bibliography

Citations to works discussed, and a sketch of the construction of a subdiscipline.

Cases

A. Gay Jensen Farms Co. v. Cargill, Inc., 309 N.W. 2d 285 (Minn. 1981)
Abercrombie v. Davies, 130 A.2d 338 (Del. 1957)
Abrams v. Baker Hughes, Inc., 292 F.3d 424 (5th Cir. 2002)
Alaska Plastics, Inc. v. Coppock, 621 P.2d 270 (Alaska 1980)
A. P. Smith Mfg. Co. v. Barlow, 98 A.2d 581 (N.J. 1953)
Basic Inc. v. Levinson, 485 U.S. 224 (1988)
Bebchuk v. CA, Inc., 902 A.2d 737 (Del. Ch. 2006)
Braswell v. United States, 487 U.S. 99 (1988)
Brehm v. Eisner, 746 A.2d 244 (Del. 1996)
Broz v. Cellular Info. Sys., Inc., 673 A.2d 148 (Del. 1996)
In re Caremark Int'l Inc. Derivative Litig., 698 A.2d 959 (Del. Ch. 1996)
Cheff v. Mathes, 199 A.2d 548 (Del. 1964)
Chiarella v. United States, 445 U.S. 222 (1980)
Coates v. S.E.C., 394 U.S. 976 (1969)
Cohen v. Beneficial Indus. Loan Corp., 337 U.S. 541 (1949)

Comolli v. Comolli, 246 S.E.2d 278 (Ga. 1978)

Crosby v. Beam, 548 N.E.2d 217 (Ohio 1989)

Dartmouth College v. Woodward, 17 U.S. 518 (1819)

Dirks v. S.E.C., 463 U.S. 646 (1983)

Dodge v. Ford, 170 N.W. 668 (Mich. 1919)

Donahue v. Rodd Electroype Co., 328 N.E.2d 505 (Mass. 1975)

Eisenberg v. Flying Tigers Line, Inc., 451 F.2d 267 (2d Cir. 1971)

EP Medsystems, Inc. v. Echocath, Inc., 235 F.3d 865 (3d Cir. 2000)

First Nat'l Bank of Boston v. Bellotti, 435 U.S. 765 (1978)

Fought v. Morris, 543 So.2d 167 (Miss. 1989)

Goodwin v. Agassiz, 186 N.E. 659 (Mass. 1933)

Grimes v. Donald, 673 A.2d 1207 (Del. Sup. Ct. 1996)

Hall v. Geiger-Jones Co., 242 U.S. 539 (1919)

Helwig v. Vencor, Inc., 251 F.3d 540 (6th Cir. 2001)

Ira S. Bushey & Sons, Inc. v. United States, 398 F.2d 167 (2d Cir. 1968)

Isaac Riddle v. The Proprietors of the Locke and Canals on the Merrimack
     River, 7 Mass. 169 (1810)

Jones v. H. F. Ahmanson & Co., 460 P.2d 464 (Cal. App. 1969)

Kamin v. American Express Co., 383 N.Y.S.2d 807 (N.Y. Sup. Ct. 1976)

Kidd v. Thomas A. Edison, Inc., 239 F. 405 (1917)

Lochner v. New York, 198 U.S. 45 (1905)

Martin v. Peyton, 158 N.E. 77 (N.Y. 1927)

In re MAXXAM, Inc. 659 A.2d 760 (Del. Ch. 1995)

McCulloch v. Maryland, 17 U.S. (4 Wheat.) 316 (1819)

Meinhard v. Salmon, 164 N.E. 545 (N.Y. 1928)

Novak v. Kasaks, 216 F.3d 300 (2d Cir. 2001)

Pac. Gas & Elec. Co. v. Pub. Utils. Comm'n, 475 U.S. 1 (1986)

Regenstein v. J. Regenstein Co., 97 S.E.2d 693 (Ga. 1953)

Revlon v. MacAndrews & Forbes Holdings, Inc., 506 A.2d 173 (Del. 1986)

Ringling Bros. Barnum & Bailey Combined Shows v. Ringling, 53 A.2d 441
     (Del. 1947)

Robertson v. Cockrell, 325 F.3d 243 (5th Cir. 2003)

Rosenstein v. CMC Real Estate Corp., 522 N.E.2d 221 (Ill. App. Ct. 1988)

Santa Clara County v. Southern Pacific R.R. Co., 118 U.S. 395 (1886)

Sea Land Services, Inc. v. Pepper Source, 941 F.2d 519 (1968)

S.E.C. v. Chenery Corp., 318 U.S. 80 (1943)

S.E.C. v. Ralston Purina Co., 346 U.S. 119 (1953)

S.E.C. v. Texas Gulf Sulfur, 401 F.2d 833 (2d Cir. 1968), *cert. denied sub nom.*
     Coates v. S.E.C., 394 U.S. 976 (1969)

S.E.C. v. W. J. Howey Co., 328 U.S. 293 (1946)

Smith v. Van Gorkom, 488 A.2d 858 (Del. 1985)

In re Silicone Gel Breast Implants Products Liability Litigation, 887 F.Supp. 1447 (N.D. Ala. 1995)

In re Silicon Graphics Sec. Litig., 183 F.3d 970 (9th Cir. 1999)

Southern-Gulf Marine Co. No. 9, Inc. v. Camcraft, Inc., 410 So.2d 1181 (La. Ct. App. 1982)

United States v. O'Hagan, 521 U.S. 642 (1997)

Unocal Corp. v. Mesa Petroleum Co., 493 A.2d 946 (Del. 1985)

Villar v. Kernan, 695 A.2d 1221 (Maine 1997)

Walkovszky v. Carlton, 23 N.Y.2d 714 (1968)

In re Walt Disney Co. Derivative Litigation, 907 A.2d 693 (Del. Ch. 2005), *aff'd In re* Walt Disney Co. Derivative Litigation, 906 A.2d 27 (Del. June 8, 2006)

Weinberger v. UOP, Inc., 457 A.2d 701 (Del. 1983)

Wilkes v. Springside Nursing Home Inc., 353 N.E.2d 657 (Mass. 1976)

Yeager v. Paul Semonin Co., 691 S.W.2d 227 (Ky. Ct. App. 1985)

Zapata Corp. v. Maldonado, 430 A.2d 779 (Del. 1981)

Scholarship

Ahdieh, Robert B. "From 'Federalization' to 'Mixed Governance' in Corporate Law: A Defense of Sarbanes-Oxley." *Buffalo Law Review* 53 (2005): 721–56.

Aglietta, Michel, and Robert Cobbaut. "The 'Financialization' of the Economy, Macroeconomic Regulation and Corporate Governance," in Robert Cobbaut and Jacques Lenoble (eds.), *Corporate Governance: An Institutional Approach.* Leiden: Kluwer Law International, 2003: 87–115.

Alexander, Janet C. "Do the Merits Matter? A Study of Settlements in Securities Class Actions." *Stanford Law Review* 43 (1991): 497–598.

Alexander, Janet C. "Unlimited Shareholder Liability Through a Procedural Lens." *Harvard Law Review* 106 (1992): 387–445.

Allen, William T., Jack B. Jacobs, and Leo E. Strine, Jr. "Realigning the Standard of Review of Director Due Care with Delaware Public Policy: A Critique of *Van Gorkom* and Its Progeny as a Standard of Review Problem." *Northwestern University Law Review* 96 (2002): 449–66.

Arlen, Jennifer. "The Potentially Perverse Effects of Corporate Criminal Liability." *Journal of Legal Studies* 23 (1994): 833–67.

Arlen, Jennifer, and Reinier Kraakman. "Controlling Corporate Misconduct: An Analysis of Corporate Liability Regimes." *New York University Law Review* 72 (1997): 687–754.

Arlen, Jennifer, and Deborah M. Weiss. "A Political Theory of Corporate Taxation." *Yale Law Journal* 105 (1995): 325–90.

Arrow, Kenneth J. *Essays in the Theory of Risk Bearing.* Chicago: Markham Publishing, 1971.

Ayres, Ian, and Stephen Choi. "Internalizing Outsider Trading." *Michigan State Law Review* 101 (2002): 313–408.

Bainbridge, Stephen M. "Abolishing Veil Piercing." *Journal of Corporation Law* 26 (2001): 479–535.

Bainbridge, Stephen M. "The Board of Directors as Nexus of Contracts." *Iowa Law Review* 88 (2002): 1–34.

Bainbridge, Stephen M. "Community and Statism: A Conservative Contractarian Critique of Progressive Corporate Law Scholarship." Review of *Progressive Corporate Law,* by Lawrence E. Mitchell. *Cornell Law Review* 82 (1997): 856–904.

Bainbridge, Stephen M. "Director Primacy: The Means and Ends of Corporate Governance." *Northwestern University Law Review* 97 (2003): 547–606.

Bainbridge, Stephen M. "Exclusive Merger Agreements and Lock-Ups in Negotiated Corporate Acquisitions." *Minnesota Law Review* 75 (1990): 239–334.

Baker, J. H. *An Introduction to English Legal History.* 2nd ed. London: Butterworths, 1979.

Balotti, R. Franklin, and A. Gilchrist Sparks, III. "Deal-Protection Measures and the Merger Recommendation." *Northwestern Law Review* 96 (2002): 467–88.

Bebchuk, Lucian A. "The Case for Facilitating Competing Tender Offers: A Reply and Extension." *Stanford Law Review* 35 (1982): 23–50.

Bebchuk, Lucian A. "The Case for Increasing Shareholder Power." *Harvard Law Review* 118 (2005): 833–914.

Bebchuk, Lucian A. "Federalism and the Corporation: The Desirable Limits on State Competition in Corporate Law." *Harvard Law Review* 105 (1992): 1437–510.

Bebchuk, Lucian A. "A New Approach to Corporate Reorganizations." *Harvard Law Review* 101 (1988): 775–804.

Bebchuk, Lucian A. "Toward Undistorted Choice and Equal Treatment in Corporate Takeovers." *Harvard Law Review* 98 (1985): 1693–808.

Bebchuk, Lucian A., and Allen Ferrell. "Federalism and Corporate Law: The Race to Protect Managers from Takeovers." *Columbia Law Review* 99 (1999): 1168–99.

Bebchuk, Lucian A., and Jesse M. Fried. *Pay Without Performance: The Unfulfilled Promise of Executive Compensation.* Cambridge, MA: Harvard University Press, 2004.

Bebchuk, Lucian A., and Assaf Hamdani. "Vigorous Race or Leisurely Walk: Reconsidering the Competition Over Corporate Charters." *Yale Law Journal* 112 (2002): 553–615.

Bebchuk, Lucian A., and Mark J. Roe. "A Theory of Path Dependence in Corporate Ownership and Governance." *Stanford Law Review* 52 (1999): 127–70.

Berle, Adolf A. "For Whom Corporate Mangers Are Trustees: A Note." *Harvard Law Review* 45 (1932): 1365–72.

Berle, Adolf A., and Gardiner C. Means. *The Modern Corporation and Private Property.* New York: Macmillan Company, 1933.

Bernstein, Peter L. *Against the Gods: The Remarkable Story of Risk.* New York: John, Wiley & Sons, 1996.

Black, Bernard, Brian Cheffins, and Michael Klausner. "Outside Director Liability." *Stanford Law Review* 58 (2006): 1055–159.

Black, Bernard, and Reinier Kraakman. "A Self-Enforcing Model of Corporate Law." *Harvard Law Review* 109 (1996) 1911–981.

Blair, Margaret M., and Lynn A. Stout. "Team Production in Business Organizations: An Introduction." *Journal of Corporation Law* 24 (1999): 743–50.

Blair, Margaret M., and Lynn A. Stout. "A Team Production Theory of Corporate Law." *Virginia Law Review* 85 (1999): 247–327.

Blair, Margaret M., and Lynn A. Stout. "Trust, Trustworthiness, and the Behavioral Foundations of Corporate Law." *University of Pennsylvania Law Review* 149 (2001): 1735–810.

Boatright, John R. "Business Ethics and the Theory of the Firm." *American Business Law Journal* 34 (1996): 217–38.

Bogle, John C. *The Battle for the Soul of Capitalism.* New Haven, CT: Yale University Press, 2005.

Bowers, Helen M. "Fairness Opinions and the Business Judgment Rule: An Empirical Investigation of Target Firms' Use of Fairness Opinions." *Northwestern University Law Review* 96 (2002): 567–78.

Brandeis, Louis. *Other People's Money and How the Bankers Use It.* New York: Frederick A. Stokes, 1914.

Bratton, William W., Jr. "Berle and Means Reconsidered at the Century's Turn." *Journal of Corporation Law* 26 (2001): 737–70.

Bratton, William W., Jr. "Corporate Debt Relationships: Legal Theory in a Time of Restructuring." *Duke Law Journal* 1989 (1989): 92–172.

Bratton, William W., Jr. "The Economic Structure of the Post-Contractual Corporation." *Northwestern Law Review* 87 (1992): 180–215.

Bratton, William W., Jr. "The New Economic Theory of the Firm: Critical Perspectives from History." *Stanford Law Review* 41 (1989): 1471–527.

Bratton, William W., Jr. "The 'Nexus of Contracts' Corporation: A Critical Appraisal." *Cornell Law Review* 74 (1989): 407–65.

Braucher, Jean. "Contract versus Contractarianism: The Regulatory Role of Contract Law." *Washington and Lee Law Review* 47 (1990): 697–739.

Bruck, Connie. *The Predator's Ball: The Junk-Bond Raiders and the Man Who Staked Them.* New York: American Lawyer/Simon & Schuster, 1988.

Brudney, Victor. "O'Hagan's Problems." *Supreme Court Review* (1997): 249–69.

Buchan, James. *Frozen Desire: The Meaning of Money.* New York: Farrar, Straus, and Giroux, 1997.

Burrough, Bryan, and John Helyar. *Barbarians at the Gate: The Fall of RJR Nabisco.* New York: Harper and Row Publishers, 1990.

Carney, William J. "Appraising the Nonexistent: The Delaware Courts' Struggle with Control Premiums." *University of Pennsylvania Law Review* 152 (2003): 845–80.

Carney, William J. "The Legacy of 'The Market for Corporate Control' and Origins of the Theory of the Firm." *Case Western Law Review* 50 (1999): 215–44.

Carney, William J. "Limited Liability Companies: Origins and Antecedents." *University of Colorado Law Review* 66 (1995): 855–80.

Carney, William J. "The Production of Corporate Law." *University of Southern California Law Review* 71 (1998): 715–59.

Carney, William J., and Leonard A. Silverstein. "The Illusory Protections of the Poison Pill." *Notre Dame Law Review* 79 (2003): 179–220.

Cary, William L. "Federalism and Corporate Law: Reflections upon Delaware." *Yale Law Journal* 83 (1974): 663–705.

Choi, Stephen J., and A. C. Pritchard. "Behavioral Economics and the SEC." *Stanford Law Review* 56 (2003): 1–73.

Clark, Robert C. *Corporate Law.* Boston: Little, Brown, 1986.

Clark, Robert C. "Major Changes Lead Us Back to Basics." *Journal of Corporation Law* 31 (2006): 591–98.

Coase, Ronald. "The Nature of the Firm." *Economica* 4 (1937): 386–405.

Coffee, John C., Jr. "Market Failure and the Economic Case for a Mandatory Disclosure System." *Virginia Law Review* 70 (1984): 717–53.

Coffee, John C., Jr. "The Uncertain Case for Takeover Reform: An Essay on Stockholders, Stakeholders and Bust-Ups." *1988 Wisconsin Law Review* (1988): 435–65.

Coffee, John C., Jr. "No Exit?: Opting Out, The Contractual Theory of the Corporation, and the Special Case of Remedies." *Brooklyn Law Review* 53 (1988): 919–74.

Coffee, John C., Jr. "Shareholders Versus Managers: The Strain in the Corporate Web." *Michigan Law Review* 85 (1986): 1–109.

Coffee, John C., Jr. and William A. Klein. "Bondholder Coercion: The Problem of Constrained Choice in Debt Tender Offers and Recapitalizations." *University of Chicago Law Review* 58 (1991): 1207–73.

Coffee, John C., Jr., Louis Lowenstein, and Susan Rose-Ackerman, eds. *Knights, Raiders, and Targets: The Impact of the Hostile Takeover.* New York: Oxford University Press, 1998.

Coffey, Michael P. "In Defense of Limited Liability—A Reply to Hansmann and Kraakman." *George Mason University Law Review* 1 (1994): 59–90.

Crusto, Mitchell F. "Extending the Veil to Solo Entrepreneurs: A Limited Liability Sole Proprietorship Act." *2001 Columbia Business Law Review* (2001): 381–430.

Cunningham, Lawrence A. "Commonalities and Prescriptions in the Vertical Dimension of Global Corporate Governance." *Cornell Law Review* 84 (1999): 1133–94.

Cunningham, Lawrence A. "The Essays of Warren Buffett: Lessons for Corporate America." *Cardozo Law Review* 19 (1997): 1–214.

Cunningham, Lawrence A. "The Sarbanes-Oxley Yawn: Heavy Rhetoric, Light Reform (And It Just Might Work)." *Connecticut Law Review* 35 (2003): 915–88.

Demsetz, Harold. "The Structure of Ownership and the Theory of the Firm." *Journal of Law and Economics* 26 (1983): 375–90.

Dewey, John. "The Historic Background of Corporate Legal Personality." *Yale Law Journal* 35 (1926): 655–73.

Dorff, Michael B. "Softening Pharaoh's Heart: Harnessing Altruistic Theory and Behavioral Law and Economics to Rein in Executive Salaries." *Buffalo Law Review* 51 (2003): 811–91.

DuBois, Armand B. *The English Business Company After the Bubble Act 1720–1800.* New York: Common Wealth Fund, 1938.

Easterbrook, Frank H. "Antitrust and the Economics of Federalism." *Journal of Law and Economics* 26 (1983): 23–50.

Easterbrook, Frank H., and Daniel R. Fischel. The *Economic Structure of Corporate Law.* Cambridge, MA: Harvard University Press, 1991.

Easterbrook, Frank H., and Daniel R. Fischel. "Limited Liability and the Corporation." *University of Chicago Law Review* 52 (1985): 89–117.

Easterbrook, Frank H., and Daniel R. Fischel. "The Proper Role of a Target's Management in Responding to a Tender Offer." *Harvard Law Review* 94 (1981): 1161–204.

Easterbrook, Frank, and Daniel R. Fischel. "Voting in Corporate Law." *Journal of Law and Economics* 26 (1983): 395–427.

Edelman, Paul H., and Randall S. Thomas. "Corporate Voting and the Takeover Debate." *Vanderbilt Law Review* 58 (2005): 453–98.

Eichenwald, Kurt. *Conspiracy of Fools: A True Story.* New York: Broadway Press, 2005.

Eisenberg, Melvin A. "The Architecture of American Corporate Law: Facilitation and Regulation." *Berkeley Business Law Journal* 2 (2005): 167–84.

Eisenberg, Melvin A. *The Structure of the Corporation: A Legal Analysis.* Boston: Little Brown, 1976.

Ellis, Richard B. *Aggressive Nationalism: Law and Politics in the Early Republic* (forthcoming).

Elson, Charles M., and Christopher J. Gyves. "In re *Caremark*: Good Intentions, Unintended Consequences." *Wake Forest Law Review* 39 (2004): 691–706.

Elson, Charles M., and Robert B. Thompson. "*Van Gorkom*'s Legacy: The Limits of Judicially Enforced Constraints and the Promise of Proprietary Incentives." *Northwestern University Law Review* 96 (2002): 579–93.

Ereigh, Viscount. *The South Sea Bubble.* New York: G. P. Putnam's Sons, 1933.

Estes, Ralph. *Tyranny of the Bottom Line: Why Corporations Make Good People Do Bad Things.* San Francisco: Berrett-Koehler Publishers, 1996.

Fischel, Daniel R. *Payback: The Conspiracy to Destroy Michael Milken and His Financial Revolution.* New York: HarperCollins Publishers, 1996.

Fischel, Daniel R. "The 'Race to the Bottom' Revisited: Reflections on Recent Developments in Delaware's Corporation Law." *Northwestern University Law Review* 76 (1982): 913–45.

Fisher, William W., III, Morton J. Horwitz, and Thomas A. Reed, eds. *American Legal Realism.* New York: Oxford University Press, 1993.

Folk, Ernest L. *Folk on the Delaware General Corporation Law: A Commentary and Analysis.* 3rd ed. Little Brown, 1972/1992.

Franco, Joseph A. "Why Antifraud Prohibitions are Not Enough: The Significance of Opportunism, Candor and Signaling in the Economic Case for Mandatory Securities Disclosure." *2002 Columbia Business Law Review* (2002): 223–362.

Fried, Jesse M. "Informed Trading and False Signaling with Open Market Repurchases." *California Law Review* 93 (2005): 1323–86.

Gabaldon, Theresa A. "The Lemonade Stand: Feminist and Other Reflections on the Limited Liability of Corporate Shareholders." *Vanderbilt Law Review* 45 (1992): 1387–456.

Galanter, Marc. "Planet of the APS: Reflections on the Scale of Law and its Users." *Buffalo Law Review* 53 (2006): 1369–417.

Galbraith, John Kenneth. *The Economics of Innocent Fraud: Truth for Our Time.* Boston: Houghton Mifflin, 2004.

Geelhoed, E. Bruce. *Charles E. Wilson and Controversy at the Pentagon, 1953 to 1957.* Detroit: Wayne State University Press, 1979.

Gerding, Erik F. The Next Epidemic: Bubbles and the Growth and Decay of Securities Regulation." *Connecticut Law Review* 38 (2006): 393–450.

Gervais, Pierre. "The Cotton Factory in a Pre-Industrial Political Economy: An Exploration of the Boston Manufacturing Company 1815–1820." Charles Warren Seminar. Charles Warren Center, Harvard University, 2003.

Gervais, Pierre. "What Is the 'Industrial Revolution'?" Charles Warren Seminar. Charles Warren Center, Harvard University, 2003.

Getzler, Joshua, and Mike Macnair. "The Firm as an Entity Before the Companies Acts," in P. Brand, K. Costello, and W. N. Osborough (eds.), *Adventures of the Law: Proceedings of the Sixteenth British Legal History Conference, Dublin 2003.* Dublin: Four Courts Press, 2005: 267–88.

Gevurtz, Franklin A. "The Historical and Political Origins of the Corporate Board of Directors." *Hofstra Law Review* 33 (2004): 89–173.

Gilmore, Grant. *The Ages of American Law.* New Haven, CT: Yale University Press, 1977.

Gilson, Ronald J. "A Structural Approach to Corporations: The Case Against Defensive Tactics in Tender Offers." *Stanford Law Review* 33 (1981): 819–91.

Gilson, Ronald J. "Value Creation by Business Lawyers: Legal Skills and Asset Pricing." *Yale Law Journal* 94 (1984): 239–313.

Gilson, Ronald J., and Reinier H. Kraakman. "Delaware's Intermediate Standard for Defensive Tactics: Is There Substance to Proportionality Review?" *Business Lawyer* 44 (1989): 247–74.

Gilson, Ronald J., and Reinier H. Kraakman. "The Mechanisms of Market Efficiency." *Virginia Law Review* 70 (1984): 549–643.

Gilson, Ronald J., and Reinier H. Kraakman. "The Mechanisms of Market Efficiency Twenty Years Later: The Hindsight Bias." *Journal of Corporation Law* 28 (2003): 715–42.

Gordon, Robert W. "Critical Legal Histories." *Stanford Law Review* 36 (1984): 57–125.

Greenfield, Kent. "Does Corporate Law Protect the Interests of Shareholders and Other Stakeholders?: September 11th and the End of History for Corporate Law." *Tulane Law Review* 76 (2002): 1409–29.

Greenfield, Kent. "Ultra Vires Lives! A Stakeholder Analysis of Corporate Illegality (With Notes on How Corporate Law Could Reinforce International Law Norms)." *Virginia Law Review* 87 (2001): 1279–379.

Greenfield, Kent. "Using Behavioral Economics to Show the Power and Efficiency of Corporate Law as Regulatory Tool." *U. C. Davis Law Review* 35 (2002): 581–644.

Griffith, Sean J. "Uncovering a Gatekeeper: Why the SEC Should Mandate Disclosure of Details Concerning Directors' and Officers' Liability Insurance Policies." *University of Pennsylvania Law Review* 154 (2006): 1147–208.

Grossman, Sanford J., and Joseph E. Stiglitz. "On the Impossibility of Informationally Efficient Markets." *American Economic Review* 70 (1980): 393–408.

Grundfest, Joseph A. "The Limited Future of Unlimited Liability: A Capital Markets Perspective." *Yale Law Journal* 102 (1992): 387–425.

Hamermesh, Lawrence A. "A Kinder, Gentler Critique of Van Gorkom and Its Less Celebrated Legacies." *Northwestern University Law Review* 96 (2002): 595–605.

Hansmann, Henry B. "Reforming Nonprofit Corporation Law." *University of Pennsylvania Law Review* 129 (1981): 497–623.

Hansmann, Henry B. "When Does Worker Ownership Work? ESOPs, Law Firms, Codetermination, and Economic Democracy." *Yale Law Journal* 99 (1990): 1749–816.

Hansmann, Henry B., and Reinier H. Kraakman. "Do the Capital Markets Compel Limited Liability? A Response to Professor Grundfest." *Yale Law Journal* 102 (1992): 427–36.

Hansmann, Henry B., and Reinier H. Kraakman. "The End of History for Corporate Law." *Georgetown Law Journal* 89 (2001): 439–68.

Hansmann, Henry B., and Reinier H. Kraakman. "The Essential Role of Organizational Law." *Yale Law Journal* 110 (2000): 387–440.

Hansmann, Henry B., and Reinier H. Kraakman. "Toward Unlimited Shareholder Liability for Corporate Torts." *Yale Law Journal* 100 (1991): 1879–934.

Hansmann, Henry B., Reinier H. Kraakman, and Richard Squire. "Law and the Rise of the Firm." *Harvard Law Review* 119 (2006): 1333–403.

Holmes, Oliver Wendell. *The Common Law.* Boston: Little Brown, 1881.

Horwitz, Morton J. *The Transformation of American Law, 1870–1960: The Crisis of Legal Orthodoxy.* New York: Oxford University Press, 1992.

Hovenkamp, Herbert. "The Classical Corporation in American Legal Thought." *Georgetown Law Journal* 76 (1998): 1593–689.

Hovenkamp, Herbert. *Enterprise and American Law, 1836–1937.* Cambridge, MA: Harvard University Press, 1991.

Hurst, James Willard. *The Legitimacy of the Business Corporation in the Law of the United States, 1780–1970.* Charlottesville, VA: University Press of Virginia, 1970.

Investment Company Institute and the Securities Industry Association. "Equity Ownership in America." A survey prepared by the Investment Company Institute and the Securities Industry Association, 2002.

Jacobs, Jack B. "The Uneasy Truce between Law and Equity in Modern Business Enterprises Jurisprudence." UCLA School of Law, Program in Business Law and Policy Occasional Paper Series, January 2006.

Jardim, Anne. *The First Henry Ford: A Study in Personality and Business Leadership.* Cambridge, MA: MIT Press, 1970.

Jensen, Michael C. "The Takeover Controversy, Analysis and Evidence," in John C. Coffee, Jr., Louis Lowenstein, and Susan Rose Ackerman, eds., *Knights, Raiders, and Targets.* New York: Oxford University Press, 1988: 314–54.

Jensen, Michael C., and William H. Meckling. "Theory of the Firm: Managerial Behavior, Agency Costs and Ownership Structure." *Journal of Financial Economics* 26 (1976): 305–60.

Joo, Thomas W. "Race, Corporate Law, and Shareholder Value." *Journal of Legal Education* 54 (2004): 351–64.

Kaufman, Andrew L. *Cardozo.* Cambridge, MA: Harvard University Press, 1998.

Kaufman, Jason. "Origins of the Asymmetric Society: Political Autonomy, Legal Innovation, and Freedom of Incorporation in the Early United States." 2006 (on file with author).

Kelly, Marjorie. *The Divine Right of Capital: Dethroning the Corporate Aristocracy.* San Francisco: Berrett-Koehler Publishers, 2001.

Kennedy, Duncan. *Legal Education and the Reproduction of Hierarchy: A Polemic Against the System.* New York: New York University Press, 2004. (Originally self-published in 1983.)

Kindleberger, Charles P. *Manias, Panics, and Crashes: A History of Financial Crises.* New York: Basic Books, 1978. 5th edition with foreword by Robert Aliber and Robert Solow. New York: Wiley, 2005.

Kindleberger, Charles P., and Jean-Pierre Laffargue. *Financial Crises: Theory, History, and Policy.* Cambridge: Cambridge University Press, 1982.

Klein, William A. "The Modern Business Organization: Bargaining Under Constraints." *Yale Law Journal* 91 (1982): 1521–64.

Klingman, William K. *1929 the Year of the Great Crash.* New York: Harper and Row Publishers, 1989.

Kornhauser, Lewis A. "The Nexus of Contracts Approach to Corporations: A Comment on Easterbrook and Fischel." *Columbia Law Review* 89 (1989): 1449–60.

Kraakman, Reinier, et al. *The Anatomy of Corporate Law: A Comparative and Functional Approach.* Oxford: Oxford University Press, 2004.

Kuykendall, Mae. "Reflections on a Corporate Law Draftsman: Ernest L. Folk's Lessons for Writing and Judging Corporate Law." *Rutgers Law Review* 35 (2004): 391–481.

Landauer, Carl. "Beyond the Law and Economics Style: Advancing Corporate Law in an Era of Downsizing and Corporate Reengineering. Review of *Progressive Corporate* Law, edited by Lawrence E. Mitchell, and *Strong Managers, Weak Owners,* by Mark J. Roe." *California Law Review* 84 (1996): 1693–718.

Langevoort, Donald C. "Behavioral Theories of Judgment and Decision Making in Legal Scholarship: A Literature Review." *Vanderbilt Law Review* 51 (1998): 1499–540.

Lee, John W., III. "Class Warfare 1988–2005 over Top Individual Income Tax Rates: Teeter-Totter from Soak-the-Rich to Robin-Hood-in-Reverse." *Hastings Business Law Journal* 2 (2006): 47–164.

Litowitz, Douglas. "Are Corporations Evil?" *University of Miami Law Review* 58 (2004): 811–41.

Litowtiz, Douglas. "The Corporation as God." *Journal of Corporation Law* 30 (2005): 501–38.

Llewellyn, Karl N. *The Bramble Bush: On Our Law and Its Study.* New York: Oceana Publications, 1930/1960.

Lloyd, Robert M. "*Pennzoil v. Texaco,* Twenty Years after: Lessons for Business Lawyers." *Transactions: The Tennessee Journal of Business Law* 6 (2005): 321–59.

Lopez, Frank R. "Corporate Social Responsibility in a Global Economy after September 11: Profits, Freedom, and Human Rights." *Mercer Law Review* 55 (2004): 739–77.

LoPucki, Lynn M. "The Death of Liability." *Yale Law Journal* 106 (1996): 1–92.

Macey, Jonathan R. "*Smith v. Van Gorkom*: Insights About C.E.O.s Corporate Law Rules, and the Jurisdictional Competition for Corporate Charters." *Northwestern University Law Review* 96 (2002): 607–29.

Makiel, Burton. *A Random Walk Down Wall Street: The Time Tested Strategy for Successful Investing.* 8th ed. New York: W. W. Norton and Company, 2003.

Mann, Richard A., Michael O'Sullivan, Larry Robins, and Barry S. Roberts. "Starting from Scratch: A Lawyer's Guide to Representing a Start-Up Company." *Arkansas Law Review* 56 (2004): 773–869.

Manne, Henry G. "Insider Trading: Hayek, Virtual Markets, and the Dog that Did not Bark." *Journal of Corporate Law* 31 (2005): 167–85.

Manne, Henry G. "Mergers and the Market for Corporate Control." *Journal of Political Economy* 73 (1965): 110–20.

Manne, Henry G. "Our Two Corporation Systems: Law and Economics." *Virginia Law Review* 53 (1967): 259–84.

Manning, Bayless. "The Business Judgment Rule and the Director's Duty of Attention: Time for Reality." *Business Lawyer* 39 (1984): 1477–501.

Manning, Bayless. "From Learned Profession to Learned Business." *Buffalo Law Review* 37 (1988): 658–70.

Manning, Bayless. "Reflections and Practical Tips on Life in the Boardroom after Van Gorkom." *Business Lawyer* 41 (1985): 1–14.

Manning, Bayless. "The Shareholder's Appraisal Remedy: An Essay for Frank Coker." *Yale Law Journal* 72 (1962): 223–65.

Marsh, Harold, Jr. "Are Directors Trustees? Conflict of Interest and Corporate Morality." *Business Lawyer* 22 (1966): 35–75.

McChesney, Fred S. "A Bird in the Hand and Liability in the Bush: Why Van Gorkom Still Rankles, Probably." *Northwestern University Law Review* 96 (2002): 631–49.

Micklethwait, John, and Adrian Wooldridge. *The Company: A Short History of a Revolutionary Idea.* New York: Modern Library, 2003.

Millon, David. "Frontiers of Legal Thought I: Theories of the Corporation." *Duke Law Journal* (1990): 201–62.

Mitchell, Lawrence E. *Corporate Irresponsibility: America's Newest Export.* New Haven, CT: Yale University Press, 2001.

Mitchell, Lawrence E. "The Death of Fiduciary Duty in Close Corporations." *University of Pennsylvania Law Review* 138 (1990): 1675–731.

Mitchell, Lawrence E. "The Fairness Rights of Corporate Bondholders." *New York University Law Review* 65 (1990): 1165–229.

Mitchell, Lawrence E. "Fairness and Trust in Corporate Law." *Duke Law Journal* 43 (1993): 425–91.

Mitchell, Lawrence E. "Groundwork of the Metaphysics of Corporate Law." *Washington and Lee Law Review* 50 (1993): 1477–88.

Moll, Douglas K. "Shareholder Oppression and Dividend Policy in the Close Corporation." *Washington and Lee Law Review* 60 (2003): 841–924.

Moll, Douglas K. "Shareholder Oppression and 'Fair Value': Of Discounts, Dates, and Dastardly Deeds in the Close Corporation." *Duke Law Journal* 54 (2004): 293–383.

Nader, Ralph, Mark Green, and Joel Seligman. *Constitutionalizing the Corporation: The Case for the Federal Chartering of Giant Corporations.* Washington, DC: Corporate Accountability Research Group, 1976.

Nader, Ralph, and Wesley J. Smith. *No Contest: Corporate Lawyers and the Perversion of Justice in the United States.* New York: Random House, 1996.

Neal, Steven. *Happy Days Are Here Again: The 1932 Democratic Convention, the Emergence of FDR—and How America Was Changed Forever.* New York: William Morrow, 2004.

Nevins, Allan, and Frank Ernest Hill. *Ford: Expansion and Challenge 1915–1933.* New York: Charles Scribner's Sons, 1957.

Note. "Incorporating the Republic: The Corporation in Antebellum Political Culture." *Harvard Law Review* 102 (1989): 1883–903.

Note. "Protecting Shareholders against Partial and Two-Tiered Takeovers: The 'Poison Pill' Preferred." *Harvard Law Review* 97 (1984): 1964–83.

Partnoy, Frank. "Barbarians at the Gatekeepers?: A Proposal for a Modified Strict Liability Regime." *Washington University Law Quarterly* 79 (2001): 491–547.

Partnoy, Frank. "A Revisionist View of Enron and the Sudden Death of 'May.'" *Villanova Law Review* 48 (2003): 1245–80.

Partnoy, Frank. "Why Markets Crash and What Law Can Do About It." *University of Pittsburgh Law Review* 61 (2000): 741–817.

Pistor, Katharina, and Chenggang Xu. "Incomplete Law." *New York University Journal of International Law and Politics* 35 (2003): 931–1013.

Posner, Richard A. *Cardozo: A Study in Reputation.* Chicago: University of Chicago Press, 1990.

Powers William C., Jr., Raymond S. Troubh, and Herbert S. Winokur, Jr. "Report of Investigation by the Special Investigative Committee of the Board of Directors of Enron Corp." February 1, 2002. Available at: www.lib.umich.edu/govdocs/dnOZ/dnozcrim.html#enron.

Presser, Stephen B. "Thwarting the Killing of the Corporation: Limited Liability, Democracy, and Economics." *Northwestern University Law Review* 87 (1992): 148–79.

Radin, Margaret J. *Reinterpreting Property.* Chicago: University of Chicago Press, 1993.

Ribstein, Larry E. "Efficiency, Regulation and Competition: A Comment on Easterbrook and Fischel's *Economic Structure of Corporate Law.*" *Northwestern University Law Review* 87 (1992): 254–86.

Ribstein, Larry E. "The Important Role of Non-Organization Law." *Wake Forest Law Review* 40 (2005): 751–92.

Rock, Edward, and Michael Wachter. "Dangerous Liaisons: Corporate Law, Trust Law and Interdoctrinal Legal Transplants." *Northwestern University Law Review* 96 (2002): 651–73.

Roe, Mark J. "Delaware's Competition." *Harvard Law Review* 117 (2003): 588–646.

Roe, Mark J. "Legal Origins, Politics and Modern Stock Markets." *Harvard Law Review* 120 (2006): 460–527.

Roe, Mark J. *Strong Mangers, Weak Owners: The Political Roots of American Corporate Finance.* Princeton, NJ: Princeton University Press, 1994.

Romano, Roberta. "After the Revolution in Corporate Law." *Journal of Legal Education* 55 (2005): 342–59.

Romano, Roberta. "Answering the Wrong Question: The Tenuous Case for Mandatory Corporate Laws." *Columbia Law Review* 89 (1989): 1599–618.

Romano, Roberta. "Comment on Easterbrook and Fischel, 'Contract and Fiduciary Duty.'" *Journal of Law and Economics* 36 (1993): 447–51.

Romano, Roberta. "Competition for Corporate Charters and the Lesson of Takeover Statutes." *Fordham Law Review* 61 (1993): 843–64.

Romano, Roberta. *The Genius of American Corporate Law.* Washington, DC: AEI Press, 1993.

Romano, Roberta. "A Guide to Takeovers: Theory, Evidence and Regulation." *Yale Journal on Regulation* 9 (1992): 119–79.

Romano, Roberta. "Law as Product: Some Pieces of the Incorporation Puzzle." *Journal of Law and Economic Organization* 1 (1985): 225–83.

Romano, Roberta. "Metapolitics and Corporate Law Reform." *Stanford Law Review* 36 (1984): 923–1016.

Romano, Roberta. "The Shareholder Derivative Suit: Litigation without Foundation?" *Journal of Law, Economics, and Organization* 7 (1991): 55–87.

"Roundtable Discussion: Corporate Governance." *Chicago-Kent Law Review* 77 (2001): 235–64.

Rubin, Edward L. "Trial by Battle, Trial by Argument." *Arkansas Law Review* 56 (2003): 261–94.

Schlag, Pierre. *The Enchantment of Reason.* Durham, NC: Duke University Press, 1998.

Schlegel, John Henry. *American Legal Realism and Empirical Social Science.* Chapel Hill: University of North Carolina Press, 1995.

Schlegel, John Henry. "Walt Was Right." *Journal of Legal Education* 51 (2001): 599–609.

Schuck, Peter H. *Agent Orange on Trial: Mass Toxic Disasters in the Courts.* Cambridge, MA: Harvard University Press, 1986.

Schumpeter, Joseph A. *Capitalism, Socialism, and Democracy.* 3rd ed. New York: Harper and Row Publishers, 1950.

Seligman, Joel. "The New Corporate Law." *Brooklyn Law Review* 59 (1993): 1–62.

Seligman, Joel. "The Historical Need for a Mandatory Corporate Disclosure System." *Journal of Corporation Law* 9 (1983): 1–61.

Shiller, Robert J. *Irrational Exuberance.* Princeton, NJ: Princeton University Press, 2000.

Shleifer, Andrei. *Inefficient Markets: An Introduction to Behavioral Finance.* Oxford: Oxford University Press, 2000.

Silbey, Susan S., and Patricia Ewick. "The Double Life of Reason and Law." *University of Miami Law Review* 57 (2003): 497–512.

Skeel, David A., Jr. "Book Review: Corporate Anatomy Lessons." Review of *The Anatomy of Corporate Law: A Comparative and Functional Approach,* by Reinier Kraakman. *Yale Law Journal* 113 (2004): 1519–77.

Skeel, David A., Jr. *Icarus in the Boardroom: The Fundamental Flaws in Corporate America and Where They Came From.* Oxford: Oxford University Press, 2005.

Sommer, Joseph H. "The Birth of the American Business Corporation: Of Banks, Corporate Governance, and Social Responsibility." *Buffalo Law Review* 49 (2001): 1011–97.

Stewart, James B. *Den of Thieves.* New York: Simon and Schuster, 1991.

Stout, Lynn A. "Are Takeover Premiums Really Premiums?: Market Price, Fair Value, and Corporate Law." *Yale Law Journal* 99 (1990): 1235–95.

Stout, Lynn A. "In Praise of Procedure: An Economic and Behavioral Defense of *Smith v. Van Gorkom* and the Business Judgment Rule." *Northwestern University Law Review* 96 (2002): 675–93.

Stout, Lynn A. "The Mechanisms of Market Inefficiency: An Introduction to the New Finance." *Journal of Corporation Law* 28 (2003): 635–69.

Symposium: "Revisiting the Mechanisms of Market Efficiency." *Journal of Corporation Law* 28 (2003): 499.

Symposium: "Theory Informs Business Practice, Roundtable Discussion: Corporate Governance." *Chicago Kent Law Review* 77 (2001): 235, 238.

Tocqueville, Alexis de. *Democracy in America.* New York: Alfred A. Knopf, 1945.

Tusk Mitchell, Dalia. "Shareholders as Proxies: The Contours of Shareholder Democracy." *Washington and Lee Law Review* 63 (2006): 1575–76.

Twining, William L. *Karl Llewellyn and the Realist Movement.* London: Weidenfeld and Nicolson, 1973.

Viano, Michael, and Jenny R. Arnold. "Corporate Criminal Liability." *American Criminal Law Review* 43 (2006): 311–39.

Wall Street. Movie directed by Oliver Stone. Twentieth Century Fox, 1987.

Walker, C. E. "The History of the Joint Stock Company." *Accounting Review* 6 (1931): 97–105.

Wasserstein, Bruce. *Big Deal: Mergers and Acquisitions in the Digital Age.* New York: Warner Books, 1998.

Weiss, Elliott J. "Some Thoughts of an Agenda for the Public company Accounting Oversight Board." *Duke Law Journal* 53 (2003): 491–515.

Weiss, Elliott J., and John S. Beckerman. "Let the Money Do the Monitoring: How Institutional Investors Can Reduce Agency Costs in Securities Class Actions." *Yale Law Journal* 104 (1995): 2053–128.

Weiss, Elliott J., and Lawrence J. White. "Of Econometrics and Indeterminacy: A Study of Investors' Reactions to 'Changes' in Corporate Law." *California Law Review* 75 (1987): 551–607.

Westbrook, David A. *City of Gold: An Apology for Global Capitalism in a Time of Discontent.* New York: Routledge, 2003.

Westbrook, David A. "Corporation Law after Enron: The Possibility of a Capitalist Reimagination." *Georgetown Law Review* 92 (2003): 61–127.

Westbrook, David A. "*Galanter v. Weber.*" *Buffalo Law Review* 53 (2006): 1445–51.

Westbrook, David A. "Pierre Schlag and the Temple of Boredom." *University of Miami Law Review* 57 (2003): 649–84.

Westbrook, David A. "Telling All: The Sarbanes-Oxley Act and the Ideal of Transparency." *Michigan State Law Review,* 2004, 441–62.

Williams, Cynthia A. "The Securities and Exchange Commission and Corporate Social Transparency." *Harvard Law Review* 112 (1999): 1197–311.

Williamson, Oliver E., and Sidney G. Winter, eds. *The Nature of the Firm: Origins, Evolution, and Development.* New York: Oxford University Press, 1993.

Winter, Ralph K. *Government and the Corporation.* Washington, DC: American Enterprise Institute, 1978.

Winter, Ralph K. "State Law, Shareholder Protection, and the Theory of the Corporation." *Journal of Legal Studies* 6 (1977): 251–92.

Yablon, Charles M. "Justifying the Judge's Hunch: An Essay on Discretion." *Hastings Law Journal* 41 (1989): 231–79.

Pedagogical Materials

American Law Institute. *Restatement of the Law of Agency.* St. Paul, MN: American Law Institute Publishers, 1933.

American Law Institute. *Restatement of the Law of Agency.* 2nd ed. St. Paul, MN: American Law Institute Publishers, 1958.

Allen, William T., and Reinier Kraakman. *Commentaries and Cases on the Law of Business Organizations.* New York: Aspen Publishers, 2003.

Bainbridge, Stephen M. *Corporation Law and Economics.* New York: Foundation Press, 2002.

Bauman, Jeffrey D., Elliot J. Weiss, and Alan R. Palmiter. *Corporations Law and Policy: Materials and Problems.* 5th ed. St. Paul, MN: West Group, 2003.

Carney, William J. *Corporate Finance: Principles and Practice.* New York: Foundation Press, 2005.

Cary, William L., and Melvin Eisenberg. *Cases and Materials on Corporations.* 5th ed. Mineola, NY: Foundation Press, 1980.

Choper, Jesse H., John C. Coffee, Jr., and Ronald J. Gilson. *Cases and Materials on Corporations.* 6th ed. New York: Aspen Publishers, 2004.

Cox, James D., and Thomas Lee Hazen. *Corporations.* 2nd ed. New York: Aspen Publishers, 2003.

Eisenberg, Melvin. *Cases and Materials on Corporations.* 9th ed. Mineola, NY: Foundation Press, 2005.

Epstein, David G., Richard D. Freer, and Michael J. Roberts. *Business Structures.* St. Paul, MN: West Group Publishing, 2002.

Hamilton, Robert W. *The Law of Corporations in a Nutshell.* St. Paul, MN: West Group Publishing, 2000.

Hamilton, Robert W., and Jonathan R. Macey. *Cases and Materials on Corporations Including Partnerships and Limited Liability Companies.* 8th ed. St. Paul, MN: West Group Publishing, 2003.

Hazen, Thomas Lee, and Jerry W. Markham. *Corporations and Other Business Enterprises: Cases and Materials.* St. Paul, MN: West Group, 2003.

Hazen, Thomas Lee, and Jerry W. Markham. *Mergers, Acquisitions, and Other Business Combinations: Cases and Materials.* St. Paul, MN: West Group, 2003.

Klein, William A., and John C. Coffee, Jr. *Business Organization and Finance.* Mineola, NY: Foundation Press, 2004.

Klein, William A., J. Mark Ramseyer, and Stephen Bainbridge. *Business Associations: Agency, Partnerships, and Corporations.* New York: Foundation Press, 2003.

Manning, Bayless. *A Concise Textbook on Legal Capital.* Mineola, NY: Foundation Press, 1977.

Mitchell, Lawrence, ed. *Progressive Corporate Law.* Boulder, CO: Westview Press, 1995.

Mitchell, Lawrence E., and Michael Diamond. *Corporations a Contemporary Approach: Cases and Materials for a Course in Corporate Law.* Durham, NC: Carolina Academic Press, 2004.

Palmiter, Alan R. *Corporations: Examples and Explanations.* 4th ed. New York: Aspen Publishers, 2003.

Presser, Stephen B. *An Introduction to the Law of Business Organizations: Cases, Notes and Questions.* St. Paul, MN: West Group, 2005.

Oesterle, Dale A. *The Law of Mergers and Acquisitions.* 3rd ed. St. Paul, MN: West Group, 2005.

Romano, Roberta. *Foundations of Corporate Law.* New York: Foundation Press, 1993.

Smith, D. Gordon, and Cynthia Williams. *Business Organizations: Cases, Problems, and Case Studies.* New York: Aspen Publishers, 2004.

Solomon, Lewis D., Russell B. Stevenson, Jr., and Donald E. Schwartz. *Corporations Law and Policy: Materials and Problems.* St. Paul, MN: West Group Publishing, 1982.

Index

About the Author

David A. Westbrook is professor and Floyd H. & Hilda L. Hurst Faculty Scholar at the University at Buffalo Law School, State University of New York. After completing his legal education, Westbrook practiced corporate law in Washington, D.C. Over the past decade, he has taught, lectured internationally, and published widely on advanced topics in finance, in addition to giving the basic course on corporations. He is the author of *City of Gold: An Apology for Global Capitalism in a Time of Discontent* (Routledge 2003) and the forthcoming *Navigators of the Contemporary: Why Ethnography Matters*. Westbrook lives in the historic village of East Aurora, New York, with his wife and three children.